/ / ‒

SCRIPTURE IN TRADITION

SCRIPTURE IN TRADITION

*The Bible and its Interpretation
in the Orthodox Church*

JOHN BRECK

ST VLADIMIR'S SEMINARY PRESS
CRESTWOOD, NEW YORK
2001

The benefactors who have made this publication possible wish to dedicate it in thanksgiving for their children, Michael, David, King, Olivia, Karl and Sophia.

Library of Congress Cataloging-in-Publication Data
Breck, John, 1939-
Scripture in tradition: the Bible and its interpretation in the Orthodox
  Church /John Breck.
    p. cm.
Includes bibliographical references.
ISBN 0-88141-226-0
  1. Bible—Hermeneutics.   2. Orthodox Eastern Church—Doctrines.
3. Chiasmus.   I. Title.
BS476.B595 2001
220.6'088'219—dc21   2001041986

SCRIPTURE IN TRADITION

Copyright © 2001 by
John Breck

ST VLADIMIR'S SEMINARY PRESS
575 Scarsdale Rd., Crestwood, NY 10707
1-800-204-2665

ISBN 0-88141-226-0

PRINTED IN THE UNITED STATES OF AMERICA

For M.P.K.
and to the memory
of C.E.K.

Contents

Preface

For more than a quarter of a century I have been privileged to work with Orthodox theological students in the area of biblical studies, particularly New Testament. In theological schools from Alaska to New York to France and Romania, I have met and taught students who are preparing for the priesthood or other positions of responsibility within the Church. Their levels of preparation as they enter seminary vary a great deal. A small number majored in Religious Studies while in college. Many others left a first career in another field to take up an entirely new vocation. In parts of the United States and Western Europe, only a minority are "cradle-Orthodox," raised in families whose lives have always revolved about the Church. Most are "converts" from another Christian confession or from a vague agnosticism, who have discovered Orthodoxy and find themselves called to the priestly ministry. With few exceptions they are bright, dedicated and highly motivated.

The one factor that causes some dismay is that so many enter seminary with a very limited knowledge of the Holy Scriptures. Not only are they unaware of methods and approaches for interpreting the Bible. More troubling, they are often unfamiliar with its basic content. Even those who have grown up in the Church and participated regularly in its cycle of services often know only what those services have conveyed to them. They are familiar with the Sunday lectionary for the Gospels. Yet even though they have repeatedly heard portions of the Epistles, a lack of context has usually made those passages incomprehensible and therefore meaningless.

Once theological students are exposed to the riches of Scripture, however, they seem to develop a special taste for it, a desire to sound its depths and to incorporate it into every phase of their ministry. This in turn places a special burden on teachers of the Bible. It means, in the first place, that we need to introduce our students to the content of biblical writings. But it also obliges us to offer them tools by which they can unlock that treasure for others, through their sermons, in church-school, for catechetical instruction, and in their ministry of witness to the poor, the sick and the suffering members of their congregations and in the world about them.

About a decade ago, in the early 1990s, I realized that I was failing more and more to provide the kind and quality of tools our students required. Increasingly my classroom lectures were becoming exercises in analysis, dealing primarily with questions of "Introduction": when, where, why and how the various canonical writings came into being. This was partially a reaction against an artificial "spiritual" approach to the Bible adopted for pious reasons by many Orthodox Christians. While well-meaning, it tends toward a reading of the Scriptures that is subjective and arbitrary. The Orthodox have always been rather suspicious of historical-critical method applied to the biblical texts, feeling that its rational, analytical manner can only arouse skepticism and doubt about fundamental elements of the faith. My aim in class, therefore, was largely to open students' eyes and minds to a variety of approaches, especially ones grounded in the modern historical and literary sciences. On the whole, they seemed quite capable of holding together the objective and subjective, the critical and spiritual readings of God's Word.

Nevertheless, we can easily get entangled in our own methodologies. Gradually I came to realize that I was becoming as one-sided as the more literalist or fundamentalist attitudes I had tried to modify. As a result, for the past few years my interest and the focus of my teaching have shifted away from historical-critical, narrative and other types of biblical analysis currently in vogue throughout the world, in traditionally Orthodox countries (Greece, Russia, Romania) as well as in the West. Thanks to the availability of outstanding patristics series such as the *Sources chrétiennes,* and the renewed interest in the Church Fathers they have spawned, it is now possible to provide students with texts that include a critical apparatus, together with good translations and extensive bibliographies on patristic exegesis.

Rediscovering the ancient Fathers, with their critical eye and remarkable talent for discerning multiple layers of meaning in the biblical text, has been a blessing to me, both personally and in the classroom or lecture hall. It has led me to restructure my courses in Scripture so as to approach the text with what is essentially a patristic hermeneutic. This is an interpretive stance or attitude that seeks to uncover in the biblical writings both the literal-historical meaning as the author understood it, and another, "spiritual" level of meaning, which speaks directly to the life-situation of the reader.

The two need to be held together. Modern biblical scholarship has provided invaluable insight into the background, composition and original meaning of individual writings. Discernment is certainly needed to sift the chaff from the wheat. That does not mean, however, that we should dismiss the work of biblical specialists—whatever their confessional background—who have provided us with tools such as the Nestle-Aland Greek New Testament, the Interpreter's and Anchor Bible dictionaries, and a vast array of books and articles that clarify what we call the "literal" sense of the text.

At the same time, it is evident that the literal sense in itself is incomplete. A further step in the hermeneutic process has to be taken, to translate the results of exegesis into a living and life-giving witness for people of today. Our study of the Bible, in other words, should lead us from the literal sense to the spiritual sense: from the original meaning of a passage to its significance as the Word of God for the salvation of those who receive it with faith. It is with this concern that I found myself moving from a purely historical-critical approach to the Bible to one based more specifically on the methods and insights of the ancient Church Fathers.

This shift in perspective provides the rationale for this present book. Its purpose is to introduce theological students, pastors and others who may be interested, to certain "new" approaches to Scripture. These approaches, though—from typology and allegory, to analysis of the literary form known as chiasmus—have existed for thousands of years. Since the Enlightenment, they have largely remained a treasure hidden in a field. If readers of this book come to appreciate something of the patristic legacy which is theirs, then it will serve its modest purpose, and I shall be grateful.

Several of these chapters on "The Bible and Its Interpretation in the Orthodox Church" are revisions of essays that have appeared in theological journals, especially *St Vladimir's Theological Quarterly* and *Pro Ecclesia*. In a rather different form, chapters two, three and four were originally prepared for two series of lectures delivered in October 1999, at the Institute for Orthodox Christian Studies, Cambridge, England, and, in May 2000, at the Theological Faculty of the University of Sibiu, Romania. I wish to express my gratitude to the Rev Dr John Jillions, Principal of the Cambridge Institute, and to the Rev Professor Vasile Mihoc of the University of Sibiu, for their kind invitations to address their student bodies and for the very cordial welcome they extended to me.

My most special thanks, however, goes to my mother, Margaret P. Kleiber, and to her late husband Carl, for their gracious and loving support over my lifetime. This book, dedicated to them, is a small token of my deep appreciation and affection.

Fr John Breck
Feast of St Nicholas, 2000

Introduction

It is a well-known, if to some minds curious fact that Orthodox biblical scholars today rarely write commentaries on books of the Bible.[1] Introductions to the New Testament are more common,[2] and large numbers of Orthodox studies on particular scriptural themes have appeared over the past decades in Greece, Romania and Russia, as well as in Western Europe and the United States. The scientific format of modern biblical commentaries, however, has never really appealed to the Orthodox, however much teachers of Scripture may rely on them in course preparation, priests may use them when preparing sermons, and the laity may refer to them in working up materials for Bible study.

This lack of historical-critical commentaries is due in part to the fact that Orthodox scholars have often had difficulty obtaining Western books and journals on exegesis, archaeology and other disciplines necessary to produce such works. This is especially true of those who lived in the former Soviet Union. The more basic reason, however, is the fact that Orthodox biblical interpretation has usually taken a *homiletic* rather than strictly exegetical approach to the Word of God. In fact, biblical commentaries abound in Orthodox tradition. They are simply not recognized as such today, because they assume what is often termed (pejoratively) a "pre-critical" attitude toward the biblical narrative.

Ever since the middle of the last century certain scholars, often labeled reactionary, have signaled the demise of the historical-critical method as applied to books of the Bible.[3] They express dismay at the rationalizing tendencies of

1 A noteworthy exception is the commentary series begun by Prof. Paul Tarazi of St Vladimir's Seminary, Crestwood, New York. To date, Fr Tarazi has completed commentaries on First Thessalonians and Galatians, published by the St Vladimir's Seminary Press.
2 See, for example, the introductions by J. Karavidopoulos of the University of Thessalonika, by S. Tofana of the Romanian theological faculty in Cluj, and by Fr. Tarazi (Old and New Testaments).
3 Such reaction is to be found even in Germany, the foremost center for historical-critical studies during the past two centuries. See, e.g., Gerhard Maier, *Das Ende der Historisch-Kritischen Methode* (Wuppertal, 1974); English tr., *The End of the Historical-Critical Method* (St Louis: Concordia, 1977).

biblical specialists today and want to return to what they understand to be a more traditional interpretation of the sacred Scriptures. Many of them seem to be laboring under the impression that historical and text-critical method was first developed in the wake of the Enlightenment. In fact, the early Church Fathers, particularly Irenaeus and Origen, adopted for their interpretation of Scripture an approach that in their time was clearly analogous to the way exegesis is done today. They used critical tools to establish the text (that is, to determine the most accurate readings based on a comparison of ancient manuscripts) and to draw from the text its literal, historical meaning: the meaning "intended" by the biblical author. The difference, perhaps, lies in their single-minded concern to interpret the Bible as the life-giving Word of God. For the Fathers, exegesis was never an end in itself. It always served the Church's mission to proclaim a Word of salvation. This is why their approach to biblical interpretation was homiletic rather than scientific. Their primary aim was to preach the Gospel rather than to analyze it.

Because of its apparent pre-critical limitations, patristic exegesis plays a very small role in shaping and informing the biblical commentaries that are produced today. This includes the many annotated versions of the Bible that have appeared recently. A welcome corrective to this trend can be found in the InterVarsity series, *Ancient Christian Commentary on Scripture*, edited by Prof. Thomas Oden of Drew University. This series will eventually offer patristic commentary from East and West on the entire Bible, making available to the modern reader insights from the most important spiritual leaders of the early Church. The tide is shifting, it seems. Yet there remains a regrettable ignorance among theologians, in the Western churches but also within Orthodoxy, regarding the hermeneutic presuppositions and exegetical methods adopted by the ancient patristic writers.

It is because of this situation that the first part of this book takes up the issue of patristic hermeneutics and the place of Scripture within the historical Orthodox Church. The ancient Fathers, and particularly the early Greek theologians, shared a certain *vision* of the place and meaning of Scripture that has been largely lost in recent times. More important than particular exegetical conclusions they reach with respect to any given passage is this vision which perceives the presence and activity of God in every aspect of Israel's history and in every facet of the Church's life. Theirs was an inspired vision, a God-given perception which they termed *theôria*. This vision enabled them to discern the deeper meaning of the biblical message and to interpret that meaning for their flock. Avoiding the pitfall of "verbal inerrancy," they knew that every word of the text was produced by a "synergy" or cooperative effort between the human author and the Holy Spirit. Whether or not they found a "spiritual" sense in every phrase of the text, they were convinced that every word was inspired by God for the purpose of guiding the faithful along the way toward life in the Kingdom of Heaven. To their mind, exegesis has one purpose only: to enable the people of God to hear his Word and to receive it for their salvation.

The writings of these early Church exegetes make up a vital aspect of what we term Holy Tradition. This is a much misunderstood concept. The popular view holds it to be either a complement to Scripture or an alternative to it. A simplistic view of the Roman Catholic position finds there two "pillars" that uphold the Church: Scripture and Tradition, with the latter being primary. An equally simplistic view sees the Protestant churches rejecting Tradition altogether as an unfortunate development that places human interpretation ahead of God's Word. Although these are caricatures, they accurately reflect a certain dichotomy, even a severe tension, between Scripture and Tradition that has existed in Western Christendom since before the sixteenth century. To an outside observer, it appears as though this tension has led to two extremes: on the one hand, the Magisterium; on the other, *sola scriptura.*

The Eastern Church Fathers stressed the fact that the Bible is not *sui generis* but that it was born and shaped within a community of faith. The primary influence in the formation of the New Testament canon was not, as is often thought, the negative factor of the Church's struggle against heresy. It was rather the profoundly positive experience of the living God, who reveals himself and continues to act for the salvation and glorification of his people. This experience was first pondered, formulated and proclaimed as oral tradition(s). Gradually, select aspects of that body of tradition took written form. They appeared as occasional letters which addressed specific doctrinal and pastoral issues within various church communities, and as theological interpretations of Jesus' life, teaching and overall mission that made up a wide variety of gospels. Further selection—understood to be guided by the Holy Spirit—led slowly to creation of the "canon" or body of normative writings that preserved the *regula veritatis*: the fundamental beliefs that united Christians in a single ecclesial Body. (To gain a perspective on this development, it helps to recall that the first complete list of New Testament writings was formally made only in the year 367, in a festal epistle penned by St Athanasius. In the Syriac-speaking churches, 2 Peter, 3 John and Jude were not received as canonical until well into the fifth century; and Revelation was admitted only in the ninth century.)

Scripture, in other words, took shape within the matrix of ancient Church Tradition. Rather than seeing the two as either complementary or mutually exclusive, we need to consider them from the perspective of their historical development. Tradition has been aptly described as the life of the Holy Spirit within the Church, the presence of divine, sanctifying Life within the Body of believers. It may be likened to a great river, whose main current is Scripture. Scripture is the normative or "canonical" witness that serves as the touchstone by which all traditions are measured and all authentic Tradition is discerned. Orthodoxy sees the relationship between the two in a way that can be described not as Scripture *or* Tradition, or Scripture *and* Tradition, but Scripture *in* Tradition. This is because Scripture *is* Tradition, in the sense that the New Testament writings are a part of Tradition and constitute its normative element. Those writings came forth from the Church's life and proclamation, and they have continued through the ages to be the measure, rule or "canon" of Christian faith.

The purpose of this book is to describe and illustrate how Eastern patristic tradition interpreted the canonical writings, and how Orthodoxy continues even today to ground its theological reflection in Scripture as read through the lens of patristic *theôria*. That lens, as we shall see, provides a vision of God and his saving purpose as they are revealed to the Church, and through the Church to the world, by the "two hands of the Father": Christ and the Holy Spirit.

Part I introduces the reader to the role of the Bible in Orthodox theology and worship. It develops various "principles" or guidelines to interpretation based on the hermeneutics of the Church Fathers and provides illustrations of those principles from the writings of early Christian exegetes such as Justin Martyr, Irenaeus of Lyons, Origen, and Cyril of Alexandria. The section concludes with suggestions for an appropriate "spiritual" reading of the Scriptures: a reading grounded in the inspirational activity of the Holy Spirit within the Church.

Part II takes up the issue of "chiasmus" in the Scriptures: the use of concentric parallelism on the part of the biblical author that provides valuable insight into the "literal" sense of a biblical text. Following an introduction to the nature and importance of chiasmus in biblical interpretation (ch. 5), three essays illustrate its usefulness for determining the authenticity of a particular passage or textual reading, and for clarifying the evangelist's meaning in a familiar but often misunderstood element of his tradition. The first uses chiastic analysis to demonstrate, against most recent interpretations, that the final chapter of John's Gospel (ch. 21) is an integral part of the original composition. The second considers an important variant reading in 1 John that bears on the question of pneumatology and illustrates the importance of the

Byzantine textual tradition. And the last demonstrates—again, as a corrective to much current exegesis—that the passage Luke 1:26-38 (the Annunciation) included vv. 34-35 in its original redaction.

Part III focuses on elements of Orthodox christology and pneumatology that are central to current ecumenical debate. Chapter 9 considers the continuing relevance of the Nicene-Constantinopolitan Creed, including the difficult and contentious issue of the *filioque*. Chapter 10 takes up a related topic: the importance of Orthodox incarnational theology for proclaiming the mystery of redemption. Chapter 11 then discusses the indispensable role of God the Son in disclosing the "face" or personal identity of the Holy Spirit. Each of these chapters seeks in part to offer a corrective to current attempts on the part of many Western theologians to separate the person of Jesus from the eternal Son of God (a modern form of Nestorian dualism), and to reduce the Spirit to a creative, prophetic power, rather than to "worship and glorify him together with the Father and the Son," as a hypostatic mode of God's very being, a "person" of the Holy Trinity.

The last chapter turns, like chapter 4, to the practical, spiritual consequences of the Church's dogmatic teachings, grounded as they are in personal and communal experience. It focuses on the respective roles of Christ and the Spirit in the hesychast tradition known as "Prayer of the Heart." Here as throughout this book, our chief aim is to demonstrate the relationship that exists between the biblical witness on the one hand, and ecclesial experience and theological reflection on the other, a relationship expressed by our title, "Scripture *in* Tradition." All doctrinal and liturgical developments within the life of the Church—its faith and its worship, including "prayer of the heart"—are properly grounded in Holy Scripture. Yet Scripture itself derives from Tradition, while it serves as the canon or rule by which all authentic Tradition is measured.

Finally, the *Appendix* consists of a review essay, originally published in *Pro Ecclesia* (4/1, 1995), that critiques a recent book by the Dutch Catholic theologians E. Schillebeeckx and C. Halkes, *Mary: Yesterday, Today, Tomorrow*. It is included here to illustrate how Orthodox Mariology, based on the witness of Scripture, preserves against current theological trends the traditional understanding of Mary as *Theotokos* or "Mother of God."

Part One

Aims and Methods of
Orthodox Biblical Interpretation

1

The Bible in the
Orthodox Church

1. Scripture in Tradition

"The Paraclete, the Holy Spirit, whom the Father will send in my name, will teach you all things, and bring to your remembrance all that I have said to you... He will guide you into all the truth... He will glorify me, for he will take what is mine and declare it to you" (Jn 14:26; 16:13f).

This quotation from Jesus' Farewell Discourse provides the foundation for Orthodox biblical interpretation. It specifies the relationship that exists between Scripture and Tradition, together with the way by which the words of the biblical witness become the living and life-giving Word of God.

Orthodox hermeneutics—the principles and methods for interpreting Scripture—takes as a point of departure the affirmation of 2 Timothy 3:26, "All scripture is inspired by God." That inspirational work involves what we term a *synergy*, a cooperative effort between, on the one hand, the Holy Spirit of God, and, on the other, the human instrument who receives divine revelation and translates it into the gospel proclamation.

As the inspired author composes his work, he draws upon elements of *tradition*, both oral and written. Although his writing reflects his own creative thought, it is largely based on the *paradosis*, the witness of Jesus' followers which was passed from the first to the second Christian generation. Consequently, the Gospel or Epistle the apostolic author produces is given both shape and content by *Holy Tradition*. Tradition is the matrix in which the Scriptures are conceived and from which they are brought forth. Tradition, however, has been well described as the "living memory of the Church" (Fr. Sergius Bulgakov). It is the Church, in other words, that produces the canonical Scriptures. This means in the first place the writings of the New Testament. Yet the Hebrew Scriptures are also to be understood and interpreted in relation to Jesus Christ, who is both their source and their fulfillment. He is their *source* because he is the Logos, the eternal Word of God, who serves both as the agent of creation and as the ultimate content or referent of the prophetic oracles. And he is the *fulfillment* of the Hebrew Scriptures because at the deepest level of meaning they point forward to him and to his saving work. Christ, therefore, provides the true key to the inner meaning of the Law and the Prophets. Accordingly, Christ himself is our "hermeneutic principle" or principle of interpretation, in that it is he who reveals the true sense of all inspired Scripture. It is from this perspective that Orthodox Christianity holds both Old and New Testaments to be "books of the Church." Together they constitute the Church's "canon" or "rule of truth" that alone determines what are and what are not authentic elements of Holy Tradition.

In order for the biblical canon to determine the actual content and limits of Tradition, though, it must be interpreted in a certain way. The Bible is not "self-interpreting." This is evident from the fact that so many conflicting understandings exist concerning the meaning of any given passage. In fact, the biblical writings can only be properly interpreted *in the light of Holy Tradition*. Tradition provides the original content of Scripture. It comprises the oral and written *paradosis*, meaning "what is handed down" from the beginning in the form of eyewitness testimony and early Christian reflection on the mystery of Christ. Tradition may even be identified with the "apostolic gospel," understood in the broadest and deepest sense of that expression, to which each individual biblical writing bears a partial yet unique witness. Rather than see Scripture as the original and primary medium of revelation, and Tradition as mere human reflection upon its witness, we need to give full weight to the fact that *Scripture as written text is born of Tradition*. Consequently, Tradition provides the hermeneutic perspective by which any biblical writing is to be properly interpreted.

This means, however, that Orthodoxy operates within a closed "hermeneutic circle." That expression originally referred to the interaction between the interpreter, who comes to the Bible with certain presuppositions or preunderstandings, and the biblical text itself. There is no such thing as interpretation without presuppositions.[1] Put simply, we approach the Bible to acquire or deepen our faith, yet we do so with a certain level of faith that determines the way we will read the biblical writings. We seek understanding and faith through reading God's Word; yet we can only truly understand that Word through eyes of faith. Faith depends on the Word; yet proper interpretation of the Word requires faith. Therein lies the "hermeneutic circle."[2]

1   See R. Bultmann, "Is Exegesis Without Presuppositions Possible?" *Existence and Faith* (New York, 1960), 289-296; and his study "The Problem of Hermeneutics," *Essays Philosophical and Theological* (London: SCM, 1955), 234-261.
2   Rather than see this circular process as a hindrance to biblical exegesis, scholars today envision it as a "hermeneutic spiral" that describes the interaction between text and interpreter. See Grant Osborne, *The Hermeneutic Spiral* (Downers Grove, IN: InterVarsity Press,

This kind of circularity also exists in the dynamic between Scripture and Tradition. Scripture is the canon or norm by which all traditions are judged and authentic, inspired Tradition is determined. Yet the canonical Scriptures are created within the Church and by the Church as the normative expression of her "living Tradition." Scripture determines what constitutes genuine Tradition, yet Tradition gives birth to and determines the limits of Scripture.

To many people's minds, this way of envisioning the circular relationship between Scripture and Tradition appears untenable. The Protestant Reformers attempted to break this form of the hermeneutic circle by advancing the teaching known as *sola scriptura*, holding that Scripture alone determines faith and morality: what we believe and how we behave as Christian people. This was to a large extent in reaction to medieval Roman Catholicism which had separated Scripture and Tradition into separate domains, giving priority to the latter.

The ancient Christian exegetes of both East and West whom we identify as Fathers of the Church approached the matter from a more holistic point of view. Their writings were shaped by a particular hermeneutic perspective which they characterized by the term *theôria*. The expression refers to an "inspired vision" of divine Truth as revealed in the person of Jesus Christ and in the biblical witness to him.[3] That inspired vision—which itself is an essential part of Holy Tradition—enabled the Fathers to perceive depths of meaning in the biblical writings that escape a purely scientific or empirical approach to interpretation. Rather than attempt to break the hermeneutic circle, their passionate aim was to preserve it: to determine authentic Tradition by its conformity to the canon, while reading and interpreting the canonical Scriptures through the lens of Holy Tradition.

To the patristic mind, what makes this seemingly circular approach not only possible but necessary is the presence and activity of the Holy Spirit, the Spirit of Truth, who guides the Church and her inspired authors both to

1991). Such a spiral is inevitable in the process of interpretation and in fact plays a positive role in acquisition of knowledge of God. In their conservative Protestant approach to the question, W.W. Klein, C.L. Blomberg and R.L. Hubbard, *Introduction to Biblical Interpretation* (Dallas/London: Word Publishing, 1993), 114, make the point: "As we learn more from our study of Scripture we alter and enlarge our preunderstanding in more or less fundamental ways. In essence, this process describes the nature of all learning: it is interactive, ongoing, and continuous. When believers study the Bible they interact with its texts (and with its Author), and, as a result, over time they enlarge their understanding."

3   For a discussion of *theôria* in the Greek Fathers, see J. Breck, *The Power of the Word* (NY: St Vladimir's Seminary Press, 1986), chs. 2-3; and B. de Margerie, *An Introduction to the History of Exegesis, vol. I, The Greek Fathers* (Petersham, MA: St Bede's Publications, 1993), 165-186.

preserve and to transmit the essential elements of Tradition, and to produce
the canonical or normative writings which Tradition spawns and shapes in
terms of their content. Without this inspirational work of the Spirit, both
Scripture and Tradition would be purely human products, devoid of any
claim to ultimate truth or authority. It is the work of the Spirit that enables
the Church both to generate and to interpret her own canon or rule of truth,
and thereby to preserve intact, as she must, the true hermeneutic circle constituted by *Scripture in Tradition*.

The "Paraclete" sayings of John 14-16 also specify the way in which the
words of Jesus become the source of faith and life for each new generation of
Christian believers. The Spirit "brings to remembrance" the words and acts of
Jesus (Jn 14:26), and thereby the Spirit "glorifies" him in the Church's life, faith
and celebration. An Orthodox hermeneutic proceeds from the premise,
grounded in the biblical understanding of *anamnesis*, that "remembrance" is
more than a simple "recalling" of past events. *Anamnesis* signifies *reactualization*,
a reliving of the event within the community of faith. Yet beyond that, the
work of the Spirit in bringing the Word to remembrance also *fulfills* that Word.
On the one hand, the saving power of Jesus' life and mission are *reactualized* in
the experience of faith through eucharistic celebration of the great feasts of the
liturgical year: his nativity, baptism, transfiguration, and triumphant entry into
Jerusalem, as well as his crucifixion, death, resurrection, and ascension, together
with the Pentecostal outpouring of the Holy Spirit. On the other hand, those
saving acts are *brought to completion or fulfillment* by virtue of the power inherent in the scriptural Word that bears witness to them. As the Protestant
Reformers so rightly stressed, the Word of God itself is efficacious; it possesses
the power to save those who have ears to hear and hearts to receive its message.
"My word that goes forth from my mouth," declares the Lord of Israel, "shall
not return to me empty, but it shall accomplish that which I purpose, and prosper in the thing for which I sent it!" (Isaiah 55:11)

The saving power of God's Word is lived and experienced within the
Church, in the lives of women and men who welcome it with faith. And there
it is *proclaimed*, in order that its life-giving message might be heard by believers and nonbelievers alike. Yet in order to be received as the Bread of Heaven
and a wellspring of Living Water that nourish and transform human life, the
Word of God must be *celebrated* as well as proclaimed. This means that the
public reading and preaching of the Scriptures must be accomplished within
the broader framework of the Church's sacramental life. The reading and
exposition of Scripture properly constitute the liturgical "synaxis," the gathering of seekers, catechumens and the faithful for the purpose of edification.

The synaxis, however, is situated in a larger liturgical context that normally comes to completion with the celebration of the sacrament, particularly eucharistic communion.

The most striking biblical image for this complementarity of Word and Sacrament is perhaps St Luke's story of the encounter between the two disciples and the risen Jesus on the road to Emmaus (Lk 24:13-35). As the disciples journey toward the village, the stranger who accompanies them reveals the true sense of the Hebrew Scriptures, which point to the necessity for the Son of God, the Messiah of Israel, to suffer, die and rise again for the salvation of God's people. Although the disciples' hearts "burn" within them, the stranger remains unrecognized. Only when they sit together at table—as he assumes the role of *pater familias*, blessing God then breaking and distributing the bread—are their eyes opened, and they recognize him to be the risen Lord. For the Word to be truly *heard* it must be *celebrated*: read and proclaimed, yes; but also reactualized, internalized and consumed.

This emphasis on the fulfillment of the Word of God through liturgical celebration marks the uniqueness of an Orthodox hermeneutic. It is this emphasis, too, that provides what we can call the "doxological" aspect of the Church's ongoing work of interpretation. Such interpretation occurs through both preaching and singing, since both the sermon and the words of liturgical hymns comment on the text of Scripture and serve to convey its essential meaning to God's people. In the context of the liturgy the Word of God is preached and celebrated for the edification and spiritual nurture of those gathered in the church assembly. At the same time, that life-giving Word is *actualized* in the experience of the people, who, if they truly have ears to hear, respond to it with joy and thanksgiving.

This implies, however, that the Word of God is not a human creation; it is a divine gift. The Bible is written in human language and exhibits the limits of human perception and understanding. It contains the Word of God and gives expression to it. But the Word of God can never be reduced to the biblical text. Although it takes the form of written tradition in the Holy Scriptures, in confessional statements and in liturgical hymnography, "the Word of God" refers in the first place to a *Person*, "one of the Holy Trinity." The words proclaimed and celebrated by the gathered faithful, therefore, have meaning only insofar as they bear witness to the life-giving presence within the Church of the one who himself *is* the eternal Word and Son of God.

It is through the preaching of the Gospel and liturgical celebration that the faithful accomplish their *leitourgia*, their "liturgical service." That service consists in receiving the divine Word from God as a free gift of grace, then proclaiming and celebrating it to the glory of God and for the salvation of his people. Like the eucharistic gifts, the Word is to be received and offered back to God as a sacrifice of praise: "Thine own of Thine own, we offer unto Thee on behalf of all and for all!"[4] By means of this quintessentially liturgical gesture, proclamation of the Word through both sermons and liturgical hymnography creates a living communion between the believer and the triune God, from whom that eternal, life-giving Word comes forth.

With these observations offered by way of introduction, we should first ask how Orthodox Christians view the Scriptures and make use of them. Then we will consider the deficiencies in actual Orthodox practice, including an unfortunate neglect of the Word of God that has often occurred in Orthodox parish life and in the Church's mission. Finally, we shall turn to the question of hermeneutics proper, and ask how an authentic Orthodox understanding of Scripture and Tradition can help us recover something of the true purpose of both exegesis and preaching.

My contention is that the only way we can avoid the futility of so much contemporary study of the Bible is by situating the Word of God once again in its proper *ecclesial and liturgical context*. For it is only there that the Word can reclaim for itself its *eschatological* quality as the revelation and manifestation of the new creation, the new life of the Kingdom, present and active within the community of the Church, for the salvation of God's world. And it is only there, within the Church and its liturgy, that we can rediscover the Scriptures as a source of life and hope for ourselves, one to be received, celebrated and communicated through the Holy Spirit, to the glory of him who *is* the eternal Word of God.

2. *The Bible in the Church*

What, then, is the place of the Bible in the faith and practice of the Orthodox Church? To Western Christians, struck by the liturgical exuberance of Orthodoxy, the role of the Bible might seem minimal. In fact the Word of God is absolutely central and essential to every aspect of Orthodox life, from its liturgical celebration to its mission within the world at large.

The Church's doctrinal teachings and liturgical prayers, its language and its symbols, are all drawn directly from the canonical writings. For example, every Matins service includes the *Magnificat* and every Vespers service

4   The offertory phrase of the Byzantine eucharistic Liturgy that completes the *Anamnesis* or Memorial and provides the link between the Words of Institution and the *Epiklesis* or Invocation of the Holy Spirit.

includes the *Nunc Dimittis*, both taken from the Gospel according to St Luke. Psalms, prophecies and historical narratives are read constantly, as are the Epistles and Gospels. The only New Testament writing that is not read liturgically in Orthodox worship is the Book of Revelation. This is to be explained in part because of the obscurity of much of the book's apocalyptic imagery, and in part because when the Orthodox canon was promulgated in the mid-fourth century, Revelation was still a disputed work in Syria and elsewhere throughout the Mediterranean world. Yet the Orthodox liturgy is replete with images taken from Revelation, and since the fifth century the book's canonical authority has never been seriously questioned.

The Bible also functions iconically within Orthodox liturgical services. At the eucharistic liturgy it is processed, held aloft as in the ancient Church when the bishop made his entry into the house of worship, preceded by the deacon carrying the Book of the Gospels. The four Gospels remain constantly on the altar of our churches, bearing depictions of Christ crucified and resurrected. At the Matins service on the eve of Sundays and great feasts, following the reading of a resurrection Gospel, the book itself is brought to the center of the church and placed on a stand, where it is venerated by the faithful. If there is a "canon within the canon" in Orthodoxy, it is precisely the book of the four Gospels, which contains both the witness *of* Jesus Christ and the witness *to* him.

The Bible is equally important in the personal, daily worship of Orthodox faithful. A rule of prayer will normally include readings from both Gospel and Epistle, readings that follow the course of the liturgical year. The culminating event of what we term "the year of grace of our Lord" is Holy Pascha, or Easter. Throughout the rigorous lenten fast, Scripture provides essential nourishment, complemented by the reading of liturgical texts, lives of the saints, and teachings of the ascetics, whose own life of prayer, abstinence and love for neighbor serves as an inspirational model for those who journey through the "bright sadness" of the Lenten Spring. Pascha itself is a profoundly scriptural event; it is the Feast of Feasts when the Church celebrates and proclaims to the world that Christ is risen, destroying by his own death the powers of sin, death and corruption. It is a feast of joy, when the promise of the Gospel is realized in the midst of the celebrating community.

Yet however important the place of the Bible may be in both personal and liturgical usage, for many Orthodox that place is purely formal. They respect and venerate the Scriptures, they recognize many familiar passages, particularly from the Sunday Gospel readings, and they insist that theirs is a "biblical Church." Nevertheless, only a small minority seeks daily nourishment from

Bible reading. A mordant, in-house joke goes: "We Orthodox kiss the Bible, we don't read it." This tendency goes hand-in-hand—whether as cause or effect—with neglect of expository preaching. Exceptional preachers have always been present within the Church, from St John Chrysostom through Metropolitan Philaret of Moscow, down to the recently assassinated martyr-priest Alexander Men. Nevertheless, we Orthodox have all too often neglected or even abandoned our patristic heritage which placed primary emphasis on the *preaching* of God's Word.

This said, however, it is also true that in recent decades a far-reaching biblical renewal has occurred throughout the Orthodox world, initiated primarily through our theological seminaries: Athens and Thessalonika in Greece, Balamond in Lebanon, the St Sergius Theological Institute in Paris, together with seminaries in the United States, especially Holy Cross, St Tikhon's, and St Vladimir's. Following more than seventy years of severe persecution under communism, the Russian Orthodox Church is also struggling in both seminaries and parishes to recover its biblical and theological heritage. And the Romanian Orthodox Church today numbers among its fifteen theological faculties a significant number of biblical scholars who are making important contributions to scholarly study of the Scriptures while contributing directly towards a biblical renewal within local church communities. With increased knowledge of Holy Scripture comes more vibrant, biblically based preaching. In addition, Bible curricula are increasingly available, aimed at children and young people, at lay adults, and at the clergy in the form of continuing education.

This last concern—to provide solid biblical instruction for seminary students and parish pastors—has led many of us in recent years to try to recover an authentic Orthodox hermeneutic, one grounded in the vision of the Eastern Church Fathers yet adapted to the theological and pastoral demands of life in the modern parish. It is this development that I would like to discuss in the remainder of this chapter.

3. The Aim of Biblical Interpretation

The aim of all biblical interpretation should be to acquire *knowledge of God*. To the Church's earliest exegetes, this aim was axiomatic. It led them to seek such knowledge for themselves, but always with the intent to convey it to others in a language that is *theoprepês*, "worthy of God." This is the language of "theology," the language *of* God and *about* God, that indicates the way to eternal life.

The acute crisis that presently afflicts the field of biblical studies is due to hermeneutical approaches that have largely abandoned that aim. The primary symptom of that crisis is the fact that so little biblical research today speaks directly to the spiritual needs of our people. Students of the Bible seem bent on acquiring knowledge *about* God, the world and themselves. Rarely do they demonstrate a serious concern for that knowledge *of* God which is the ground of personal communion *with* him.

Those of us who are professional biblical scholars have only added to the crisis. We publish among ourselves, for ourselves. We are a closed and rather elite group of specialists, whose concern is more often to edify (and perhaps impress) our colleagues than to train our students and lay leaders to proclaim to the world a Word of life and hope. There are exceptions to this, of course, but they are just that: exceptions. And although we Orthodox make a special claim on the spiritual and exegetical tradition of the Church Fathers, we too have fallen into a certain academic sterility in our studies of the Bible.

It must be said, however, that this is due at least in part to the "captivity" experienced by Orthodox who live in pluralistic and highly secularized Western societies. In Orthodox circles we speak of "the pseudomorphosis of the biblical mind." That rather pompous sounding phrase means that we have succumbed, more than we care to admit, to the methods and aims of exegesis that have long been in vogue in churches of the West. We have adopted as our own, Western presuppositions and methodologies that have the effect of objectifying the Scriptures and removing them from their proper liturgical and ecclesial context. Put most simply, *we have restricted ourselves to interrogating the biblical text, rather than allowing ourselves to be addressed and challenged by the living and life-giving Word of God.*

To Orthodox eyes, Western approaches to biblical interpretation today can be characterized by terms such as "scientific," "objective," "analytical," "disintegrative." A traditional Orthodox approach, on the other hand, tends to be holistic and synthetic. The fragmentation evidenced today in biblical periodicals, for example, is due in part to the Western understanding of academic "disciplines": the arts and sciences are separated into discrete categories for purposes of in-depth analysis, and the forest often becomes lost for the trees. In the area of biblical studies specifically, this fragmentation has resulted from transporting into it methods employed by secular literary critics. There is no question that source and form criticism have been highly useful for indicating the way kerygmatic, catechetical, liturgical and other elements have been incorporated into a given text. Yet they have tended to atomize the text, undermining both its integrity and its authority. Redaction critics have attempted to recover something of the holistic impression of the text by focusing on the process of composition and the theological agenda that underlies it. Yet their work, too, has spawned a multitude of theories concerning the composite nature of biblical writings. (Is it more reasonable to suppose, for example, that Philippians 3 and 2 Corinthians 10-13 were inserted into the original compositions by some tortuous process that has left no trace whatsoever in the textual tradition, or simply to accept that the change of tone in those passages results from Paul's habitual use of A:B:A' chiastic parallelism?)

Further reactions to the disintegrative approach of much modern biblical criticism have caused the pendulum to swing far in the opposite direction. The "new literary criticism," particularly narrative and reader-response theory, have helped us immensely to understand how stories function. But the "down" side is their tendency toward relativism. Like structuralism, they abandon interest in the literal sense of a biblical text and focus rather on the meaning derived by the reader, the so-called "esthetic pole" of the "bipolar virtual entity" that constitutes a literary composition. While reader-response dynamics need to be understood, the exegete's first task must be what it traditionally has been in the hermeneutic enterprise: to determine the *literal meaning* of the passage. Otherwise the text becomes detached from the historical framework in which it was produced, and "exegesis" is reduced to a sophisticated, modern form of allegorizing.

The result with all of this, once again, is the loss of both the integrity and the authority of the biblical witness. Single themes, representing particular theological agendas, emerge as all-important. Each individual interpreter determines a favorite "canon within the canon." Reductionism becomes the order of the day; ancient traditions concerning the historical origins and theological meaning of the text are abandoned as naive and inherently improbable; and major effort goes into demolishing, on the basis of highly debatable evidence, biblical images of God, Christ and the human person that have sustained Christian faith since the beginning.

The most notable example of this kind of pseudo-science is probably the silliness of the "Jesus Seminar," with its color-coded conclusions as to what Jesus did or did not say. While some of its analyses may be historically accurate, the point is that the project as a whole represents a blatant betrayal of the biblical witness. If "inspiration" means anything, it means that the risen Lord, through the Spirit-Paraclete, is present within the community of faith, to guide both the composition and the interpretation of biblical writings, to make of them a revelation of truth and life.

Because of this ongoing hermeneutic function of the Spirit within the Church, the words attributed to Jesus in the Gospels are to be received as authoritative, whether they derive from Jesus' own teaching during the course of his public ministry, *or represent the words of the risen and glorified Lord, conveyed to the ecclesial community by the Holy Spirit after Pentecost.* This is a point of greatest importance. Nonetheless, the fact that it presupposes the activity of Christ within the world *after his ascension*—an activity which is empirically unverifiable—means that purely scientific approaches to biblical interpretation will consider it inadmissible. Exegesis which is bound by the perspective of the natural sciences can view as "authentic" only those statements that Jesus actually spoke during the period of his earthly life, prior to his crucifixion. Yet as modern scholars, including members of the Jesus Seminar, have so adroitly shown, determining with any degree of certainty whether a specific teaching attributed to Jesus was actually spoken by him, or represents instead a formulation by the "post-Easter Church," is in most cases impossible. We are left, in other words, with a stark alternative. Statements attributed to Jesus by the Gospels either originated with him during the course of his earthly ministry (and these represent a small fraction of the total), or else they derive from the theological reflection of the Gospel authors and others within the early Church. In the former case, they can be considered "authentic" insofar as they go back more or less intact to Jesus himself.[5] In the latter case they are to be read simply as theological reflection on the message of Jesus, rather than as actual elements of that message.

From an Orthodox—and biblical—perspective, there is nevertheless another way of looking at the question of "authenticity." The experience of Christian people from the beginning confirms that after his resurrection, Jesus continues to "speak" to the Church through the voice of the Spirit, who dwells within the community of faith (Jn 16:13; cf. Rev 2:7).[6] This is what makes of Tradition a *living* reality and not simply a collection of archives. During the first and second Christian generations, the authors of the canonical Gospels drew upon their own memory and the memory of their respective communities to produce their writings. That memory—preserved by the

5   Taking into account, of course, the fact that any Gospel statement uttered by Jesus was passed through the filter of translation from Aramaic into Greek; and any translation is inevitably a paraphrase rather than an exact reproduction of the words originally spoken.

6   In Orthodox worship this experience of the continuing presence of Christ within the Church is given particular expression by the Kontakion of the feast of the Ascension: "When Thou didst fulfill the dispensation for our sake, and unite earth to heaven, Thou didst ascend in glory, O Christ our God, not being parted from those who love Thee, but remaining with them and crying: I am with you and no one will be against you!"

Holy Spirit and transmitted in both oral and written form—included actual teachings of Jesus and various accounts of his activity. It also included theological reflection on the meaning of those teachings and events. The way in which the Gospel authors themselves interpreted that traditional material—how they translated, reshaped and amplified Jesus' actual words, and how they recounted and recast events of his earthly ministry—was likewise guided or "inspired" by the Spirit of Truth. On the one hand, the Spirit brings to remembrance within the Church all (*panta*) that Jesus had taught prior to his passion and death, meaning the message of salvation insofar as the disciples were able to receive it (Jn 14:26; 16:12). On the other hand, the Spirit speaks a fullness of truth (*alêtheia pasê*) that Jesus could not convey before his death and resurrection. This fullness that the Spirit speaks is nothing other than *the words of the risen, ascended and glorified Christ* (Jn 16:13-15). This is the point expressed by our opening quotation:

"I have yet many things to say to you, but you cannot bear them now," Jesus declares to his disciples in the Upper Room. "When the Spirit of Truth comes, he will guide you into all the truth; for he will not speak on his own authority, but whatever he hears he will speak... He will take what is mine and declare it to you" (Jn 16:12-15).

The crucial matter, then, is not the *historical* question: Which words did Jesus actually speak prior to his crucifixion? The crucial matter is rather the *canonical authority* invested in the entire biblical witness by God himself. For even among the *ipsissima verba Jesu*, the words Jesus actually spoke during his earthly ministry, the biblical authors were selective, guided in their choice by both the needs of local communities and the living memory of the Church. And we take it as an article of faith that the process of selecting and recasting those teachings, to provide the basis for the apostolic writings, was an *inspired* process, one guided precisely by the risen Lord acting through the Spirit of Truth.

A quest for the *ipsissima verba Jesu*, as we should have learned with the original "Quest for the Historical Jesus," is ultimately fruitless. It may be of interest from a strictly historical point of view, but it has no bearing on the matter of salvation. Whether spoken before his crucifixion or after his resurrection and exaltation, the words of Jesus are authoritative—they are words of eternal life—only because they are invested with saving power by God himself. In other words, neither their authority nor their saving power depends on their historicity—i.e., whether Jesus actually pronounced them prior to his crucifixion. They depend, rather, on their *canonicity*, their divinely established normative character.

Those associated with the Jesus Seminar would certainly reject this line of reasoning as "precritical," meaning basically "fundamentalist." But such an approach is based not only on venerable patristic tradition. It is confirmed repeatedly in the experience of the worshiping Church, where the authority of the canonical Word is made known by the living presence of the eternal Word himself. From this perspective, the Jesus Seminar appears to be merely an extreme example of a commonplace tendency in the field of biblical studies: to serve the interests of scientific inquiry rather than the purpose of God for the world's salvation.[7]

In every confessional tradition it is necessary to redress an imbalance while avoiding a pitfall. The imbalance is caused by unilaterally embracing systems of text analysis that fragment the biblical witness into objective, scientifically observable data devoid of revelatory value. The pitfall is the opposite extreme represented by fundamentalism or a naive literalism. This involves the rejection of all critical methodology, in a well-meaning but misguided attempt to preserve the text in conformity with some dogmatic presupposition foreign to it, such as verbal inerrancy.

Neither of these extremes does justice to the Scriptures, because neither appreciates the dynamic, Spirit-filled quality of God's Word. The Bible is a living book as well as a book about life. If it is read appropriately, it can become in Christian experience a vehicle for conveying life-giving knowledge of God. Yet through the working of the Holy Spirit in the interplay between text and reader, it can become as well a medium for *communion* with the God who reveals himself in and through it.

4. Typology in the Work of Interpretation

To draw together the issues we have been discussing, we can ask the following questions. How, from an Orthodox perspective, does one read the Bible appropriately? What are the presuppositions that we bring to the text, in order to glean from it a saving, healing and life-giving "knowledge of God"?

Three of the most basic of those presuppositions hold (1) that God is absolutely sovereign over the entire cosmos, as its creator and sustainer as well as its redeemer; (2) that God governs all events in the course of human history, either by his "permissive will" that allows tragedy and destruction in a fallen world, or by his "intentional will" that initiates events which lead the world toward salvation and the faithful toward eternal life; and (3) that God

---

7   Because of the current influence of the Jesus Seminar in scholarly and popular literature, as well as in television and other media, we can only second the judgment of the eminent Jewish scholar Jacob Neusner, who declared that the Seminar represents "either the greatest scholarly hoax since the Piltdown Man or the utter bankruptcy of New Testament studies—I hope the former." Quoted in *Time Magazine* (Jan. 10, 1994) 39.

has ordered "salvation-history" in terms of "Promise" and "Fulfillment": that is, he has revealed his saving will—the divine economy—by means of the former Covenant established with Israel, and he works out that economy throughout the age of the Church.

Within the framework of salvation-history, select events that occur in the experience of a people, particularly the Hebrew people, constitute "types" (*typoi*) or prophetic figures of persons, events and institutions to come, that will be fulfilled in the messianic age. The relation between the two Testaments is a "typological" relationship, in which God's promises of salvation, expressed by events in Israel's history as well as by oracles of the prophets, will be fulfilled in the person of Jesus Christ and in the life of the Church. This means that the Old Testament and the New Testament bear mutual witness to one another, and therefore they can only be properly interpreted *reciprocally*. Although the Old Testament still constitutes "the Hebrew Scriptures," it is in reality the first panel of a diptych, the whole of which reveals God's creative and redemptive activity in the person of his Son, Jesus Christ. The exegetical method developed by the Church Fathers to accomplish this interpretive task—which sees the Old Testament as a prefiguration or prophetic image of the New Testament—is therefore the method of *typology*. Today this is a highly disparaged and much misunderstood approach to biblical interpretation, and we need to look at it somewhat more closely if we are to rediscover its value as a heuristic tool.

The Old and New Testaments represent a *unified* witness to salvation-history. The relation between the two Testaments is that of Promise and Fulfillment. An inner, organic unity exists between the two, such that key persons and events of the Old Covenant find their ultimate meaning in those of the New. This relationship of Promise to Fulfillment, inherent in the historical process itself, can be described as a relation of type to antitype, or, in the vertical perspective of Hebrews and the Johannine writings, of type to archetype. To interpret the Old Testament in the light of the Gospel, then, the Orthodox exegete will have recourse to typology as one indispensable approach among others such as form and narrative criticism.

The unity between the Old and the New Testaments is grounded in the Church's perception of both the historical and the symbolic links that exist between them.[8] A distinction is usually made between two methods of

---

8 "Symbolic" (*symbolikôs*) is used here in the sense of "representation": a particular reality denotes or represents another image, often one which is eschatological or transcendent. As we shall see in the next section, the symbol is not necessarily separated from its referent by extension through time (i.e., "historically"); the supersensible referent can coincide with its visible representation. Cf. 1 Cor 10:4 and Justin, *Dial.* 86.3 (*PG* 6.681A).

deciphering those links: allegory and typology. It is usually assumed that typology stresses the connections between actual persons, events, places and institutions of the Old Testament, and parallel realities in the New Testament which complete or fulfill them. Thus Moses and Melchizedek are seen to be types or prophetic images of Christ, the true Lawgiver and High Priest. The manna in the wilderness is interpreted as a typological image of the Lord's Supper or eucharist. The Temple of the Old Covenant is seen to prefigure the Church of the New Covenant, and so on. Allegory, on the other hand, is usually defined as a quest for the "hidden" or symbolic meaning of a given Old Testament narrative, a meaning considered to be higher, fuller or more spiritual than the meaning discerned by typology. The focus of allegorical exegesis is not on historical events as such, but on the underlying spiritual meaning concealed in the *words* that speak of that event.

If typology, rather than allegory, has prevailed in Orthodox hermeneutics, it is because of the radically de-historicizing tendencies of the allegorical method as it was developed by Clement, Origen, Didymus the Blind and other representatives of the exegetical school of Alexandria during the third and fourth centuries. Interpreters of the rival school of Antioch—especially Diodore of Tarsus, Theodore of Mopsuestia, Theodoret of Cyrus, and John Chrysostom—insisted that the ultimate meaning of any event or reality must be grounded in the event itself, that is, grounded *in history*. Their quest was for what they termed *theôria*, an inspired vision of divine truth. This concern led them to identify not two senses, but rather a *double sense* within events of the Old Covenant, a sense or meaning which is both literal (i.e., historical) and spiritual. Those events or realities, through the work of God, point forward to and are fulfilled by corresponding events or realities in the New Covenant. Similarly, New Testament images can be interpreted as prototypes of transcendent, heavenly archetypes: e.g., the Church that points forward to and is fulfilled by the Kingdom of God, or the eucharist that points forward to and is fulfilled by the eschatological banquet.

With regard to Antiochene typology, the unilateral movement from past to future or from earth to heaven represents only part of the story. Most importantly, it must be understood that typology involves a *double movement*: from past to future, but also from the future to the past. That is, within the type the antitype or archetype is already proleptically present, present by anticipation, as in the formula "already but not yet (in fullness)." Therefore the eternal Logos appears already in the Old Covenant, not only as the agent of creation (Gen 1:1ff; Jn 1:3; Col 1:16; Heb 1:2), but as the divine presence who guides and sustains the covenant people. Accordingly, the Church Fathers insisted that every theophany, every divine manifestation, in the Old Testament is to be understood as a theophany of God the Son rather than of God the Father. The clearest New Testament example of this way of thinking is provided by St Paul in 1 Corinthians 10. Speaking of the rock that provided water for the Israelites during their wanderings in the wilderness, Paul declares: "and the rock was Christ!" The Son of God, in other words, was present and active in the rock, as he was in the person of Moses. The rock is a type of Christ; yet Paul's conviction is that *the type already contains and manifests the antitype.*

This means that the perspective of typology is that of an authentic salvation history. Events of the past are fulfilled by future realities; but that future or eschatological fulfillment is already manifest in the event itself. This is particularly evident in the experience of the Church. Already we live in the "eschaton," the "last days" of the New Creation; already we participate in the Kingdom and its festal joy, through eucharistic celebration; already death has been overthrown and we are given life, through the resurrection from the dead of the Author of life.

To perceive connections such as these, however, involves the interpreter in more than just an awareness of the possible links that exist between realities of the Old Testament and their corresponding antitypes in the New Testament. A spiritual vision, a God-given *theôria*, is crucial as well. It is this vision that unites typology and a certain allegorical perspective in a single hermeneutic program. We can no more hold to the radically de-historicizing aspects of allegory than could the Fathers of Antioch. There is, however, a valid and useful aspect to allegory, insofar as it perceives in the type a fullness of meaning that the biblical author could not see. The Evangelist John declares that Isaiah "saw" the glory of Jesus and spoke of him (Jn 12:41). But this means, of course, that Isaiah's prophecy pointed toward a coming messianic figure. Only from the perspective of the Church, the eschatological community of faith, can we declare that the one to whom Isaiah pointed was in fact Jesus of Nazareth. This messianic confession is based on the *typological* link between Isaiah's hope and the fulfillment of that hope in the Church's experience of Jesus. Yet that link also depends on what is properly an *allegorical* interpretation of the messianic type. To identify either the Emmanuel born of a virgin (Isa 7:14) or the Suffering Servant (Isa 52-53) with the person of Jesus requires an insight into the "hidden" sense of the text, a meaning that was not apparent to the prophet himself, or of which he, at the very most, was only dimly aware. That meaning becomes apparent *only through the inspirational activity of the Spirit within the Church,* who provides to eyes of faith an authentic *theôria,* a vision of divinely established truth or reality.

5. The Type as Both Event and Interpretation

Recent studies have modified the traditional picture of typology and allegory in significant ways. Frances Young, for example, argues that ancient exegetes did not make any sharp distinction between the two exegetical methods, and that typology as such is "a modern construct."[9] While this is something of an overstatement,[10] her understanding of biblical types is thoroughly to the point. "The word *typos*," she holds, "may be used for any 'model' or 'pattern' or 'parable' foreshadowing its fulfillment, whether an event or an oft-repeated ritual. It is not its character as historical event which makes a 'type'; what matters is its mimetic [i.e., representational] quality."[11] This means that typology functions less diachronically than synchronically. The type-antitype relationship is not primarily dependent on an historical extension through time, from past to future. Rather, the type contains a "mimetic impress" or representational quality that comes to expression through the biblical narrative, such that the antitype is already reflected by or "contained in" the type. The Promise proleptically contains its own Fulfillment, since the type bears "the 'impress' of eternal truth."[12]

This is not a new concept; in fact it goes back at least to Diodore of Tarsus. Ultimately, this perspective is rooted in St Paul's conviction concerning the presence of Christ in the Old Testament (1 Cor 10:4). Frances Young's contribution is of particular importance, however, for its clarification of the "simultaneity" characteristic of types: they transcend purely linear, historical progression (past "promise" to future "fulfillment") and reflect rather what Sebastian Brock calls a-temporal "sacred" or "liturgical" time. Within that transcendent time-frame, the type takes on a symbolic, revelatory quality

9 F. Young, *Biblical Exegesis and the Formation of Christian Culture* (Cambridge, England: University Press, 1997), 152. This is an important study that provides a fresh and highly valuable analysis of patristic exegesis.

10 The term "typology" may well have arisen in the nineteenth-century, but the distinction between typological and allegorical exegesis, as we have seen, was well known to the early Church Fathers. The Alexandrians made conscious use of allegorical method, following a venerable tradition of which the Jew Philo was one of the most notable representatives; the Antiochene Fathers, and particularly Diodore of Tarsus, employed typology and produced now lost works on the subject. Prof. Young points out quite correctly, however, that modern scholarship has approached the matter from the perspective of nineteenth-century historiography, and that the ancient exegetes made no sharp distinction between the two as exegetical methods. The Antiochenes, esp. Theodore of Mopsuestia, decried what they considered to be the excesses of allegory among the Alexandrians; yet their use of typology frequently veered off into what today we would consider to be allegorical interpretation.

11 Young, 153.

12 Young, 157.

that comes to expression less through the historical event than through the narrative or story that recounts that event; that is, through the *text of Scripture*. Therefore it can be argued that typology, like allegory, finds ultimate meaning less in historical events than in the biblical witness to them.

Nevertheless, it is essential that we not sever the historical roots of typology. Revelation necessarily occurs within the domain of what we call "history," and it does so through the medium of historical realities: events, persons, places, institutions, rituals. Those realities may not be objectively verifiable; they may even be essentially symbolic or parabolic (e.g., the etiological myths of Gen 1-11; the story of Jonah). They are not for that reason any less "real" than events of our immediate experience. Insofar as they exist in the *divinely inspired religious consciousness* of the people of God, they convey revealed truth and serve God's purposes for their salvation, even if the stories that convey them can be properly labeled myth, legend, or even metaphor.

The point is that behind the biblical narratives there is ultimate reality, ultimate truth, that at one point in history was revealed within the framework of objectively determinable human experience. For example, whatever "really happened" in Egypt at the time of the Exodus, by God's intervention in human affairs his chosen people were "actually," "historically," liberated from the yoke of bondage, made their pilgrimage through the desert wilderness (led, we would say, by Moses or by someone of the same name), and settled in the land God had promised them.

This foundational event in Israel's experience, however, also possesses transcendent, eschatological significance that was hidden to the Hebrews but revealed in the person and work of Jesus Christ. The Exodus is a type—a symbolic image, rooted in history yet transcending the dimensions of time and space—that points forward to and is fulfilled by the death and resurrection of the Son of God; just as his "exodus" (cf. Lk 9:31, *exodon*) is a typological prefiguration of the "general resurrection": the end-time liberation of the members of his Body from the bondage of sin and death. But whereas the Hebrew Exodus, as a revelatory symbol of the victory to come, *prophetically announces* ultimate liberation through Christ, Christ's own death and resurrection actually *accomplish* that liberation. The antitype does not merely repeat the type in a different form; it *fulfills* it.

The historicity of type and antitype, however, are of two different orders. The antitype (in this case, Christ's death and resurrection) proleptically infuses the type (the Hebrew Exodus) with ultimate meaning that will be fully revealed only in the experience of the women and the disciples through Christ's resurrectional appearances and in their communion with him as the ascended and glorified Lord. As *typos*, the Exodus thus contains the "impress" or symbolic significance brought to fulfillment by Christ's victory over death. But whereas the antitype is necessarily an objective, concrete reality within the domain of human experience—and is consequently a historically determinable "fact"—the type need not possess the same degree of reality or verifiability; it does not necessarily possess the same degree of historicity. For the significance of the type lies in its *symbolic quality* and in the way that quality is *interpreted* in the experience of Israel and the Church.

To the people who "went out from Egypt," the ultimate significance of the Exodus was barely adumbrated by the actual events, whatever those may have been. What is clear is the fact that the people experienced liberation through a series of events which they would later remember, recount and celebrate. For later generations of Hebrews, as for early Christians, the significance of the Exodus lay in their "memory" of it; that is, *in the ongoing recitation and interpretation of the events* rather than in the events themselves. In this way—by virtue of its recitation, interpretation and celebration—the Exodus, through the ages, has been continually experienced and reactualized. Once again, meaning—and therefore revelation—lies less in the event than in the text, the interpretive witness to the event.

Whatever "really happened" at the time the people left Egypt, therefore, does not constitute the essence of the type. The true essence of the type is the *interpretation* of those events—elaboration of their "spiritual significance"—that shaped the religious consciousness of the people. This is evident from a reading of Psalms 104(105) and 105(106) which, like Ps 77(78), recount God's saving acts on behalf of rebellious Israel. Here the Exodus is presented as a type of the liberation for which the psalmist prays in the framework of his present experience. "*Both we and our fathers* have sinned...Our fathers, when they were in Egypt, did not consider Thy wonderful works...Yet He saved them for His name's sake...He caused them to be pitied by all those who held them captive" (Ps 105/106). This recital of God's faithfulness towards his sinful and rebellious people then concludes with a cry that focuses attention on the *present:* "Save us, O Lord our God, and gather us from among the nations, that we may give thanks to Thy holy name and glory in Thy praise!"

This interpretation of the historical events surrounding the Exodus—whatever those events may "really" have been—constitutes what early followers of Jesus saw to be the prophetic announcement or type of his own death and resurrection. The crucial matter, once again, is not the historical events in themselves, for these theoretically could have been interpreted, and therefore transmitted, in very different ways, ways that would have no correspondence whatever with the "Christ-event." What remains crucial in the Old Testament witness is the *scriptural interpretation* of events in Israel's history that serve as types of realities to come. Accordingly, the author of Hebrews draws on an interpretation of the Exodus provided by the psalmist (Ps 94/95:7-11), in order to present Jesus as the antitype of the faithful Moses, and the Christian people as those in whom the promises made to Israel can be fulfilled (Heb 3-4). What matters here is not the events as such, but the interpretation of those events by the psalmist, speaking in the name of Israel.

The type, then, consists of *interpreted events* whose historicity is of secondary importance. Since the apostolic and patristic writers were convinced that "all Scripture is inspired by God," it was not at all important that the events *per se* be objectively, scientifically verifiable. Yet this should not be construed to imply that "history doesn't matter," that it is immaterial whether the Exodus occurred or not. To the mind of the psalmist as much as to that of the apostles, whatever actually happened in Egypt during the thirteenth century B.C. did in fact lead to Israel's liberation and its constitution as the Lord's chosen people. While the type is interpretation, it is interpretation of God's actual, *historical* intervention in human affairs. The concept of "type," therefore needs to be broadened. It needs to embrace both the concrete, objective reality of God's saving activity within the sphere of human existence—i.e., the salvation event—and the *interpretation* of that event which becomes an element of Tradition in the form of Old Testament writings.

The interpretation has priority over the event in the sense that the antitype is perceived only in light of that interpretation. Whatever the accuracy of the details concerning the "spiritual rock" which gave forth water in the wilderness (Ex 16; Num 20), Paul bases his argument in 1 Corinthians 10 on this scriptural witness plus a later midrash that pictured the rock actually following the Israelites in their desert wanderings. That account is surely legendary. Nevertheless, it served the apostle's purposes by showing that Christ was continually present among the Israelites throughout their wilderness experience as (to use Johannine language) an inexhaustible, supernatural source of "living water." Paul is not concerned with historical accuracy. That is not even an issue for him, since he takes the tradition he has received at face value. His real concern is with the *interpretation* of the rock, and that on two levels: first, as its significance is elaborated in Hebrew tradition, and second as it speaks typologically to the Corinthians. Just as God's blessings on Israel in the form of water and manna were no guarantee of the people's salvation, so partaking of baptism and the eucharist—Christian antitypes of the water and manna—are no guarantee that the Corinthians will be spared God's wrath if they continue to "indulge in immorality" (1 Cor 10:1-12).

To the mind of the apostle, as to the later patristic writers, however, both levels of interpretation—that of Hebrew tradition and Paul's own—presuppose the historicity or concrete, objective reality of the event in question. Details of the event might be lost and the entire story might be so overlaid with legendary material (all of which represents further interpretation) that it is impossible to recover "what actually happened." What is clear, however, is the fact that both apostolic and patristic authors were convinced that "something did happen," that God, or rather the eternal Son of God, was present and active in Israel's history, to guide the chosen people along the tortuous pathway toward their salvation. And he did so by means of what we would term historical realities: actual events within Israel's experience.

Insofar as they are recounted, those events are bound up with interpretation, just as all events are, including those of today. No one believes the evening TV news shows are purely objective; everyone acknowledges that they are as much entertainment as they are "news" of a factual nature. This does not mean that their stories are lies or sheer fabrications. They are interpretations of history, shaped in a particular way to evoke a particular response on the part of the televiewers. The same is true with Paul's interpretation of Old Testament events, just as it was with the interpretation the psalmists gave to the Exodus event. The response they attempted to evoke from their readers was perhaps different and more noble than the response sought by news anchors. But the dynamic is the same. Events of the past have meaning for us today only by virtue of the interpretation given to those events by our contemporaries. "How are they to hear without a preacher?" Paul asks rhetorically (Rom 10:14). "To hear" in this sense is to grasp the meaning of specific events *through the oral or written witness* and to interiorize that meaning to the point that it establishes faith and commitment.

The Exodus had meaning for Israelites and Jews thanks to the interpretation given it by the psalmists and other interpreters of tradition, just as it had meaning for early Christians by virtue of its interpretation at the hands of Paul and other apostolic authors. It is essential that the event have an objective, historical grounding; but the crucial matter remains the way that historical event—which is God's activity within the sphere of human existence—is explained and proclaimed.

Thus the Exodus—historically grounded both as event and as symbolic type—finds fulfillment in its antitype, the *historical events* of Christ's passion and his victory over death. Both must be rooted in history, that is, in experiential reality ("If Christ has not been raised...," Paul opines, 1 Cor 15:17). Yet both find their ultimate meaning *beyond* history: the Exodus in God's saving activity among his people Israel *and* in their hope of the messianic kingdom; and the Resurrection in Christ's victory over death *and* in the eternal life he offers to all believers, "to the Jew first, and also to the Gentile." *Although rooted in history (the domain of fallen human existence), the type transcends history, insofar as it bears the "impress" of its own eschatological fulfillment.*

The type, then, is "double." Necessarily grounded in historical reality—because that is where salvation must be worked out if it is to concern us as historical beings—the type bears and reveals eternal truth, eternal reality. Its uniqueness and significance lie in the fact that it serves as the intersection between life in this world and life in the Kingdom beyond. This is why Diodore had to insist that the type contains a *double sense*, at once historical and transcendent, literal and spiritual.

This entire approach, of course, appears to be totally at odds with modern methods of biblical interpretation that are based on historical or narrative criticism. The consensus among Orthodox exegetes, however, is that a proper typological approach can complement in a very fruitful way the more conventional scientific approaches.[13]

The relation between type and antitype is not susceptible of proof in the usual sense of the term. It can only be attested or witnessed to on the basis of ecclesial experience. The quest for a patristic *theôria*, undertaken with the tools of typology and allegory, is possible only because of a fundamental conviction that underlies it, a conviction firmly rooted in the biblical witness. It is the conviction that God himself orders and governs events and realities within history, and invests those events and realities with ultimate meaning. If St Paul's affirmation, "the rock was Christ," is not mere fantasizing—if it corresponds to a truth essential to faith because it is essential to salvation-history—this is because God is present and active within all of creation. It is he who determines the order and meaning of things. The task of the exegete is to discern that order and interpret its meaning, and to do so under the inspirational guidance of the Holy Spirit.

A further element of Orthodox biblical interpretation, which we shall return to in the next chapter, also seems to be at odds with the approach and attitude adopted by most interpreters of the Bible today. It concerns an inner

---

13 As Frances Young has insisted, typology should be understood as one aspect of a broader allegorical approach, properly understood. Allegory, of course, has to be applied to Jesus' parables and to similar forms. Modern exegetes do so instinctively, just as they often have recourse to the model of "promise" and "fulfillment." Most loathe to admit, nevertheless, that they employ methods usually classified as "pre-critical."

conviction that roots the work of exegesis firmly within the life of the ecclesial community. This is the conviction, shared universally by patristic tradition, that *one cannot interpret the Scriptures faithfully or accurately unless one lives in accordance with them.* In Johannine language, to know the truth we must walk in the truth. Or in the words of the apostle Paul, to have "the mind of Christ," we must live "in Christ."

The Scriptures, in other words, can only truly be understood and expounded *from within.* Their proper—that is, their true or "orthodox"—interpretation requires on the part of the interpreter a life of personal repentance, ascetic struggle and worship. Truly "to hear" the Word of God requires that one be in a living and life-sustaining communion with him who is the Word. This is the key to understanding Jesus' enigmatic statement in Mark 4:11, "To you has been given the secret of the Kingdom of God, but for those outside everything is in parables." To penetrate that secret, however, does not require some special gnosis, nor does it require special election in the sense of predestination. The *mysterion* or secret of the Kingdom is *offered to all* without exception, as the "living water" offered without price (Rev 22:17). To be received, it need merely be believed. Yet belief must be expressed by the whole of one's life: by repentance, prayer and works of love, and not merely by rational assent to certain doctrinal propositions.

All authentic interpretation of Scripture, then, will arise from the interaction between faith, love and prayer. These are gifts and fruits of the Spirit, bestowed upon the biblical interpreter, that can transform the work of exegesis from rational analysis into genuine *theology:* a living witness to the life-giving God.

2

Principles of Patristic Hermeneutics

From the perspective of the Orthodox Church, Holy Scripture is characterized by an absolute unity, integrity and truth.

With regard to its unity, Orthodox Tradition holds firmly to the view, discussed in chapter one, that the Old Testament, like the New Testament, is a "Christian book." The two Testaments constitute a *unified* witness to the divine Logos or eternal Word, who came into the world to work out the salvation of "the children of God" (Jn 1:12-13; 20:31). In addition, this witness and the inspiration that underlies it is understood to be *integral* or complete, insofar as every passage of Scripture reflects the same truth, and therefore every passage is capable of clarifying other passages that are more obscure. For example, St Paul's reflections on the saving work of Christ in Romans 5:9, "we are justified by his blood, therefore we shall be saved by him," can be used to clarify and amplify the affirmation in 1 John 1:7, "the blood of Jesus his Son cleanses us of all sin." Or the mysterious allusion in Isaiah 7:14 (a virgin will bear a child, Emmanuel) can be interpreted in the light of Matthew 1:23, where the Virgin Mary fulfills Isaiah's prophecy by bearing the eternal Son of God.

Every passage of the Old Testament as well as the New bears direct or indirect witness to the person and work of Jesus Christ, who is Truth itself in incarnate form ("I am the Way, the Truth and the Life," he declares, Jn 14:6). Therefore the biblical writings that bear a unique witness to that Truth constitute the "canon"—the norm or "rule of truth"—which serves as the indispensable basis of Christian doctrine and morality.

To Jesus and the apostles, "Holy Scripture" consisted of the Hebrew Bible, what we call "the Old Testament." In the perspective of the Church Fathers, the affirmation that the Old Testament is a "Christian book" is justified by the fact that they considered every theophany or manifestation of God in Israel's history to be not of God the Father but of God the *Son*, the Second Person of the Holy Trinity. In the Psalms they heard the voice of Christ (for example, Ps 21/22) as well as the voice of sinful humanity (Ps 50/51). The Law of Moses is perceived by the Church Fathers to be the foundation of the New Law given to the Christian community by Christ. Christ is thus the New Moses, who utters the great Sermon on the mountain that represents a new Mount Sinai. This is the New Law of the Kingdom, with its antitheses that proclaim a new morality and a new righteousness, greater than those of the Pharisees. (Recall the formula of the so-called "Matthean antitheses" that Jesus repeats so often: "You have heard it said... But I say to you..."). In the patristic perspective, the infant Emmanuel of Isaiah 7, the Suffering Servant of Isaiah 52-53, the innocent one who loves a prostitute (Hosea), and the effusion of the Spirit prophesied by Joel are all types (*typoi*) or figures that point forward to the coming in the flesh of the eternal Son of God, and when properly interpreted, they indicate the meaning of his person and the purpose of his earthly mission.

It is these relationships that lead us to affirm that the movement from the Old Testament to the New Testament is a movement from "promise" to "fulfillment," from the prophetic figure to its realization in the person of Christ. Recounting the history of the divine economy from Creation to Redemption (which is the New Creation), the Bible as a whole offers a unified, integral and true witness to the work of the Holy Trinity for the life and the salvation of God's world.

This patristic perspective concerning the unity of the two Testaments is grounded in the way the New Testament authors themselves interpreted the Old Testament books. That is, the hermeneutic principles or rules of interpretation developed by the Fathers of the Church represent an extension and development of certain methods of interpretation that the apostles used to understand and proclaim the messianic significance of the Law and the Prophets.

The apostolic authors searched through their Scriptures—the Old Testament—in order to find there various types or prophetic figures which they recognized to be realized or fulfilled in Jesus' person and ministry. In doing so, they merely elaborated on a procedure Jesus himself had employed. Jesus evoked certain images and certain titles, known in the Hebrew Scriptures and in the writings of intertestamental Judaism, in order to reveal the meaning of his life and work. He attributed to himself, for example, the title "Son of Man." This is an apocalyptic figure found in Daniel 7 and in pseudepigraphic writings such as Ethiopic Enoch (1 Enoch). "Son of Man" designates a heavenly being who was expected to come at the end of time, to judge the living and the dead, and to usher in the Kingdom of God. (It is only from the time of St Ignatius of Antioch [† c. 110] that the title Son of Man came to be used to designate Jesus' human nature). Yet as Jesus uses the title Son of Man in regard to himself, he infuses it with new meaning. Since the Aramaic *bar nasha* can mean simply a human being, the ambiguity inherent in the title allows Jesus to expand and deepen it, so that it alludes both to his heavenly origin and to his coming Passion (Jn 1:51; Mk 9:12).

According to the Gospel of John especially, Jesus also called himself the "Son of the Father." The evangelist Mark refers to him as Son of God, a quasi-messianic title originally attributed to the king of Israel, although it is not clear whether Jesus used the designation to refer to himself. Implicitly, Jesus did identify himself with the "Servant of the Lord," the *ebed Yahweh* of Isaiah 52-53, who would be humiliated to the point of death, taking upon himself the sins of God's chosen people. As the "Suffering Servant," Jesus the Innocent One would be justified by God (by the resurrection) and elevated into glory (Isa 52:13; 53:10-12; cf. Jn 12:32, an allusion to his elevation, but in a double sense: he is to be lifted up on the Cross, then raised into the glory of the Father). In order to reveal the meaning of his life and death in language and images familiar to his contemporaries, Jesus thus applied to himself various well-known Old Testament and intertestamental images and messianic titles. Thereby he affirmed that those images and titles found their ultimate fulfillment in his own life and saving work.

In similar fashion, the authors of the New Testament writings attributed to Jesus other Old Testament images and titles. Already in the semi-monastic community of Qumran, at least a century before Christ's birth, the enigmatic figure of Melchizedek (Gen 14) was considered to be of celestial origin. Because he appeared to have no human genealogy, king Melchizedek was conceived as the archetype of the messianic king (cf. Ps 109/110:4). The author of the Epistle to the Hebrews finds the fulfillment of this archetype in the person of Jesus, the eternal Son of God, who will be "a priest forever according to the order of Melchizedek" (Heb 5:10).

Other New Testament authors also attributed to Jesus images and titles drawn from the Old Testament and intertestamental Judaism. In each case, their intention was to proclaim that it is Jesus alone who fulfills the messianic prophecies. St Paul, for example, sees in Jesus Christ the incarnation of divine Wisdom. Already in the books of Proverbs and the Wisdom of Solomon the Wisdom figure was depicted as personified and preexistent, dwelling with God before the creation of the world. This same image very likely inspired the evangelist John in his depiction of Jesus Christ as the Logos or eternal Word of God.

Matthew presents Jesus as the fulfillment of a great number of Old Testament prophecies. His virginal birth fulfills the promise of Isaiah 7:14; his descent into Egypt and his return to Galilee confirm that it is he who constitutes the "true Israel"; and with the other evangelists, Matthew sees in Jesus' Passion the fulfillment of promises made by God to Israel throughout the course of the chosen people's history.

As for the apostle Paul, Christ is already present in the Old Testament, most strikingly in the form of the rock that served the people of Israel as a source of living water during their desert wanderings (1 Cor 10:1-4). In Galatians 4:21-31, the apostle uses a method he terms "allegorical" in order to identify Hagar with the Old Covenant and Sarah with the New Covenant. (In this passage Paul actually uses a form of typology, despite the fact that he refers to it as *allêgoroumena*, Gal 4:24).

Typology, the theme of "promise and fulfillment," and the appeal to ancient messianic titles all served the apostolic authors in their efforts to proclaim that God's promises to Israel and to the world are accomplished—they are fulfilled and elevated to still greater heights—by the saving mission of Jesus of Nazareth, the crucified and glorified Son of God. It is those authors who laid the foundation for the elaboration of various hermeneutic perspectives and procedures which were developed in later generations by the Fathers of the Church, both Latin and Greek.

Following in the footsteps of the apostolic authors, post-apostolic theologians continued to work out exegetical methods to discern and explicate the relation between Jesus and Old Testament tradition. These methods have been discussed in a number of recent works, and I do not want to repeat that information.[1] My aim here is much more modest: I would like simply to underscore several basic yet important *hermeneutic principles* which underlie and govern the exegetical work of the Holy Fathers.

What, then, are the various hermeneutic principles or presuppositions that patristic authors utilized in their attempts to interpret Scripture and to expound the "christological" meaning of the Old Testament?

The answer concerns less a systematic set of rules than a *spiritual perspective* referred to by the term *theôria*. *Theôria*, as we noted in the previous chapter, signifies an inspired vision or contemplation of divinely revealed Truth, granted both to the apostolic writer *and to future interpreters* by the Holy Spirit.

---

1   See esp. B. de Margerie, *An Introduction to the History of Exegesis, vol. I, The Greek Fathers* (Petersham, MA: Saint Bede's Publications, 1993); J. Breck, *The Power of the Word* (Crestwood, NY: St Vladimir's Seminary Press, 1986); and M. Simonetti, *Biblical Interpretation in the Early Church* (London: T&T Clark, 1994).

The patristic understanding of *theôria* is closely tied to a particular view of *inspiration*. We recall that biblical scholars of the fourth-century exegetical school at Antioch held that the events of Scripture contain a "double sense," both literal and spiritual. Each of these derives from divine inspiration, as the Spirit of God indwells and guides the sacred author in composing his work. The Antiochenes understood the literal sense to refer to the "intention of the Biblical author." This means the message the writer himself perceived through the inspirational activity of the Spirit and sought to communicate to his readers. The spiritual sense, on the other hand, referred to the Word which God speaks *through the written text* in each present moment, each new generation, of the Church's life. Yet the spiritual sense, for the Antiochene Fathers, remains firmly rooted in the events of history. Flowing out of the literal sense, the *sensus plenior* serves to reactualize at every new historical moment the salvific value of God's work in the past: among the people of Israel and, supremely, in the life, death and resurrection of Jesus Christ.

Pace Origen, the Antiochenes saw *every* scriptural passage as containing a double meaning, both literal and spiritual. The concept of *theôria* includes the inspired vision of the biblical author that led him to shape his witness as he did, in order to express its literal sense. But it also includes the inspired perception *of the later interpreter* concerning the inner meaning of Scripture that reveals both its literal and its spiritual sense. Thus by virtue of *theôria*, the prophets of Israel could see God at work in historical persons, institutions and events of their day, as he prepared his people for the coming of the Messiah. And New Testament authors could see in Jesus of Nazareth not merely a charismatic miracle-worker who survived crucifixion, but the resurrected and glorified Son of God.

In the perspective of John 14-16 and the Church Fathers, therefore, it is the Holy Spirit who preserves within the Church the truth and authority of Holy Tradition, including the witness of Scripture. Tradition, once again, should be understood as the "living memory of the Church." This is a memory which—through the Scriptures, the liturgy and the sacraments—has the effect of *reactualizing* in the midst of the ecclesial community the work of salvation accomplished by Jesus Christ. On the one hand, this living memory takes us back, by means of the scriptural witness, to the events of Jesus' life, death and resurrection. In the words of the Danish theologian Søren Kierkegaard, we thereby become "contemporaneous with Christ."[2] On the other hand, by means of the liturgy and sacraments, that memory makes those past events *present* in the experience of the Church. The crucifixion of

2 *Philosophical Fragments* (new English ed., Hong and Hong, vol. VII of "Kierkegaard's Writings," Princeton University Press.).

Christ becomes present for us today, as do his resurrection, his glorification and his sending of the Holy Spirit at Pentecost. This is why the Church can proclaim at the great feast of Easter or Holy Pascha, "*Today*" we have died with Christ and risen with him, to share already here and now in the eschatological future of his Kingdom.

> Yesterday I was buried with Thee, O Christ.
> Today I arise with Thee in Thy resurrection.
> Yesterday I was crucified with Thee.
> Glorify me with Thee, O Savior, in Thy Kingdom!
> (Paschal Matins, Ode 3)

The hermeneutic principles developed—or perhaps more accurately, *intuited*—by the Church Fathers are founded on this inspired, contemplative vision known as *theôria*. Consequently, these principles constitute an important part of Holy Tradition, for they, too, were formulated under the guidance of the Spirit of Truth. Their purpose is to provide the Church with an accurate and authoritative interpretation of the Scriptures, by which the Spirit can guide Christian people into the fullness of the truth which Christ himself embodies (Jn 16:13).

Drawing on our discussion in chapter one, we can reduce the most important presuppositions and principles of patristic exegesis to the following eight points.

1. The expression *Word of God* is used today, particularly in Protestant circles, to refer to the Bible and its exposition, especially in the form of preaching. To the Church Fathers, on the other hand, "the Word of God" refers in the first place to the eternal Logos, the God-Man who became incarnate as Jesus of Nazareth and is glorified in the Church as "one of the Holy Trinity." The Word of God, therefore, is ultimately a *person*, the second Person of the Trinity, who communicates his revelation to the world primarily through the canonical Scriptures. The expression "Word of God," thus refers to three distinct but intimately related realities: the Person of the divine Logos, the written witness *to* him in the form of the apostolic writings, and proclamation *of* him as an invitation to faith and life *in* him.

2. The Word of God in all its forms can be properly understood and interpreted only from a *trinitarian* perspective. The Father, the Son and the Spirit share a common will and activity in inspiring the composition and interpretation of biblical writings, just as they do in the work of creation and redemption. Through the apostolic witness, the Spirit reveals Jesus Christ to be the source of eternal truth and life. As the indwelling power of God within the Church, who inspires the Church's proclamation to the world, the Spirit leads us to faith in God the Son. And the Son in turn draws us into eternal

communion with God the Father. Yet there is reciprocity in this movement. For the Son also prays the Father to send the Spirit upon the body of believers in a continuing Pentecostal effusion, to strengthen, enlighten and sanctify them. Revelation proceeds *from* the Father *through* the Son and becomes intelligible *in* the Holy Spirit, while our response of receptivity, grounded in faith, proceeds *in* and *from* the Spirit, *through* the Son, *to* the Father. The gospel proclamation becomes "the power of God for salvation" (Rom 1:16), therefore, only through the concerted economy of the Son and the Spirit, whom St Irenaeus described as "the two hands of the Father."

3. This means that the Word of God in the form of Scripture or proclamation, like the Incarnate Logos himself, must be understood as a *theandric* or divine-human reality. To the Orthodox mind, the Scriptures are God's Word to his human creatures, and not merely human words about God. Nevertheless, that Word is the product of a *synergy* or cooperation between God and his human agents. God did not dictate the biblical writings; he inspired sinful and limited human beings to compose them. Both the apostolic author and the later interpreter, *under the guidance of the Holy Spirit*, speak out of their respective historical, cultural and linguistic contexts. The Scriptures reflect this human aspect by the different perspectives represented by each of the four Gospels, by irreconcilable differences in chronology (for example, the date of the Last Supper or of the cleansing of the Temple), and by the fact that they contain at least one major teaching that the Church later rejected, namely the affirmation in Heb 6:4-6 that there is no forgiveness for sins committed after baptism.

These human elements that appear in the Scriptures make it clear that the Word of God must be *interpreted anew* in every generation of the Church's life. That does not mean that the teaching of Scripture changes. It means that the Spirit enlightens each new generation of Christian people, in the language and circumstances of their time, in order to guide them into "all the truth." Therefore Orthodox Christians pray before reading the Gospel at the Divine Liturgy: "Illumine our hearts, O Master who lovest mankind, with the pure light of Thy divine knowledge. Open the eyes of our mind to the understanding of Thy Gospel teachings." The words of the biblical writings are often obscure and difficult to understand. Yet they contain the fullness of truth. It is the work of the Holy Spirit, in conjunction with the apostolic authors and later interpreters in the Church, to illumine that truth and to make it accessible to everyone at every time in history.

4. The *Church* is the proper locus for the interpretation as well as for the proclamation and liturgical celebration of the Word of God. Exegesis is a function

of the worshiping, witnessing community of faith. While personal interpretations of Scripture are welcome and encouraged, those interpretations forfeit their claim to authority if they sever their connection with the ecclesial Body and its Tradition. This does not mean that the exegete's conclusions are predetermined by the doctrinal teachings of the Church. After all, those teachings themselves are the fruit of patristic exegesis. Nevertheless, Orthodox exegetes accept as integral to their calling the need to submit their reflections to the *phronêma ekklêsias*, the "mind of the Church." This implies that exegetes will conform their interpretation to the doctrinal and moral teachings of Holy Tradition, that they will assume their exegetical labors as a *diakonia* or service to the Church, and that they will carry them out in the interests of the Church and its mission within the world.

To be sure, this principle appeared far more evident to the Church Fathers than it does to most exegetes today. The language of theology, like that of liturgy, is ever expanding and developing. New discoveries in the field of literary criticism, but also in the realms of archaeology and other historical disciplines, often seem to call into question findings of earlier generations. It must be admitted, however, that those discoveries have never yet offered "proof" that undermines key elements of Christian dogma. Sociological studies of life in first-century Palestine may lead some interpreters to describe Jesus as nothing more than an itinerant prophet; modern embryology may to some minds offer decisive evidence against the possibility of a virgin birth ("Where did the other twenty-three chromosomes come from?"); and comparisons of Paul's letters with the various gospel accounts may lead some to the conclusion that Paul, and not Jesus, is the true founder of Christianity. Intellectual honesty, however, requires anyone to admit that the conclusions drawn on the basis of these kinds of scientific studies are subjective. They involve leaps of faith—or unfaith—insofar as the conclusions are not inherent in the discoveries themselves but are rational extrapolations based on those discoveries.

Science, like every other discipline (art, music, theology) operates within a limited sphere of reality. It can neither prove nor disprove *transcendent* realities, even when they interact with the physical world. Biblical images such as demons and angels are not subject to scientific inquiry, since the tools of science are simply not adapted to investigate their presence and activity. The same must be said for the presence and activity of God within the world and human experience. Nor are the tools of exegesis adequate to determine the truth or falsity of biblical claims regarding the person of Jesus: his divine origin, the redemptive value of his death, his resurrection, and so forth. Exegesis can help us to better grasp the literal sense of the text: the author's own understanding of his experience and the tradition he has received. But it cannot verify or refute that witness; it cannot pass judgment on the accuracy of its claims. Its verification depends on faith, which by definition is not susceptible to scientific proof.

Therefore the (Orthodox) exegete will perform his or her task within the limits of the discipline, then submit the results to the "mind of the Church," that is, to Holy Tradition. This is because we hold it as an article of faith (!) that Tradition offers the key to a fuller understanding of reality than do the empirical sciences. The exegete's task is not to break the hermeneutic circle, but to hold it intact. This can be done by taking the fruit of one's exegetical labors and preserving only what conforms to the mind or spirit of the Church as expressed in those teachings which the Church itself affirms to be authoritative and therefore *true*. To accept such a procedure, however, requires a further leap of faith: the conviction that our exegetical labor, like all genuine biblical interpretation, is guided and inspired by the Spirit of Truth.

5. If the exegete is called to submit ultimately to the "mind of the Church," it is because of the relationship that exists between *Scripture* and *Tradition*. The two, Scripture and Tradition, are to be understood neither as complementary nor as conflicting authorities. While it rejects the notion of scriptural *autarkeia* or "self-sufficiency" expressed in the phrase *sola scriptura*, Orthodoxy fully accepts the *canonical* or normative quality of Scripture for deciding matters of belief and behavior.

On the other hand, it recognizes that Scripture is a product or fruit of Tradition. The biblical witness has normative or canonical authority only insofar as it *receives* the gospel message, *interprets* it correctly, then *transmits* it so that others might *believe*. The clearest and most striking example of this point is given by the apostle Paul in 1 Cor 15:1-11. He, "the least of the apostles," received and transmitted through his preaching the witness that "Christ died for our sins in accordance with the Scriptures." It is on the basis of this proclamation, grounded in and faithfully reflecting the received message (*paradosis*), that the Corinthians came to believe in the gospel of the risen Christ. The parallelism established by the four chief verbs is significant: "I transmitted what I received...I preached and you believed." This is the dynamic that constitutes "living Tradition." Tradition is not merely a body of information passed on from one person to another; it always involves *interpretation* in the form of analysis (exegesis) and proclamation (preaching). Paul *receives* the gospel message, which he *believes* for his own salvation. Yet he also *interprets* and *transmits* that message in a new form, conforming it to the particular needs and receptive capacities of his audience. The verbs "transmit/deliver" (*paredôka*) and "preach/proclaim" (*kêryssomen*) express those actions that

transform Tradition from a body of historical data into a life-giving Word
which elicits the faith that leads to salvation.

6. The Old and New Testaments represent a unified witness to salvation-history. The relation between the two Testaments is that of *Promise and
Fulfillment*. An inner, organic unity exists between them, such that key persons
and events of the New Testament are foreshadowed by those of the Old, and
those of the Old Testament find their ultimate meaning in those of the New.
This relationship of Promise to Fulfillment is expressed concretely as a relation
of type to antitype or of type to archetype. To interpret the Old Testament in
the light of Christ, the Orthodox exegete, like the Church Fathers themselves,
will make use of *typology*. We discussed this method in chapter one, noting
many examples by which the New Testament fulfills the hopes and expecta-
tions of Israel. We also noted the emphasis laid by Antiochene exegetes on the
simultaneity which is characteristic of typology, insofar as the type "contains"
the antitype and the eschatological fulfillment is already "impressed" on the
original figure.[3] Typology—as a specific form of the overarching symbolic or
allegorical approach to Scripture—needs to be supplemented by other methods, including historical, archaeological and linguistic research, literary analysis, and so forth. Yet typology remains a key element in any quest to discern the
pattern of God's activity within history and the relation between the two Cove-
nants: God with Israel and Christ with the Church.

7. A further principle developed by the Holy Fathers was inherited directly
from the Jewish Rabbis. It was known by Jesus and used by him as a basic tool
for interpreting the Scriptures as they relate to himself and his work. This is
the principle known today as *exegetical reciprocity*. By this we mean that all of
Scripture is uniformly and integrally inspired, in the sense described at the
beginning of this chapter. Thus Jesus can apply to himself various messianic
titles from the Old Testament. And he can confound the reasoning of the
Pharisees by arguing—on the basis of Psalm 109/110—that the true Messiah
is the Lord and Son of God rather than (merely) the son of David (Mt
22:41-46). Another example would be Revelation 12, which depicts a woman
clothed with the sun, who bears a son whose existence is threatened by the
dragon with seven heads and ten horns. Modern criticism would tend to see
in the woman an image of the Church and in the dragon a figure of Rome,

---

3   We refer again in this regard to the work of Frances Young, *Biblical Exegesis and the Forma-
    tion of Christian Culture, op. cit.* See as well the perceptive analysis of Young and others
    made by Xenia Werner in her unpublished Master's thesis, *Marian Typology: An Analysis of
    Hymnography and Iconography*, (St Vladimir's Orthodox Theological Seminary, May
    1999), esp. part I.

with her seven hills, who persecutes the Church. Referring to passages such as the so-called "proto-gospel" of Genesis 3:15, on the other hand, patristic authors would tend rather to see the woman as an image of the Virgin Mary, who gives birth to the Messiah, while the dragon corresponds to Satan and his persecution both of Christ and the Church.

Since all of Scripture is uniformly inspired, and all of it points to Christ, then any passage can be interpreted so as to reveal its messianic message. Furthermore, any obscure passage can be enlightened and clarified by any other passage that is more clear. Hence there is "reciprocity" between all biblical statements, irrespective of who the author of those statements was or what the original, literal sense of those statements might have been.

8. Finally, we need to consider the most basic and essential pathway that leads from the literal sense to the spiritual sense, or *sensus plenior*. This leads us back to the theme of *theôria*, the contemplative vision of divine truth and reality communicated by the inspirational activity of the Holy Spirit. In the experience of the Church Fathers, God reveals himself most fully, not through rational analysis of scriptural texts, but through prayer that occurs in the depths of the heart. Prayer is the fruit of the Spirit who dwells within the temple of the heart, understood in biblical tradition as the center of thought as well as of emotion. Prayer is thus a divine operation, the work of God within us. In prayer, God speaks to God: the Holy Spirit addresses the Father, to provide our intercessions, supplications and praise with substance and authority. To pray "in Spirit and in Truth" (Jn 4:23) is to pray to the Father in the power of the Holy Spirit, through him who is the Truth, Jesus Christ the eternal Son of God.

The same must be said for the work of biblical interpretation. It, too, requires a synergy or cooperation between ourselves and the triune God. And ultimately, it too is the fruit of the Spirit, who dwells within us. To paraphrase the apostle Paul, we might say: "We do not know how to read the Bible as we ought" (cf. Rom 8:26). That is, in our fallen, sinful state we can have access through reason to the literal sense of a text: its original meaning in the mind of the author and its recipients. The work of translating that message into God's Word for us today, however, is accomplished by God himself. In the Person of the Holy Spirit, God dwells within the human mind and heart, as he dwells within the universal community of the Church. He speaks to ears that are willing to hear, as he spoke to the prophets of old. Like the prophets, we "hear" that word, we take it into ourselves, and we meditate upon it, in order to draw out its particular meaning for us in our present day and circumstances.[4] Then we articulate that word to others, in

---

4 For a particularly interesting discussion of the way inspiration operates in the experience of the prophets, both ancient and contemporary, see J. Lindblom, *Prophecy in Ancient Israel*

the form of sermons, meditations, and perhaps biblical commentaries. Anyone can grasp the literal sense of a text, provided they have the proper literary tools and the proper training. To make the pilgrimage from the literal sense to the "fuller sense," the *sensus plenior*, however, requires that we submit ourselves, in humility and ascetic struggle, to the guiding influence of the Spirit of Truth. St John Chrysostom and other Church Fathers insisted that no one can truly interpret Scripture who does not willingly submit to it. We cannot know the Truth if we do not humble ourselves and open ourselves before its power, beauty and majesty. The only way we can "know the Truth" is to seek it, to love it, and to live as thoroughly and faithfully as we can in conformity with it.

A final hermeneutic principle or presupposition adopted by the Holy Fathers, then, is the need for *ascetic effort*, for an ongoing inner struggle, to attain an attitude of repentance and humble obedience before God. This is indispensable if we are to *hear* God's Word and to acquire the ability to interpret it fully and properly. For those who accept such a struggle, who willingly engage in spiritual warfare, the difficult task of interpreting and proclaiming the Word of God can be transformed into an act of love and a service of praise.

These hermeneutic principles or perspectives adopted by patristic authors point to a basic and important conclusion. To recover the richness and authority accorded it by the Holy Fathers, biblical interpretation needs once again to take its proper place as a *function of the liturgical life of the Church*. In order for this to happen, however, those who interpret the Scriptures—lay persons, pastors and professional exegetes—need to acquire, like the Church Fathers themselves, a profound appreciation for both the *doxological quality* and the *diaconal focus* of their task. For the ultimate purpose of biblical interpretation is to serve both as a sacrifice offered to the praise and glory of God, and as a faithful witness to God's self-revelation, offered for the salvation of his people.

(Oxford: Blackwell, 1962). See as well Paul J. Achtemeier, *The Inspiration of Scripture* (Philadelphia: Westminster, 1980); and J. Breck, *Spirit of Truth: The Origins of Johannine Pneumatology* (Crestwood, NY: St Vladimir's Seminary Press, 1991), esp. ch. 2.

3

Examples of Patristic Exegesis

In the last chapter we discussed eight principles or presuppositions that govern a patristic approach to the interpretation of Holy Scripture. It would be worthwhile rephrasing them in summary form before we move on to specific examples that serve to illustrate them.

(1) The ultimate referent of the expression "Word of God" is neither the biblical text nor its exposition; it is the Person of the eternal Logos, the Second Person of the Holy Trinity.

(2) Therefore Scripture needs to be understood from a trinitarian perspective: inspired by the Spirit, Scripture reveals the person and work of the Son of God, whose mission in turn is to reveal to us the "face" of God the Father and to open the way towards our eternal communion with him.

(3) The witness of Scripture is the fruit of a *synergy* or cooperation between God and the human author. As a *theandric* or divine-human reality, Scripture contains elements that are historically, culturally and linguistically conditioned. Consequently, it must be reinterpreted in every new generation of the Church's life, under the inspirational guidance of the Holy Spirit.

(4) The Word of God serves God's purpose for the salvation of the world. This means that its interpretation is properly *ecclesial*, serving the mission of the Church. Exegesis has as its ultimate end to communicate saving knowledge of God; accordingly, the purpose of exegesis is essentially *soteriological.*

(5) Regarding the relationship between the Bible and Tradition, the Church holds that the New Testament writings are normative elements of Holy Tradition. This Tradition, which includes both received witness (*paradosis*) and the personal contribution of the author, provided the content of those writings. Scripture, inspired and given authority by the Holy Spirit, is the canon or norm by which all true Tradition is determined. All Tradition is not contained in Scripture, but nothing constitutes authentic Tradition that contradicts the canonical Scriptures or is incompatible with them.

(6) The relation between the Old Testament and the New Testament is one of Promise to Fulfillment. Historical events and prophetic words in Israel's

experience are figures or types of realities fulfilled in the New Covenant of Jesus Christ. Therefore the Old Testament is to be interpreted *typologically*. Authentic typology involves a double movement: from past to future (from type to antitype), but also from the future to the past (the antitype is proleptically present in the type). Therefore the Fathers will affirm that the type is characterized by a "double sense," both literal and spiritual, in that it already contains and to some degree manifests or reveals its eschatological fulfillment.

(7) Scripture, according to the patristic vision, is uniformly and integrally inspired by the Holy Spirit. Therefore it can be interpreted according to the rule of exegetical reciprocity. This holds that any obscure biblical passage can be interpreted in light of another biblical passage which is more clear, irrespective of the author, date of composition or historical circumstances represented by the writing(s) in question.

(8) Finally, to interpret Scripture properly and to discern within it its depths of truth, it is necessary for the exegete to interpret it *from within*. Scripture, in other words, prescribes a way of life—"Christ in us," in the apostle's terms. This means life lived in conformity with the Scriptures: with their moral injunctions, but also with their spiritual vision. We cannot truly understand the Word of God, the Holy Fathers insist, unless we make that Word our own and commit ourselves to it with faith and with love.

The first Christian exegetes were the apostolic writers themselves. It is they who, taking the lead from their Master, adopted and modified Rabbinic methods of interpretation so as to read the Old Testament in the light of the person and work of Jesus Christ. Thereby they laid the foundation for all subsequent exegesis within the Church. In what follows we want to consider several examples of the way early Christian thinkers interpreted the Holy Scriptures, noting in particular their use of typology as a key to unlocking the spiritual meaning of the Old Testament. These examples are not intended to represent the full range of patristic interpretation, nor is the analysis in any way exhaustive. Our purpose is simply to provide a few examples of the various approaches to biblical interpretation adopted by early Christian exegetes, and to demonstrate how each of them stands in continuity with interpretive methods used by Christ himself and the authors of the canonical books.

As we move from biblical times into the second and third Christian generations, we find some of the most interesting and useful examples of exegetical method in authors such as St Justin the Martyr and St Irenaeus of Lyons. These two in particular form a bridge between the exegetical work of the apostles and that of the major biblical theologians of the later patristic period such as Origen, John Chrysostom and Cyril of Alexandria.

The philosopher *Justin*, arguably the greatest of Greek Christian apologists, was beheaded in Rome around the year 165. Of his many and varied writings, only two apologies and the *Dialogue with the Jew Trypho* survive in complete form. It is this last work that provides us with the most insight into Justin's approach to Scripture.

Justin's use of typology is particularly interesting in his elucidation of the story of Noah and the Flood. He sees this catastrophic event in Israel's prehistory as foreshadowing both the final judgment and the person of Christ, who constitutes a "new Noah."

> At the flood, the mystery of the world's salvation was at work. The just man Noah, together with the other flood personages, namely, his wife, his three sons and their wives, made eight in number thereby symbolizing the eighth day on which our Christ was raised from the dead, that day being always implicitly the first. Christ, the first-born of all creation, has become in a new sense the head of another race, regenerated by Him, through water, through faith, and through the wood which contained the mystery of the cross, just as Noah was saved through the wood of the Ark, carried by the waters of the flood... And I mean here that those who receive preparation through water, faith, and wood escape the judgment of God that is to come.[1]

The biblical account makes three affirmations: (1) the world is fallen in sin; (2) God's righteous judgment leads to chastisement in the form of the flood; and (3) a "holy remnant" is saved to become the foundation of a new humanity. To this corresponds a threefold development in the new dispensation: the incarnation of Christ, the eschatological judgment, and Christian baptism. Hebrews and First Peter had already drawn a parallel between the flood and baptism, the latter fulfilling the former by granting salvation "through water" (1 Pet 3:18-22). Justin elaborates on this theme by linking to the story of Noah the three events that determine our salvation. (1) The incarnation of Jesus Christ into a fallen human world enables the Son of God himself to bear punishment for our sin. Yet like Noah, he is saved (by virtue of his resurrection) to become the author of a new humanity. As the New or Last Adam, he fathers the new creation of the children of God. (2) Corresponding to the destruction of evil through the flood is its final destruction at the eschatological Last

1 *Dial.* 88:1-3; quoted in B. de Margerie, *An Introduction to the History of Exegesis, vol. I, The Greek Fathers* (Petersham, MA: Saint Bede's Publications, 1993), 29-30. De Margerie adds (note 10): "We have in this text a first inkling of the distinction made by the later tradition, within the spiritual sense, between the tropological sense (pertaining to the Christian mystery) and the anagogical sense (regarding the hereafter)." This is an outstanding study of early Christian exegesis. In what follows I am greatly indebted to Fr de Margerie's published works, as well as to insights he has shared with me in personal conversation.

Judgment, when only a remnant will be saved. (3) Finally, Christian baptism serves as a sacramental figure of the final Judgment, as it does of the New Creation made possible through Christ's resurrection. In *Dial.* 88, Justin states, "At the flood the mystery of the world's salvation was at work."

The biblical account of the Flood is fulfilled, according to Justin, on three levels in Christian existence: *historically* in the life and mission of Jesus Christ; *eschatologically*, insofar as judgment of the world at the time of the Flood is a figure or type of the Last Judgment; and *sacramentally*, since those who die and rise in Christ through baptism participate in "newness of life" (Rom 6:4).

Justin's exegesis is based on the conviction that Jesus Christ, the Messiah and eternal Word of God, was present and acting already in the former Covenant between God and Israel. This awareness, available to all Christian people, is granted to him by the grace of the Holy Spirit. In his *Dialogue with Trypho*, he develops the argument that such grace has given Christians an understanding of the Old Testament that is superior to that of the Jews. (We need to recall that for Justin "Holy Scripture" consisted of what we call the Hebrew Bible or Old Testament; the New Testament canon was not yet fixed, and only some letters of the apostle Paul were accorded canonical status—and that only in certain areas of the Mediterranean world; cf. 2 Pet 3:16.) In *Dial.* 58, Justin declares: "I shall quote you the Scriptures—not that I am concerned to demonstrate proofs...but grace has been given me by God, which alone enables me to understand the Scriptures." This grace, he continues, is bestowed upon all those who seek it, and it accords to everyone the possibility to perceive the "deeper" meaning of God's Word.

Hebrews 8:5 already affirmed that the priests of the Old Covenant, who offer gifts according to the Law of Moses, "serve a copy and shadow (*hypodeigmati kai skia*) of the heavenly sanctuary." Justin makes a distinction between such "copies and shadows" on the one hand, and prophetic oracles on the other. The former are typological images of future realities, whereas the latter are "logoi" or "words" that constitute an oral witness. Both *typoi* and *logoi* are inspired by the Holy Spirit. As examples of types he offers once again the innocent Noah, father of a new people, as the prefiguration of Christ, head of the "new race" of Christians. To this can be added the tree of life as a type of the Cross, the Passover Lamb as a type of the anointed Christ, and the offering of wheat as a type of eucharistic bread.

Justin also seems to be the first to develop the theme of the reversal of Eve's sin by the Virgin Mary, a reversal that came to play a major role in Latin theology, with the inversion *Eva-Ave*. Eve is thus a type of the Virgin, as Noah is of her son.

In this and every typological relationship, it is the Holy Spirit who effects the connection. It is the Spirit who creates events that serve as types of future realities and who charges those types with eschatological meaning. History, therefore, not only stands under divine judgment. Its events which serve God's work of salvation are actually produced by God, working through the Spirit within the framework of human experience. Moreover, in Justin's view "history" is more than a chronological succession of causes and effects. Those Spirit-given events which constitute authentic types already contain and manifest the antitype: Christ is present in the person of Noah; "at the flood the mystery of the world's salvation was at work." The historical sense of an event is thus coupled with its deeper or fuller spiritual sense, in that historical realities contain the seeds of their own eschatological fulfillment.[2]

With regard to *logoi* or prophetic words, these too are to be attributed to the Spirit, who speaks through the prophet and inspires the content of his oracles. Those prophetic words announce the coming of Christ. Yet Justin will insist that those words in a very real sense *are Christ*, insofar as Christ himself utters them about himself. Thus Christ is both the true Prophet and the content of the prophetic oracle.

In *Dial.* 113-114, Justin notes that the Spirit, speaking through the prophet, uses what today is called the "prophetic perfect": future events are referred to as if they had already taken place.[3] "If one does not understand these rules," he declares, "one will never be able properly to understand the prophecies." Those rules—of typological interpretation—lead him to formulate a remarkable passage that succinctly illustrates how the prophetic oracles point forward to and are fulfilled in the person of Christ.

> In the books of the prophets we find it announced in writing that Jesus, our Christ, is to come, that he will be born of a Virgin, that he will grow to mature manhood, that he will heal all maladies and all infirmities, that he will raise the dead; we read that he will be misunderstood and persecuted, that he will be crucified, that he will die, that he will rise and ascend to Heaven; we read that he is and is called Son of God, that he will send men to announce these things in the whole world and that it will be the Gentiles above all who will believe in

2 Further examples of St Justin's use of typology, together with a valuable analysis of his overall exegetical method, can be found in Theodore Stylianopoulos, *Justin Martyr's Contribution to the Exegetical Tradition of the Church* (Athens, 1973).
3 For example, in Isa 40:1ff, the prophet conveys God's word of consolation and promise that the people's warfare has already ended, although the Israelites are still in captivity. Similarly, Isa 53 describes the Suffering Servant, a future messianic figure, as one who, at the time of the prophecy, had already been "despised and rejected" and had "borne our griefs and carried our sorrows."

him. The prophecies were made five thousand, three thousand, two thousand, one thousand, eight hundred years before his coming, for the prophets followed one another from generation to generation.[4]

In summary, we can note the following contributions Justin Martyr made to the development of exegetical method. (1) Together, the Old and the New Testaments constitute a unified witness to Jesus Christ and to God's work of salvation. A holistic reading of the Scriptures is therefore indispensable if we are to discern the relationship that exists between the Hebrew Bible and the apostolic writings of the early Church. (2) The history of salvation unfolds in two phases: the time of preparation and the time of fulfillment. Thus the history of Israel, with its own sacred Scriptures, has as its ultimate purpose to prepare the coming of Jesus Christ. (3) As the Word of God, Christ is present and active in the history of Israel. He reveals himself as both the Prophet and the fulfillment of prophecy, since it is his Word that the seers of Israel utter under the inspiration of the Holy Spirit. (4) The Spirit creates events (*typoi*) and inspires oracles (*logoi*), each of which contains a hidden, spiritual meaning as well as an obvious historical one. (5) God himself is the author of typological relationships. Since Christ is present in the Old Testament, a typological reading of the Law and the Prophets is necessary in order to discern that presence.

For Justin Martyr, understanding the Old Testament and its relation to the New depends on two things. Like all authentic "understanding" or illumination in the truth, the work of interpretation depends first of all on the grace of the Holy Spirit, which is a divine gift of spiritual illumination that later tradition would term *theôria*. On the other hand, proper interpretation of Scripture depends on a particular *method*, one practiced by Jesus himself and transmitted to his disciples. That method, passed on from apostolic times through the entire patristic period, is the method of typological exegesis.

Another great exegete of the second century was *Irenaeus of Lyons*, whose monumental work *Detection and Refutation of Pseudo-Knowledge*, more familiarly known as *Against Heresies* (*AH*), was published around the year 188. This, together with his *Demonstration of the Apostolic Preaching*, have earned for Irenaeus well-deserved recognition as the first major biblical theologian. He is perhaps best known for his development of a doctrine of "recapitulation" (*anakephalaiôsis*), the "summing up" of salvation-history in the humanity of the incarnate Christ (Eph 1:9-10; *AH* III.16.6).

As for Irenaeus' use of the Scriptures and method of interpretation, we can note the following.

4   Quoted in de Margerie, 37.

In the first place, he considered the Septuagint or Greek version of the Old Testament to be the most authentic witness to God's presence and activity within Israel. It is not clear, however, that he was familiar with the entire text, since his quotations are often obscure or inaccurate and suggest that he relied upon collections of biblical passages known as *testimonia*. His exegesis aims generally at refuting various gnostic distortions of what would come to be called Holy Tradition—the *regula veritatis* or rule of truth—derived both from the Hebrew Scriptures and from elements of apostolic witness that had come down to him.

Whereas Justin Martyr strove to demonstrate that Christ was already present in the events recounted in the Old Testament, Irenaeus' concern against the gnostics was to demonstrate the total continuity that exists between the old dispensation and the new, between the Hebrew Scriptures and the Christian gospel. Against the gnostic theme of the Demiurge, Irenaeus insisted that the God of Israel is also the God of the Church. Throughout Israel's history God gave the Law and inspired prophets to prepare the way for the coming of Christ. To make his point, Irenaeus, like Justin before him, relies on typological exegesis. As Simonetti expresses it, in Irenaeus' view God's purpose was to enable his human creatures "to pass *per typica ad vera et per temporalia ad aeterna et per carnalia ad spiritualia et per terrena ad caelestia.*"[5]

In arguing that God, the Father of Jesus Christ, inspired the Old Testament Scriptures, Irenaeus shows that the Hebrew Law is replete with prophetic allusions to Christ's incarnation and passion. "(T)he Son of God is sown everywhere throughout the writings (of Moses): at one time speaking with Abraham as he prepared to eat with him; at another with Noah as he gave him the dimensions of the Ark; at another as he searches for Adam; at another as he brings down judgment upon the Sodomites, or as he directs Jacob on his journey or speaks to Moses from the bush" (*AH* IV.10.1). Strictly speaking, these are not typological images. They reflect rather the common patristic conviction that all the theophanies of the Old Testament are revelations of God the Son, and not of God the Father, who remains forever beyond human perception.[6]

In the same book, however, Irenaeus has recourse to genuine typology, as in the example of Lot. Stressing Lot's innocence in the act of incest with his daughters, and the significance of his role in providing them with children,

---

5 M. Simonetti, *Biblical Interpretation in the Early Church* (Edinburgh: T&T Clark, 1994), 21.
6 These images do, however, confirm the intuition of Frances Young and others concerning the "simultaneity" of meanings present within the type: Christ is actually present in the person of the angel at the oaks of Mamre; he appears to Noah as "God" (Elohim); he is manifest in the person of "the Lord God" (Yahweh-Elohim) in the Garden of Eden; he is the divine presence within the Burning Bush, etc.

Irenaeus draws a parallel between the patriarch and Christ, the Word of God, whom he calls the "father of the human race," on the basis of Deuteronomy 32:6 (LXX). "When," Irenaeus asks, "did he pour out upon the human race the life-giving seed—that is, the Spirit of the remission of sins, by whom we are given life? Was it not when he was eating with men and drinking wine upon the earth?" (*AH* IV.31.2). Connections such as this may seem strained to the modern reader. But in the framework of Irenaeus' exegesis, it fits neatly as a vivid example of the saving presence and work of the eternal Son of God in the period prior to his incarnation as Jesus of Nazareth.

Irenaeus takes pains to stress the point that all authentic interpretation of Scripture occurs within the Church. His is a specifically *ecclesial* exegesis. It is only in the community of faith that Old Testament images are revealed as types of the coming Savior. He appeals, for example, to the parable of the treasure hidden in a field (Mt 13:44), describing it as an image of Christ, whose full manifestation occurs with the incarnation. That Christ is the content of his own parabolic image, however, is a truth revealed only to those who dwell "in Christ," that is, in his Body, the Church.

"If anyone," he declares, "reads the Scriptures [i.e., the Old Testament] attentively, he will find in them an account of Christ and a foreshadowing of the new calling. For Christ is the treasure which was hid in the field, that is, in this world...but the treasure hid in the Scriptures is Christ, since he was indicated by means of types and parables" (*AH* IV.26.1). Irenaeus concludes this passage by stressing the *soteriological* value of biblical interpretation, affirming that those who discover this hidden treasure will share in the fullness of Christ's own glory.[7]

In his *Demonstration of the Apostolic Preaching*, Irenaeus places special emphasis on Christ as the fulfillment of Old Testament prophecy. From chapters 57 to 85, he offers abundant references to events within Israel's history that serve as prophetic announcements—in the form of both *typoi* and *logoi*—of Christ's incarnation, passion, death, resurrection and glorification into heaven. Once again Christ himself is the one who speaks through the voice of the prophet. In Jeremiah, he notes, Christ "makes known his death and descent into hell, saying, "And the Lord, the Holy One of Israel, remembered His dead, who already slept in the dust of the earth, and He descended to them, to preach the good news [of] His salvation, to save them. Here He also delivers (ἀποδίδωμι) the reasons for His death, that, His descent to hell

7   For more on this theme in Irenaeus, especially the image of Christ as the "treasure hidden in the field" of the Old Testament, see John Behr, "Scripture, the Gospel and Orthodoxy," *St Vladimir's Theological Quarterly* 42/3-4 (1999), 241ff.

was salvation for the deceased."[8] This passage is of particular interest, because the quotation in question is apocryphal: it appears in various forms throughout *Against Heresies*, and once in Justin's *Dialogue*, suggesting that it circulated with a series of *testimonia*.

In his study of the exegesis of the Greek Fathers, Bertrand de Margerie isolates five basic exegetical rules proper to Irenaeus. We can summarize them briefly as follows:

(1) The "rule of truth" can be discerned only within the Church.

(2) Truth is preserved and transmitted by episcopal authority.

(3) Every interpretation must be in harmony with other passages of Scripture (Irenaeus employs the verb *consonare*, implying harmony, symphony or agreement, to stress the point that Scripture offers a unified witness that admits of no self-contradiction).

(4) Obscure passages can be interpreted by those that are clear and evident (the principle of "exegetical reciprocity").

(5) One must not abandon revealed truths in a quest for knowledge beyond our ken.

In this last rule, Irenaeus is stressing the point that we must avoid the vain speculation typical of the gnostics, for example, raising the question, "What did God do before creation?"[9]

An apologist, polemicist and exegete of extraordinary energy and talent, St Irenaeus employed a method of biblical interpretation that originated with Rabbinical scholars, was taken up by Jesus and the disciples and was further developed by Justin Martyr. It is essentially the method known as "the argument from prophecy." Accepting Justin's distinction between *typoi* and *logoi*, Irenaeus perceived throughout the Old Testament Scriptures the presence and purpose of one God, the Father of the Lord Jesus Christ. This Christ, the eternal Son of God, was foreshadowed in the events of Israel's salvation-history as he was in the oracles of the prophets: foreshadowed with a degree of specificity that would elicit skepticism on the part of most modern interpreters of the Bible. Yet in the framework of Irenaeus' ecclesial exegesis, that specificity was obvious and undeniable. Any demonstration of apostolic preaching, like any attack upon "gnosis falsely so-called," was grounded in the unshakeable conviction that the one God of Israel and the Church prepared his people for the coming of Christ by means of his "two hands" working

---

8 *Demonstration*, ch. 78; quoted from *St Irenaeus of Lyons. On the Apostolic Preaching* (Crestwood, NY: St Vladimir's Seminary Press, 1997), 89.
9 De Margerie, *op. cit.*, 52-57.

within Israel's history. Those "two hands," to which Irenaeus so frequently refers, are the Son and the Spirit, who announce the coming salvation through the voice of the prophets and fulfill that announcement with the incarnation, passion, death and resurrection of the One who is both Messiah of Israel and Lord of the Church.

With these two early Church theologians as examples, we move on now to several texts that further illustrate some of the main principles of patristic exegesis.

The first text is taken from the well known *Peri Pascha* or *Homily on Easter* (*Passover*) by *Melito, bishop of Sardis* († c. 190). As one of the earliest extant Christian sermons, it is especially significant for its orthodox—and anti-gnostic—christology, affirming Jesus to be "by nature both God and man" (*physei theos ôn kai anthrôpos*). For our purposes, the selected passage is important as an illustration of typological exegesis, developing the theme of Passover in light of the passion, death and resurrection of Christ.[10]

> The Scripture of the exodus of the Hebrews has been read, and the words of the mystery have been declared; how the sheep was sacrificed and how the people [of God] was saved...
>
> Therefore well-beloved, understand, how the mystery of the Pascha [the Passover] is both new and old, eternal and provisional, perishable and imperishable, mortal and immortal.
>
> It is old with respect to the law, but new with respect to the word [Logos]. Provisional with respect to the type, yet everlasting through grace. It is perishable because of the slaughter of the sheep, imperishable because of the life of the Lord. It is mortal because of the burial in the ground, immortal because of the resurrection from the dead.
>
> For the law is old, but the word is new. The type is provisional, but grace is everlasting. The sheep is perishable, but the Lord, not broken as a lamb but raised up as God, is imperishable. For though led to the slaughter like a sheep, he was not a sheep. Though speechless as a lamb, neither yet he was he a lamb [Isa 53:7]. For there was once a type, but now the reality has happened.[11]
>
> For instead of the lamb there was a son, and instead of the sheep a man; in the man was Christ encompassing all things.

10 Melito of Sardis, *On Pascha*, tr. and ed. by A. Stewart-Sykes (Crestwood, NY: St Vladimir's Seminary Press, 2001), 37-38, 47-48, 56, 64.
11 *Ho men gar typos egeneto ê de alêtheia hêurisketo*, literally, "for the type was present (or: came to be) but the truth was discovered." The sense of the last verb is perhaps "actualized," "realized."

> So the slaughter of the sheep, and the sacrificial procession of the blood, and
> the writing of the law encompass Christ [*kechôrêken*, implying "fulfillment"],
> on whose account everything in the previous law took place, though better in
> the new dispensation. (chs. 1-6)

In chapters 11-71, Melito offers a typological explanation of the Jewish
Passover. In chapters 39ff, he focuses specifically on Old Testament figures or
types that have been realized in the person and saving work of Christ.

> So then, just as with the provisional examples, so it is with eternal things; as it is
> with things on earth, so it is with the things in heaven. For indeed the Lord's
> salvation and his truth were prefigured in the people [of Israel], and the decrees
> of the Gospel were proclaimed in advance by the law.
>
> Thus the people was a type, like a preliminary sketch, and the law was the writ-
> ing of an analogy. The Gospel is the narrative and fulfillment of the law, and
> the church is the repository of reality.
>
> So the type was valuable in advance of the reality, and the illustration was won-
> derful before its elucidation. So the people were valuable before the church
> arose, and the law was wonderful before the illumination of the Gospel.
>
> But when the church arose and the Gospel came to be, the type, depleted, gave
> up meaning to the truth: and the law, fulfilled, gave up meaning to the Gospel.
>
> In the same way that the type is depleted, conceding the image to what is in-
> trinsically real, and the analogy is brought to completion through the elucida-
> tion of interpretation, so the law is fulfilled by the elucidation of the Gospel,
> and the people is depleted by the arising of the church, and the model is dis-
> solved by the appearance of the Lord. And today those things of value are
> worthless, since the things of true worth have been revealed. (chs. 39-43)

In a striking use of typological imagery, Melito expounds the theme of the
living presence of the Son of God in the life and experience of Old Testament
figures. This is one of the clearest examples we have of the way in which the
antitype or eschatological fulfillment is "impressed" or superimposed on the
type, creating a simultaneity of meaning—in Diodore's terms, a "double
sense," both literal and spiritual—within the Old Testament reality.

> This [Christ] is the Pascha of our salvation: this is the one who in many people
> endured many things. This is the one who was murdered in Abel, tied up in
> Isaac, exiled in Jacob, sold in Joseph, exposed in Moses, slaughtered in the
> lamb, hunted down in David, dishonored in the prophets. (ch. 69)

From this point (ch. 72-99), Melito plunges into a diatribe against the
Israelites, whom he sees as ungrateful and unjust slayers of Christ, doomed to

judgment and eternal destruction. It is a harsh indictment. Despite its rhetorical elegance, it strikes the modern reader as an unfortunate example of
anti-Semitic polemic. The tone in fact is comprehensible only in light of the
historical context out of which Melito speaks, a context of persecution
inflicted on certain Christian communities by Jewish religious authorities
throughout the second century.[12]

> And so he is lifted up on a tall tree, and a placard is attached to show who has
> been murdered. Who is it? To say is hard and not to say yet more fearful. Listen
> then, shuddering at him through whom the earth shook.
>
> He who hung the earth is hanging [upon the cross].
> He who fixed the heavens in place has been fixed in place.
> He who laid the foundations of the universe has been laid on a tree.
> The master has been profaned.
> God has been murdered.
> The King of Israel has been destroyed by an Israelite right hand. (ch. 96)

Several points can be made on the basis of these passages. First, although
Melito's christological argument is directed against gnostics, who denied
Christ's full humanity and the unity of the two Testaments, his rhetoric serves
to condemn the Jewish religious authorities and declare that the former covenant, though valid in its time, was rendered null and void by the coming of
Christ and the Christian gospel. The Word has not only fulfilled the Law.
Christ has not only fulfilled the image of the Passover lamb, in a relationship
of promise to fulfillment or type to antitype. He has in fact *replaced* both the
Law and the lamb. The type has been "depleted," Melito declares, because it
has delivered over its saving "meaning" to the "truth," that is, to Christ himself. With the revelation of God's economy in Jesus Christ, the former covenant with Israel has been annulled, revoked, abolished. This is an
extraordinary judgment, one that transforms typology by transforming the
type-antitype relationship familiar to Justin Martyr into a unilateral movement in which the future fulfillment totally nullifies the original covenant.

12 Jewish persecution of Christians is reflected in Mt 23-24, the book of Revelation, as
   well as in the *Didachê* and *Martyrdom of Polycarp*. A thoroughgoing Christian
   anti-Semitism seems to have arisen somewhat later, in the latter half of the second century. W.H.C. Frend, *The Rise of Christianity* (Philadelphia: Fortress, 1984), 241, says
   of the growing tensions, "Thus the bitterness between the old Israel and new was increasing and becoming ever more permanent. Actions such as the incitement of the
   Jews in Smyrna against Polycarp were being answered in kind by Christian leaders in
   other towns in Asia Minor. In these years the seeds of Christian anti-Semitism were
   sown, and it would seem that the closer the two communities resembled each other the
   more deadly the enmity became."

The type is evacuated of its truth and meaning (lit. "power"), and all saving grace is seen to repose now in the revealed Word of God, Jesus of Nazareth.

The Hebrew Passover, then, is replaced as well as fulfilled in the saving work of Jesus Christ. In addition, Melito stresses an intuition expressed by St Paul in 1 Cor 10, that Christ was literally *present* in the Old Testament type. Paul speaks of the rock, whereas Melito names important figures of the Old Covenant in whom Jesus suffered a sort of anticipatory passion. He was "murdered in Abel, tied up in Isaac," etc. (ch. 69). In the following chapter, Melito affirms what will become formal orthodox dogma: that Christ was "incarnate of a virgin, hanged upon the tree, buried in the earth, raised from the dead, exalted to the heights of heavens." And he affirms as well the theme of "theopaschism," the conviction that *God suffered in the flesh*. This motif, central to the christology of Cyril of Alexandria and exaggerated to the point of heresy by sixth century monophysite theology, was to become a touchstone of Orthodox faith: in his human nature, his full humanity, the Son of God suffered and died on the cross. Thus Melito can declare, "the Master has been profaned, *God has been murdered*" (ch. 96).

The great biblical scholar and theologian, *Origen of Alexandria*, presents his understanding of inspiration and "spiritual exegesis" in the fourth book of *Peri Archôn* or *On First Principles*.[13]

> Now the reason why all those we have mentioned hold false opinions and make impious or ignorant assertions about God appears to be nothing else but this, that scripture is not understood in its spiritual sense, but is interpreted according to the bare letter. On this account we must explain to those who believe that the sacred books are not the works of men, but that they were composed and have come down to us as a result of the inspiration of the Holy Spirit by the will of the Father of the universe through Jesus Christ, what are the methods of interpretation that appear right to us, who keep to the rule of the heavenly Church of Jesus Christ through the succession from the Apostles.
>
> That there are certain mystical revelations made known through the divine scriptures is believed by all, even by the simplest of those who are adherents of the word; but what these revelations are, fair-minded and humble men confess that they do not know...
>
> One must therefore portray the meaning of the sacred writings in a threefold way upon one's own soul, so that the simple man may be edified by what we

13 Texts taken from G. W. Butterworth, *Origen on First Principles* (New York: Harper Torchbooks, 1966), 271f, 275f, 277f, 285.

may call the flesh of the scripture, this name being given to the obvious interpretation; while the man who has made some progress may be edified by its
soul, as it were; and the man who is perfect is like those mentioned by the apostle: 'We speak wisdom among the perfect; yet a wisdom not of this world, nor
of the rulers of this world, which are coming to nought; but we speak God's
wisdom in a mystery, even the wisdom that hath been hidden, which God fore-
ordained before the worlds unto our glory' [1 Cor 2:6f]—this man may be edified by the spiritual law, which has 'a shadow of the good things to come' [Heb
10:1]. For just as man consists of body, soul and spirit, so in the same way does
the scripture, which has been prepared by God to be given for man's
salvation...

But since there are certain passages of scripture which...have no bodily sense at
all, there are occasions when we must seek only for the soul and the spirit, as it
were, of the passage. And possibly this is the reason why the water pots which,
as we read in the gospel according to John, are said to be set there, 'for the puri-
fying of the Jews,' contain two or three firkins apiece [Jn 2:6]. The language alludes to those who are said by the apostle to be Jews 'inwardly' [Rom 2:29],
and it means that these are purified through the word of the scriptures, which
contain in some cases 'two firkins,' that is, so to speak, the soul meaning and
the spiritual meaning; and in other cases three, since some passages possess, in
addition to those before-mentioned, a bodily sense as well, which is capable of
edifying the hearers. And six water pots may reasonably allude to those who are
being purified in the world, which was made in six days, a perfect number...

But if the usefulness of the law and the sequence and ease of the narrative were
at first sight clearly discernible throughout, we should be unaware that there
was anything beyond the obvious meaning for us to understand in the scriptures. Consequently the Word of God has arranged for certain stumbling-blocks, as it were, and hindrances and impossibilities to be inserted in the
midst of the law and the history, in order that we may not be completely drawn
away by the sheer attractiveness of the language, and so either reject the true
doctrines absolutely, on the ground that we learn from the scriptures nothing
worthy of God, or else by never moving away from the letter fail to learn anything of the more divine element.

Origen distinguishes three levels of meaning in the Scriptures that correspond to the threefold Platonic anthropology of body-soul-spirit. While these
are also biblical distinctions, their basically Platonic character is evident in
Origen's understanding, similar to that of his teacher Clement of Alexandria,
that humanity is divided into three groups of persons: the "fleshly" the "psychic" and the "spiritual." In Origen's mind, the somatic or fleshly sense of
Scripture refers to the literal, historical meaning; the psychic sense refers to
the moral meaning, discerned essentially by typology; and the spiritual sense

refers to the "sensus plenior" or deeper, hidden meaning of the text, a meaning discerned by allegorical interpretation. Only the "perfect" man is capable of perceiving and understanding this last sense. Yet on some level, every person is able to receive the revelation of the divine Logos through the Scriptures, and can thereby attain to salvation.

Like Philo and other Alexandrians, Origen is troubled by scriptural passages that seem unworthy of God, and he is at pains to explain how such passages are to be interpreted. His answer is intriguing. Some passages, he argues, have "no bodily sense at all," and therefore allow no reasonable literal interpretation. Every event, and therefore every passage of Scripture, however, does possess a spiritual meaning, one discernible by the method of allegorical exegesis. When he applies this principle to Jesus' miracle of changing water to wine, he is led to a far-fetched—some would say fantastic—analysis of numbers and measures that modern critical approaches to biblical interpretation would dismiss out of hand. Yet his method reflects a concern to respect the Pauline witness to those who are "perfect" or "inwardly Jews," that is, those who look beyond the letter to discover the hidden meaning of the passage and its significance for the soul's nurture and salvation.

In the last passage we have quoted, Origen takes this development a step further. There is a specific reason why disturbing and apparently incomprehensible passages appear in Scripture. The Word of God himself "has arranged for certain stumbling-blocks," in order that the reader might be obliged to press beyond the simple literal or historical sense of the text, to discover its true inner meaning, the meaning essential to salvation. It is these "hindrances and impossibilities" in the biblical text—placed there by God himself as he inspired the sacred author—that enable one to "move away from the letter" of the text in order to discover its "more divine element."

What is striking here is the conviction that every word and image of the Scriptures originates, directly or indirectly, with God. Like Jesus and the Rabbis, Origen never puts forth a theory of "verbal inspiration" or literal dictation of the Scriptures. Yet like them as well, he is persuaded that *God's inspirational power and influence stand behind every word of the biblical text.* Every passage, therefore, interpreted according to the methods of allegorical exegesis, is capable of revealing the divine presence and will, and of nurturing the soul with divine truth.

Alexandrian exegesis was directly influenced by the christological controversies North African theologians were caught up in during the first several centuries of the Christian era. This is nowhere more evident than in the writings of *St Cyril of Alexandria*, who can be justly considered the "father" of Orthodox christology. His monumental work *On the Unity of Christ* (*Oti Eis O Christos*) represents a ringing condemnation of Nestorian dualism and an articulate defense of the essential unity between humanity and divinity in the person of the God-man. Seven years after Cyril's death in 444, the Council of Chalcedon would produce a christological synthesis that reflected his thought, expressing it by means of four crucial adverbs that describe the relation between the eternal Son of God and the incarnate Christ: God became man *atreptôs* (without change), *asynchytôs* (without confusion), *adiairetôs* (without division) and *achôristôs* (without separation).

The treatise "On the Unity of Christ" is structured as a dialogue between Cyril (A) and an interlocutor (B), who at times plays devil's advocate by representing the Nestorian position, and at times caricatures that position to illustrate its heretical bent. Cyril's withering rhetoric reveals both his temperament and his use of biblical passages, in proof-text manner, to defend his views.[14]

> B. The serpent so recently appeared is that crooked one whose tongue is drunk on venom. Not only does he not welcome the tradition of all the initiates throughout the world (or rather that of all the God-inspired scriptures), but he even innovates as seems fit to him, and denies that the holy virgin is the Mother of God, and calls her Christ-Mother instead, or Mother-of-the-Man, not to mention the other shocking and absurd ideas he introduces to the orthodox and pure teachings of the catholic Church.

> A. You speak of Nestorius, I think. I am already somewhat familiar with his thought but as to its precise nature, my friend, I am not so sure. How can he say that the holy virgin is not the Mother of God?

> B. He maintains it is because she has not given birth to God, since the Word was before her, or rather is before every age and time being coeternal with God the Father.

> A. In that case it is clear that they must also deny that Emmanuel is God; and so it would seem that the evangelist interpreted the term pointlessly when he said, 'And being translated this means God-with-us' (Mt 1:23; Isa 7:14). And yet, because he is God made man, this is exactly how we ought to name the one that is born of the holy virgin according to the flesh, as God the Father clearly teaches through the voice of the prophet.

> B. But this is not how it appears to these people. They say that God, or rather

---

14 Text taken from John A. McGuckin, tr., *St Cyril of Alexandria On the Unity of Christ* (New York: St Vladimir's Seminary Press, 1995), 52-55.

the Word of God, has been with us in the form of helping us. For he saved everything under heaven through the one that was born of a woman.

A. But tell me, was he not with Moses delivering the Israelites from the land of Egypt and from their tyranny, as it is written: 'With strong hand and outstretched arm'? (Ps 36:12). And after this do we not find him saying to Joshua quite clearly: 'As I was with Moses so shall I be with you'? (Jos 3:7).

B. This is true.

A. Then why are neither of them called Emmanuel? Why does this name apply only to the one who was so wondrously born of a woman, according to the flesh, in these last times of the world?

B. Then how should we understand that God was born of a woman? Does it mean that the Word took up his being in her and from her?

A. Away with such a horrid and vile opinion! These are the teachings of a wanderer, of a sick mind that has strayed where it should not have gone so as to think that the ineffable being of the Only Begotten could ever be the fruit of flesh. On the contrary, as God he was ineffably begotten by nature from the Father and was coeternal with him. For those who wish to know clearly how, and in what manner, he appeared in a form like our own, and became man, the divine evangelist John explains when he says: 'And the Word became flesh and dwelt among us, and we beheld his glory, glory as of the Only Begotten of the Father, full of grace and truth' (Jn 1:14).

B. But they maintain that if the Word became flesh he no longer remained the Word, but rather ceased to be what he was.

A. This is nothing but foolishness and stupidity, the frenzy of a crazed mind. It seems that they are of the opinion that the term 'became,' inevitably and necessarily signifies change or alteration.

B. They say that this is the case, and they support their teaching on the basis of the God-inspired scriptures themselves. For he maintains that it is said somewhere about Lot's wife that: 'She became a pillar of salt' (Gen 19:26); and again about Moses' staff that: 'He threw it upon the ground and it became a serpent' (Ex 4:3); and that in all these cases a change of nature took place.

A. Well then, when people sing in the psalm: 'And the Lord became my refuge' (Ps 94:22), and again: 'O Lord you have become my refuge from one generation to the next' (Ps 90:1); what will they say about this? Has the one of whom we sing laid aside his being as God and through some transformation passed over into becoming a refuge? Has he changed by nature into something else which at first he was not?

B. Surely this approach is incongruous and unfitting to one who is God by nature. Immutable by nature, he remains that which he was and is for ever, even if
one says that 'he became a refuge' for various people.

A. What you have said is excellent, and perfectly true. So when we are considering God, if one uses the word 'became' is it not altogether impious and absurd
for someone to presume that it signifies change, rather than trying to understand it in another manner, applying some wisdom and turning instead to
what is much more fitting and applicable to the unchangeable God?

B. If we are to preserve the immutability and unalterability as innate and essential to God, in what sense, then, should we say that the Word has become flesh?

A. The all-wise Paul, steward of His mysteries and sacred minister of the Gospel proclamations, explains this for us when he says, 'Let each of you have
among yourselves that same mind which was in Christ Jesus who, though he
was in the form of God, did not count equality with God a thing to be grasped,
but emptied himself, assuming the form of a slave, coming in the likeness of
men; and being found in fashion as a man he humbled himself becoming
obedient even to death, death on a cross' (Phil 2:5-8). And indeed, the Only
Begotten Word, even though he was God and born from God by nature, the
'radiance of the glory, and the exact image of the being' of the one who begot
him (Heb 1:3), he it was who became man. He did not change himself into
flesh; he did not endure any mixture or blending, or anything else of this kind.
But he submitted himself to being emptied and 'for the sake of the honor that
was set before him he counted the shame as nothing' (Heb 12:2) and did not
disdain the poverty of human nature. As God he wished to make that flesh
which was held in the grip of sin and death evidently superior to sin and death.
He made it his very own, and not soulless as some have said, but rather animated with a rational soul, and thus he restored flesh to what it was in the beginning. He did not consider it beneath him to follow a path congruous to this
plan, and so he is said to have undergone a birth like ours, while all the while
remaining what he was. He was born of a woman according to the flesh in a
wondrous manner, for he is God by nature, as such invisible and incorporeal,
and only in this way, in a form like our own could he be made manifest to
earthly creatures. He thought it good to be made man and in his own person to
reveal our nature honored in the dignities of the divinity. The same one was at
once God and man, and he was 'in the likeness of men' (Phil 2:7) since even
though he was God he was 'in the fashion of a man' (Phil 2:8). He was God in
an appearance like ours, and the Lord in the form of a slave. This is what we
mean when we say that he became flesh, and for the same reasons we affirm
that the holy virgin is the Mother of God.

Here we have a perfect example of exegesis in the service of theology, and
specifically, of Orthodox christology. Cyril bases his interpretation of

Scripture on several hermeneutical principles we have already noted. The most important is that of "exegetical reciprocity," the conviction that Scripture, being integrally and uniformly inspired, witnesses everywhere and with equal authority to the truth about Jesus Christ. Accordingly, Cyril can call on passages from the Pentateuch, from psalms, prophets and gospels, from Pauline hymns and extracts from Hebrews (which he attributes to Paul), all in order to set forth his image of the God-man, the eternal Son of the Father, who assumed human nature in the womb of the Virgin, thus making her "Theotokos" or Mother of God. Modern exegetes would surely accuse him of "proof-texting," and in fact, that is his method. That method is justified, however, to the degree that one accepts the fundamental (but not necessarily "fundamentalist") conviction that all Scripture is inspired by God (2 Tim 3:16), and that God reveals in every layer of scriptural tradition something of the mystery of Christ and his redeeming work.

If Origen stressed the importance of Scripture for the nurturing of souls, Cyril places primary emphasis on its value for revealing the person and work of the Logos, the eternal Son of God. Both, of course, are primarily concerned with salvation. To press forward that concern, though, Cyril felt compelled to denounce and refute heretical opinions concerning Christ, and particularly those of his arch-adversary, Nestorius of Constantinople. However much one may question Cyril's political maneuverings and rhetorical overkill, his skill as a debater and as an exegete establish him as a primary defender of Orthodox tradition. His commentaries on the Gospels of Luke and John, together with his many letters and treatises such as the present one on the unity of Christ, demonstrate that he abided in full measure by the eighth principle noted above: he was a man who interpreted Scripture *from within*. His is a thoroughly "ecclesial" exegesis, produced by, in and for the Church. Thanks to his reading of the Hebrew Bible and the apostolic writings, Orthodox trinitarian theology and christology were safely preserved on a trajectory leading from Scripture, through early fourth century debates, to the Council of Chalcedon and beyond. And the Church was given an authoritative basis on which to honor and venerate Mary, the mother of Jesus, as the *Theotokos*, the "God-bearer" or "Mother of God."

In addition to biblical commentaries, homilies and dogmatic treatises, examples of patristic exegesis can be found as well in Orthodox *liturgical texts*. Some of the most interesting and enlightening of these make up the various services of "Holy Theophany," celebrated on January 6. The Western version of this feast is "Epiphany," which commemorates the appearance of the Wise

Men to the Christ child. Orthodoxy, however, celebrates on this day Christ's
theophany or manifestation at the time of his baptism in the Jordan River. A
quick reading of the Old Testament texts proposed for the feast shows clearly
how central a role typology plays in the Church's worship.[15] Other feasts,
however, are equally dependent on a typological approach to understanding
the mystery of Christ, for example his birth in the flesh celebrated as the
"Nativity of the Son of God."[16]

As a final example of typological interpretation, that to some degree summarizes the witness of the liturgical texts of both Nativity and Theophany, we
can note the following passage. This is the "dogmaticon" or celebration of the
Virgin's role in redemptive history, taken from the *Octoechos*, or book of the
eight weekly tones, for Friday Vespers in Tone 5.

15 Thirteen Old Testament readings are prescribed for the vesperal Liturgy of St Basil, celebrated
    Jan. 5 or 6, depending on the day of the week on which the feast falls. These are: Gen 1:1-13
    (the original creation is a type of the "new creation" effected by Christ's renewal of the Jordan
    waters through his baptism—a theme first expressed by St Ignatius of Antioch, *Eph* 18.2); Ex
    14:15-18, 21-23, 27-29 (Israel's victorious crossing of the Sea prefigures Christ's baptism and
    especially his passion, death and resurrection); Ex 15:22-16:1 (the wood of the tree renders the
    waters of Marah potable, providing life for the Israelites, thus prefiguring the Cross of Christ);
    Josh 3:7-8, 15-17 (Israelites, with the Ark, cross the Jordan on dry ground, foretelling the safe
    and victorious passage of Christians through death to eternal life); 2 Kgs 2:6-14 (Elijah and
    Elisha also pass over the Jordan on dry ground); 2 Kgs 5:9-14 (Naaman washes in the Jordan
    and is cleansed of leprosy: an image of cleansing by baptism); Isa 1:16-20 (the Lord commands
    Israel to "wash and be clean" through forgiveness of sins: a further image of the effects of Chris-
    tian baptism); Gen 32:1-10 (Jacob crossed the Jordan with only his staff, and God blessed him
    with abundant riches: another prophetic image of the effects of baptism and life "in Christ");
    Ex 2:5-10 (Moses saved from and through the waters by Pharaoh's daughter: a type of the bap-
    tized Christian); Jud 6:36-40 (Gideon's fleece and divine intervention through water foretell
    baptismal initiation); 1 Kgs 18:30-39 (water and fire upon Elijah's altar symbolize and fore-
    shadow baptism and the gift of the Holy Spirit: in Orthodox liturgical experience, the sacra-
    ments of Baptism and Chrismation); 2 Kgs 2:19-22 (Elisha and the healing of the waters
    against death and barrenness prefigure the effects of Christian baptism); Isa 49:8-15 (God an-
    nounces Israel's return from exile and restoration to the promised land, prefiguring the Chris-
    tian journey from faith and baptism to life in the Kingdom of God). See as well the fifteen Old
    Testament readings appointed for the Vesperal Divine Liturgy of Holy Saturday.
16 In addition to the Old Testament passages read at the vesperal Liturgy, repeated usage is
    made of Ps 109/110:1, 3-4, "The Lord said to my Lord, 'Sit at my right hand until I make
    your enemies your footstool'...From the womb before the morning star I have begotten
    you: the Lord has sworn and will not change his mind." Notice that this translation de-
    pends on the Greek (LXX) rather than on the Hebrew (MT). Early Christians had no diffi-
    culty seeing in the double reference to Lord the Father's address to the Son, and in the
    predestined one (Israel's king), an image of Christ's eternal generation from the Father.
    The figurative language of the psalm ("womb...begotten") was taken literally as an affirma-
    tion of Christ's preexistence. The Kontakion of the feast thus concludes with the remark-
    able affirmation, "For unto us is born a little Child, the pre-eternal God."

In the Red Sea of old
A type of the Virgin Bride was prefigured.
There Moses divided the waters;
Here Gabriel assisted in the miracle.
There Israel crossed the sea without getting wet;
Here the Virgin gave birth to Christ without seed.
After Israel's passage, the sea remained impassable;
After Emmanuel's birth, the Virgin remained a virgin.
O ever-existing God who appeared as man,
O Lord, have mercy on us!

Note especially the cosmic dimension of the divine economy expressed by this hymn. The Red Sea is perceived as a prefiguration of the Virgin Mother. The dividing of the Sea, like the conception of the divine Son, was accompanied by an agent acting in the name of God: there Moses divided the waters, here the angel Gabriel announces the miracle of the Messiah's virginal birth. The composer of the hymn draws a striking parallel between the water of the Sea and the liquid state of human seed: there Israel crossed without getting wet, here the Virgin conceives without seed. The hymn goes on to affirm the perpetual virginity of Mary, comparing it once again to the Red Sea: after Israel passed through the waters, they remained impassable to the Egyptians; after Emmanuel's passage from the womb of his mother, she remained a virgin, "impassable" or inaccessible to human intercourse. Finally, the doxology takes up and proclaims the familiar theme, stressed particularly in the liturgical services of Christ's Nativity, of the paradox—or more accurately, the antinomy—between time and eternity, the human and the divine: "O ever-existing God who appeared as a man, have mercy on us!"

In these and countless other texts that have been preserved for us, we find both a conscious and an intuited use of exegetical principles that bear eloquent testimony to "the faith of our Fathers." That faith, centering upon the divine-human person of the eternal Word of God, is essentially trinitarian. Within the biblical witness, as within history itself, it hears the voice of God the Father and perceives the work of his "two hands," the Son and the Holy Spirit. Accordingly, the Church Fathers will insist that any correct exegesis—that is, any *true* interpretation—of the Old and New Testaments must be made in concert both with the Spirit who inspired the sacred authors and with the Son to whom their witness points. Born of Holy Tradition, the canon of the Church must be interpreted within the framework and from the perspective of the Church's life and teachings. That perspective recognizes and acknowledges the divine presence and purpose throughout history, in the most insignificant events of Israel's experience as well as in God's "mighty acts." Salvation history, from the creation to the parousia, is guided, directed and fulfilled by the Father, through the Son and in the Holy Spirit. That redemptive activity, however, is only visible to eyes of faith. By its very nature it eludes the probing inquiry of the rational sciences, however helpful those sciences may be for textual criticism and clarification of the literal meaning of a given passage. Therefore, the interpreter will seek beyond the literal sense of the passage in order to discern its deeper, hidden meaning: the meaning that conveys its ultimate truth. This is the meaning known in the Church as the *sensus plenior* or fuller spiritual sense.

Although human participation is of course indispensable in the process of interpretation, that spiritual sense is revealed *by God himself* through an inspired vision or *theôria*, accorded to both the author and the interpreter of a canonical writing. The biblical *author* produces his work on the basis of his own experience and personal reflection, and from within his own linguistic, cultural and historical context. Yet he does so in concert or *synergy* with the Holy Spirit, who "inspires" his reflection and directs it toward faithful proclamation of "all the truth." The later *interpreter* of that writing accomplishes his or her task by calling upon human resources of intelligence, discernment, memory and faith. Yet that interpreter is also subject to the guiding influence of the Spirit in seeking to draw from the biblical witness both its literal and its spiritual meaning. In the final analysis, although Paul plants and Apollos waters, it is God who gives the growth (1 Cor 3:6). *It is God, working through the Spirit of Truth, who inspires the biblical witness, invests it with ultimate, redemptive meaning, and guides its interpretation from generation to generation within the community of faith.*

Any attempt to fathom and explain the Word of God apart from this perspective and this conviction can only reduce the Bible to a dead letter. If the Fathers of the Church were willing to sacrifice their lives in defense of the Word of God, it is because they recognized within the biblical witness the presence, power and authority of the living Word himself. As the Fathers well knew, no exegete, no interpreter, no "simple reader" of Holy Scripture, can accomplish his or her task truly and faithfully unless, in the words of the apostle Paul, they turn to the Lord in the freedom of the Spirit, so that the veil which obscures its life-giving message might be lifted (2 Cor 3:15ff). This act of "turning," which is in effect an act of continual repentance, opens the interpreter to "the power of God for salvation" (Rom 1:16f), a power that can transfigure the faithful reader of Scripture into the very "likeness" of God, "from glory to glory" (2 Cor 3:18).

4

In Quest of an Orthodox
Lectio Divina

1. *From Exegesis to* Lectio Divina

The last, and perhaps most important, hermeneutic principle we discussed in chapter two concerned the need to read the Scriptures "from within." To interpret the Word of God accurately, to perceive the depths of its message and its power to transform human life, one must "live" the Word. In the first place, this means to live in him who *is* the Word, Jesus Christ. It is to assume "life in Christ," to follow the commandments of Christ and, through ongoing repentance and works of love, to conform oneself to St Paul's remarkable affirmation, "it is no longer I who live, but Christ who lives in me!" (Gal 2:20).

It is also possible to "live" the Word of Scripture. In the perspective of the Church Fathers, this means to "hear" the Word in the true sense of that expression. In biblical languages, "to hear" implies "to obey" (*shamea, akouô/hypakouô*). To hear the Word in this sense is to open oneself to it, on the level of the heart as well as the mind. It is to hear the voice of God in Scripture and to accept its challenge in the sphere of human relationships. Finally, this degree of hearing leads to an actual praying of the Word. The Word of Scripture becomes in Christian experience both a source and a means of worship. Scripture provides the content of personal devotions as well as corporate liturgical celebration; but beyond that, it serves as a medium of revelation. As John Behr has observed, "Scripture is not simply a record of the history of our search for God, it is rather a record of God's quest for us, or more precisely, it is *itself* this quest—God acts through His Word."[1]

In what follows, we want to shift our focus from patristic exegesis to the role of Holy Scripture in the personal, spiritual life of Orthodox believers. More specifically, we want to explore ways in which the traditional practice known as *lectio divina* can help us to recover the contemplative reading of

---

1 J. Behr, "Scripture, the Gospel, and Orthodoxy," *St Vladimir's Theological Quarterly* 42/3-4 (1999), 229.

Scripture that was virtually second nature to the ancient Fathers and to other holy people throughout the life of the Church.

An important point, however, needs to be made at the outset. From an Orthodox perspective, every aspect of what can be termed "spiritual experience" is essentially *ecclesial.* This is because our very identity is defined by our participation, our "membership," in the Body of Christ. Any "personal" reading of Scripture, then, takes place within the Church, as a function of the life of the Church. Like prayer, it draws us into a living communion with the universal Body of Christian believers. Our quest will lead to a *lectio divina* faithful to Orthodox tradition, therefore, only to the extent that it confirms and deepens our commitment to the ecclesial Body of both the living and the dead who constitute the communion of saints.

Scripture is, of course, a familiar element in Orthodox experience. It provides the basic content of our liturgical services, our personal devotions and our mission to the world. The writings of the Church Fathers are filled with exhortations to read the Scriptures in their entirety and to commit significant passages to memory. The conviction underlying these exhortations holds that Scripture is a major medium of revelation and therefore one of the most important means by which we can attain knowledge of God and communion with him.

The classics of Orthodox spirituality—such as the *Ladder of Divine Ascent* by St John of Sinai, the *Ascetic Discourses* of St Isaac the Syrian, the Macarian *Homilies* or the collection known as the *Philokalia*—all urge frequent reading of Scripture, for both monastics and laypeople. Yet they say practically nothing about *how* to read Scripture in order to gain the most spiritual benefit and enlightenment from it. This reticence regarding method can perhaps be explained by the fact that their major concern is with the ascetic struggle itself, of which the reading of Scripture is merely one aspect. Then again, their authors are keenly aware that the spiritual benefit which accrues from such reading is a divine gift. Authentic knowledge and grace gained through meditation of God's Word, the Fathers emphasize, are acquired not by rational analysis of the biblical text, but by the Holy Spirit working in and through the text.

This reluctance on the part of the Fathers to prescribe methods for the reading of Scripture may explain in part why the Bible has often been neglected within Orthodoxy, at least outside of a formal liturgical setting. We have to admit that among Orthodox Christians in general today there is an appalling ignorance of the Bible, and especially of the Old Testament. This is true of laypeople; it is also the case with many first-year seminarians and even some members of the clergy. In order to reverse this trend, we need to demonstrate to our faithful that Scripture is indeed God's Word addressed to us and not merely our words about God; that it offers an inspired vision of the ultimate meaning and end of human life; and that it conveys a unique depth of knowledge and illumination which form the basis of our eternal communion with God.

Many Orthodox recoil from the idea that we have something to learn from other Christian traditions. They would react with skepticism and irritation to the suggestion that we might benefit from familiarizing ourselves with a method of spiritual reading usually associated with Roman Catholicism. Yet that is just what I would like to propose in the following pages. We shall find that the particular approach to the reading of Scripture known as *lectio divina* is a feature not only of Western or Latin Christianity. On the one hand, its roots go back to early Greek patristic writings. On the other, it is thoroughly compatible with a traditional Orthodox practice of reading and meditating on Scripture with the aim of acquiring knowledge of God and participation in his divine Life.

Our concern, then, is with the process that leads from reading and study of the biblical text to an "interiorizing" of the text through meditation, what French scholars term "la manducation de la Parole" or "consuming" the Word of God.[2]

This process begins with exegesis or interpretation of the original meaning of a biblical passage, and it ends with what can be properly called "praying the Scriptures." It involves, first of all, a rational movement from the literal or historical sense of a given passage to discernment of its higher or fuller spiritual sense, the *sensus plenior*. In a second stage, it requires that we appropriate that higher sense or meaning in such a way as to effect a change, an ongoing conversion at the level of the heart or vital center of our being.

Recalling our earlier discussion, we can distinguish between the literal and spiritual senses of Scripture in the following way. The literal or historical sense of the text is the sense uncovered by the work of exegesis. The exegete aims basically to discern the "intention of the biblical author," that is, the

---

2   The name most frequently associated with this "manducation" is that of Marcel Jousse, whose courses on spiritual anthropology included profound reflections on the "interiorization" of the Word, especially through memorization. See esp. Jousse, *La Manducation de la Parole* (Paris: Gallimard, 1975). The notion itself, however, goes back at least to the twelfth century. Guigues II le Chartreux spoke of *masticatio* as the first stage of meditation. See Enzo Bianchi, *Prier la Parole. Une introduction à la 'Lectio divina'* (Bégrolles-en-Mauges: Abbaye de Bellefontaine, 1983), 66.

author's own understanding and interpretation of a datum of revelation which he sought to convey through his writing. The spiritual or higher sense, on the other hand, can be understood as the message God addresses *through the text itself* to the Church and world in each successive generation. It is God's Word for us, today: a Word expressed through the medium of human words, under the inspirational guidance and power of the Holy Spirit.

To the patristic mind, both the composition of biblical works *and their interpretation* are inspired by God, acting through the Spirit of Truth. If Christ is our ultimate hermeneutic principle, the Spirit is the agent by whom that principle comes to expression both in the apostolic writings and in the right interpretation of those writings within the life of the Church. It is this same Spirit, as the apostle Paul reminds us, who *prays within us*, creating a relationship of faithfulness and saving love between God and his covenant people (Rom 8:26-27; 5:5-11). As we shall see, the Spirit-inspired interpretation of Scripture can and should be the fruit of this Spirit-inspired prayer.

To undertake a *spiritual* reading of Scripture, therefore, means to read the biblical writings *in the Holy Spirit*, that is, under the guidance of God himself and with the illumination only he can provide. Like the term "spirituality," "spiritual reading" is a vacuous expression if it does not refer to the presence and activity of the Spirit within the experience of the believer.

This emphasis on a "spiritual" reading of Scripture, however, has often led writers who are influenced by the Church's monastic tradition to reject, or at least to minimize, the significance of historical-critical, narrative and other forms of modern exegesis.[3] In what follows, we want to emphasize a basic principle of patristic—and therefore of Orthodox—hermeneutics, namely, *the spiritual sense of a passage is grounded in and unfolds from the literal, historical sense.* To discern the spiritual meaning of a passage, therefore, it is essential that we begin by understanding its original, literal meaning. This is the task of the exegete. It is a task which is indispensable not only for determining historical circumstances and the intention of the author. It is necessary as well for laying the groundwork which will enable us to discern within the biblical text God's Word for today.

To recover an authentic *lectio divina*, then, our spiritual reading, and the prayer that accompanies it, must be informed by the results of responsible

3   Although he insists on the importance of critical tools and methods for understanding the literal sense of biblical passages, E. Bianchi betrays a certain anti-critical bias when he states, "It is not particularly necessary to look for the meanings the Word had at the time it was first written; it is more important to hear it as if it had been spoken today for the first time" (ibid., p. 62).

exegesis. For Orthodox Christians, this means exegesis that stands in faithful continuity with the contemplative vision (*theôria*) and theological perspective of Greek patristic tradition.

2. Lectio Divina *in Western Tradition*

In order to pursue the question of a spiritual reading of Scripture within Orthodoxy, we need to clarify what we mean by the expression "lectio divina," particularly as it is used in the Latin Christian tradition. The term signifies a meditative reading of the Holy Scriptures whose aim is to lead the reader into union with God. Those who write about it insist that its concerns are neither exegetical, nor hermeneutic nor homiletic. *Lectio* focuses rather on acquisition of the biblical Word as a primary means by which a person can experience communion with the living God.[4] It may be described as a method by which the soul, guided and nourished by the Word and the Spirit, moves progressively from reading itself (*lectio*) to a deep reflection on the given passage (*meditatio*), to arrive at the goal of the exercise, which is prayer (*oratio*), a "praying of the Scriptures."

A meditative, prayerful reading of the Word of God was practiced in Judaism as well as in the early Church. In Psalm 118 (119) the psalmist expresses his joy at meditating on Torah, both day and night: "I find delight in Thy commandments, which I love. / I revere Thy commandments which I love, and I will meditate on Thy statutes." // (vss. 47f). The Book of Nehemiah describes the post-Exilic institution of a Liturgy of the Word, a week-long recitation of "the book of the Law of Moses," coupled with homiletic exposition, which took place during the seventh month of the year. On the twenty-fourth day of that month a special reading included recitation of God's saving works in Israel, and the people responded with celebration and acts of repentance as they entered into a new covenant of faithful obedience to God and his commandments (Neh 8-9). Then again, the Qumran Rule of the Community prescribes that a third of the night be devoted to the reading of Torah and to prayer: "The Congregation shall watch in community for a third of every night of the year, to read the Book and to study the Law and to bless together" (I QS VI.6).[5]

---

4   See, for example, "Lectio Divina et Lecture Spirituelle," *Dictionnaire de Spiritualité*, tome IX (1976), cols. 470-510; the classic study by Enzo Bianchi, *Prier la Parole, op. cit.*; and Thelma Hall, r.c., *Too Deep for Words. Rediscovering Lectio Divina* (New York: Paulist Press, 1988).

5   Translation by Geza Vermes, *The Complete Dead Sea Scrolls in English* (London & New York: The Penguin Press, 1997), 105.

We may suppose that the earliest Christians devoted themselves both to communal liturgical reading and to personal, meditative study of the Word of God contained in apostolic letters, various written forms of the apostolic gospel ("the Gospel according to..."), and collections of the sayings of Jesus such as the hypothetical "Q" or "sayings source" common to Matthew and Luke. Among these early Christians, meditation on Torah would be largely replaced by prayerful reflection on the commandments of Christ, especially the new commandment that summarizes and enfolds all others: "love one another, even as I have loved you" (Jn 13:34).

It is only with Origen, however, that we find the first clear reference to spiritual reading as such (*theia anagnôsis*).[6] As the practice leading towards a more formal *lectio divina* developed throughout the third and fourth centuries, it came to involve a daily meditation on Scripture, coupled with ascetic struggle, which issues in prayer.[7] As later representatives of Latin tradition refined and systematized the practice, its purpose took on a sharper focus as well. The ultimate end of *lectio* was to lead to *illuminatio* or even *deificatio*, that is, *theôsis* or participation in the life of God.

That end, however, as the Fathers of both East and West affirmed, is attained only through willing acceptance of a spiritual combat or "unseen warfare." This involves constant struggle against the passions and weaknesses of the flesh that distract both mind and soul, and thereby hinder the person in his or her pilgrimage that leads from purification, through illumination, to deification. To the patristic mind, there can be no authentic *lectio divina* that is not firmly grounded in this ongoing struggle against the darker side of the self. For the purpose of *lectio* is to cast light into the darkest recesses of the soul, to illumine the mind with the true knowledge of God that leads to intimate and eternal communion with him.[8]

6 *Epistula ad Gregorium Thaumaturgum 4* (Sources chrétiennes 148 [1969], 192); see Jacques Rousse, art. "La lectio divina," *Dict. de Spiritualité*, col. 473.

7 Clement of Alexandria (*paed.* 2.10, *PG* 8.512B), St Basil the Great (*ep.* 2.4, *PG* 32.229B), and St John Chrysostom (*hom.* 21.2 *in Eph*, *PG* 62.9), for example, specifically link daily personal reading of Scripture with prayer (*euchês kai anagnôsis*).

8 Accordingly, the Byzantine eucharistic liturgy includes this prayer before the reading of the Gospel: "Illumine our hearts, O Master who lovest mankind, with the pure light of Thy divine knowledge. Open the eyes of our mind to the understanding of Thy gospel teachings. Implant also in us the fear of Thy blessed commandments, that trampling down all carnal desires, we may enter upon a spiritual manner of living, both thinking and doing such things as are well-pleasing to Thee." And the prayer closes with the affirmation that Christ himself is the source and inspirational power behind this spiritual warfare, just as he is the One who leads the contemplative soul from darkness to light and from death to life. "For Thou art the illumination of our souls and bodies, O Christ our God, and unto Thee

The practice of *lectio divina* was virtually abandoned after the high Middle Ages, at least among the laity. During the twelfth century, Latin monastic leaders such as Hugues de Saint-Victor († 1141) and Guigues II le Chartreux († 1188) systematized the practice and prescribed it for their monks. Yet from the sixteenth century, inside as well as outside of monastic circles, it fell into disuse, to the point that today even many monks know little or nothing about it.[9]

One rarely emphasized element of that tradition needs to be rediscovered along with the practice as a whole. It is the importance, stressed especially by Hugues de Saint-Victor, of the practical outcome of *lectio*. To the usual steps—*lectio, meditatio, oratio, contemplatio*—Hugues added, between the last two, *operatio* or the performance of good works.[10] This adds a vital element to any spiritual itinerary, based as it is on the paraenetic passages of St Paul's letters and injunctions such as Ephesians 2:10, "For we are [God's] workmanship, created in Christ Jesus for good works (*ergois agathois*), which God prepared beforehand, that we should walk in them." For *lectio* to issue in *contemplatio*, the inner struggle of the reader needs to be coupled with humble service, a genuine *operatio* or *diakonia*, that represents a living participation in Christ's redemptive work for the world's salvation.

3. *Toward an Orthodox* Lectio Divina

Although *lectio* is usually associated with Roman Catholic monastic practice and piety, it apparently originated in some form with Greek patristic writers, beginning with Origen. Origen himself seems merely to have taken over the practice from Judaism. Its systematic development into a precise spiritual itinerary leading through various stages that culminate in prayer or

we ascribe glory, together with Thy Father, who is from everlasting, and Thine all-holy, good, and life-creating Spirit, now and ever and unto ages of ages."

9 An important exception is those of Benedictine-Cistercian (Trappist) tradition. See T. Hall, *Too Deep for Words*, 7-9; E. Bianchi, *Prier la Parole*, 20. Although the Rule of St. Benedict does not specifically mention *lectio divina*, certain portions suggest that the practice was known by the monks to whom it is addressed. From the Prologue: "Let us arise, then, at last, for the Scripture stirs us up, saying, 'Now is the hour for us to rise from sleep.' Let us open our eyes to the deifying light, let us hear with attentive ears the warning which the divine voice cries daily to us, 'Today if you hear His voice, harden not your hearts.' And again, 'He who has ears to hear, let him hear what the Spirit says to the churches.' And what does He say? 'Come, My children, listen to Me; I will teach you the fear of the Lord. Run while you have the light of life, lest the darkness of death overtake you.'" *St Benedict's Rule for Monasteries*, tr. by Leonard J. Doyle (Collegeville, MN: The Liturgical Press, 1948), 2.

10 Rousse, *Dict. de Spiritualité*, col. 485.

contemplation is, of course, to be attributed to Latin theologians and monastic leaders, particularly of the later Middle Ages.

When Eastern Church Fathers speak of stages along the way toward deification, it is usually in the context of a discussion concerning the passions and the need for ascetic struggle to preserve oneself from them. St Maximus the Confessor, for example, suggests a spiritual movement, from dispassion through contemplation of the natural order, that culminates in knowledge of God, meaning communion with divine life. "The intellect, once totally free from passions, proceeds undistracted to the contemplation of created beings, making its way towards knowledge of the Holy Trinity."[11]

Nowhere do the Greek Fathers propose a systematic approach or technique for the reading of Scripture.[12] Yet their writings are filled with exhortations to "take up and read." A few examples, culled mainly from the *Philokalia*, suffice to make the point.

On the value of Scripture:

"The distinctive features of the first method of prayer are these. When a person stands at prayer, he raises hands, eyes and intellect heavenwards, and fills his intellect with divine thoughts, with images of celestial beauty, of the angelic hosts, of the abodes of the righteous. In brief, at the time of prayer he assembles in his intellect all that he has heard from Holy Scripture and so rouses his soul to divine longing as he gazes towards heaven, and sometimes he sheds tears." [St Simeon the New Theologian († 1022), IV, 68]

"Just as God in His essence cannot be the object of man's spiritual knowledge, so not even His teaching can be fully embraced by our understanding. For though Holy Scripture, being restricted chronologically to the times of the events which it records, is limited where the letter is concerned, yet in spirit it

11 *First Century on Love 86*, in *The Philokalia* vol. II, ed. by G.E.H. Palmer, Ph. Sherrard and K. Ware (London: Faber & Faber, 1981 [vol. I, 1979; vol. III, 1984; vol. IV, 1995]), 63. Subsequent quotations from the *Philokalia* are taken from this series and are cited by volume and page number.

12 Peter of Damascus (twelfth c.?) includes among his Twenty-Four Discourses a discussion of Holy Scripture (ch. XXIII, *Philokalia* III, 263-268). Although advice about reading Scripture is given throughout, the aim of the discourse is to explain why a given biblical passage may gradually reveal a number of different meanings: "...the person who has made some progress in the practice of the moral virtues...does not know all the mysteries hidden by God in each verse of Scripture, but only as much as the purity of his intellect is able to comprehend through God's grace. This is clear from the fact that we often understand a certain passage in the course of our contemplation, grasping one or two of the senses in which it was written; then after a while our intellect may increase in purity and be allowed to perceive other meanings, superior to the first" (p. 264). Again, there is no systematic approach to the actual reading of the text.

always remains unlimited as regards the contemplation of intelligible realities." [St Maximus the Confessor († 662), II, 207]

At the Transfiguration, Christ's "whitened garments bear a symbol of the words of Holy Scripture, since at that moment they became luminous, clear and distinct to the disciples, and were comprehended apart from every dark riddle and symbolic shadow, *disclosing the Logos who exists and is hidden in them*, at which point the disciples attained to the plain and correct knowledge of God, and were freed from any inclination toward the world and the flesh." [ibid.][13]

St Ambrose († 397), in his address to sacred ministers, also suggests that Christ is "incarnate" in Scripture, and it is there that he is to be sought:

"Why not devote yourselves to reading during the time left you in your service to the Church? Why not return to Christ, speak with Christ, listen to Christ? It is he whom you speak to when you pray, it is he whom you listen to when you read the Holy Scriptures." [PL 16.50A]

On why we should read the Scriptures:

"Spiritual knowledge comes through prayer, deep stillness and complete detachment, while wisdom comes through humble meditation on Holy Scripture and, above all, through grace given by God." [St Diadochus of Photiki († late 5th c.), I, 255]

To become holy, a person "will seek the riches of Holy Scripture and so be led to the life of perfection, gaining nourishment and joy... [W]here the moisture of the passions has dried up and there is a desert, it is possible to seek the inner truth contained in Scripture." [St Nilus the Ascetic († 430), I, 242]

"The purpose of spiritual reading is to keep the intellect from distraction and restlessness, for this is the first step towards salvation." [St Peter of Damascus (twelfth c.?), III, 155]

On how to read the Scriptures:

"Understand the words of Holy Scripture by putting them into practice, and do not fill yourself with conceit by expatiating on theoretical ideas." [St Mark the Ascetic (5th c.?), I, 116]

---

13 Maximus, *Ambiguum* 10, tr. Paul Blowers, *Exegesis and Spiritual Pedagogy*, 103 (my italics). In this important study of Maximus' exegetical method, Blowers examines Maximus' notion of three incarnations: in history, in the cosmos and in Scripture. Christ is incarnate in Scripture as the eternal Logos, and it is Christ who reveals the deeper, eschatological and symbolic meaning of Scripture: "it is precisely the historically incarnate and risen Christ who unfolds eschatologically the intelligible content of scripture, the 'symbols of his mysteries'," 124. Once again, Christ is his own "hermeneutic principle," since he is both the content of Scripture and its interpreter.

"When you read Holy Scripture, perceive its hidden meanings. 'For whatever was written in past times was written for our instruction' (Rom 15:4)." [ibid., I, 112]

A holy Elder "alternately chanted psalms and recited by heart sections of the Epistles and Gospels. He spent the whole day in this manner, chanting and praying unceasingly, and being nourished by the contemplation of heavenly things. His intellect was often lifted up to contemplation, and he did not know if he was still on earth." [*A Discourse on Abba Philimon* (6th c.?), II, 346]

"We who do no more than listen to the Scriptures, should devote ourselves to them and meditate on them so constantly that through our persistence a longing for God is impressed upon our hearts..." [St Peter of Damascus, III, 123]

In this same vein, St John Chrysostom († 407) insists on the need to read the Scriptures in their entirety:

"This is why we have become so tepid in our faith: we no longer read the Scriptures as a whole. Rather, we select certain passages as being more clear and useful, and we say not a word about the rest. This is just how heresies are introduced: we have refused to read the entire Bible; we have declared certain parts to be essential and others secondary." [*Salutate Priscillam* (Hom in Rom 16:3), PG 51.187]

From these passages, selected almost at random, we can glean a number of indications as to how the Greek Fathers understood the significance of a meditative reading of the Scriptures and its relation to prayer.

(i) Above all, it is clear that they held every proper (i.e., "orthodox-catholic") reading of Scripture to be an *ecclesial* act. The Liturgy is the first and most basic context within which the Word of God comes to expression. While personal meditation on the biblical texts is essential, there is no such thing as a "private" reading. This is because every reading must be governed by Church Tradition, with its particular dogmatic and liturgical stance. If the holy Elder could be lifted up in ecstatic contemplation by ceaseless repetition of Psalms and Gospel passages, it is because his personal vision of divine life and truth had been fundamentally shaped by the "apostolic gospel" enshrined in those passages, a gospel confessed in the Church's creeds and celebrated in its liturgical services. It is this ecclesial reference that preserves individual readings of Scripture from arbitrary interpretations which represent the opinion of the reader rather than the *phronêma ekklêsias* or "mind of the Church."

(ii) A second emphasis concerns the intimate link between the reading of Scripture and *contemplative prayer*. The apostolic writings provide knowledge of God and a vision of his Kingdom. By reading them attentively, holistically, and in their entirety—rejecting the temptation to select a "canon within the canon" or to choose only those passages that appeal to the reader theologically or spiritually—a person can be led into a particular attitude of prayer. This involves what can be described as an openness of heart to the divine presence and mystery which are both hidden and revealed within the Scriptures. As familiarity with the text grows and mature understanding increases, one is led by the Spirit of God to appropriate the very words of Scripture and make them one's own. It then becomes possible to "pray" the Scriptures, using what the Fathers understand to be the very words of God himself. We read and interiorize the Word of God in order to pray to God, as it were, "in his own words."

(iii) Yet this movement from *lectio* to *oratio*, from a reflective reading of the Scriptures to personal communion with God by "praying the Scriptures," is never to be understood as our own accomplishment. It is a *gift*, one that is uniquely dependent on divine initiative. "We do not know how to pray as we ought," the apostle Paul reminds us. Prayer, and especially the contemplative prayer that lifts the mind and heart in joyful communion with God, is a work of the Holy Spirit within us. This is why every reading of Scripture, liturgical or personal, should begin with an *epiklesis*, an invocation to the Spirit. And this is why the tradition preserves a precious word of advice, ascribed to St Ephrem the Syrian: "When you take up Holy Scripture, pray and implore God that he reveal himself to you."

(iv) St Maximus, together with the entire ascetic tradition, stresses the point that a spiritual, meditative reading of Scripture helps us to embark on an inner pilgrimage which leads toward sanctification. In order for us to assume this inward journey, however, the Scriptures must be *actualized*, that is, they must become present and living in our day-to-day experience. How in fact does this actualization occur?

By virtue of *lectio divina* and its quest for the *sensus plenior*, the biblical texts present themselves in the first instance not as historical records—the recounting of past events in the life of Israel and the early Church—but as a living and life-giving Word that God speaks to us *today*. The aim of *lectio* is knowledge of God. But that knowledge requires of us, in our present life and activity, an attitude of contrition and ongoing repentance leading to genuine humility. This is because God himself is supremely humble. In his inexhaustible love for mankind, he condescended to enter into the domain of human fallenness. In the Person of the eternal Son he assumed the fullness of human nature in order to liberate that nature, to recapitulate and restore it to its original wholeness and beauty (St Irenaeus). In order to do so, he had to assume the conditions of a Suffering Servant. He had to descend through death into the realm of death, so that as Author of Life he might destroy the powers of sin, death and corruption that hold humanity in bondage. Only then could he rise in glory, exalting with himself all those who unite themselves to him in faith and love. Truly to "know" God, then, is to know him in the depths of his own kenotic love (Phil 2:7).

To know this God, to be united with the ineffably Humble One, requires that we ourselves grow in humility. Yet growth of this order can occur only when the gospel message—with its exhortations and commandments as well as its promises—is actualized in our present experience. It is a growth that involves us unavoidably in ascetic struggle against the corrupting impulses the spiritual elders identify as "passions." It draws us ineluctably into ceaseless spiritual warfare against ourselves and against the demonic powers that corrupt our life and the social order in which we find ourselves. This kind of growth—growth "in the Spirit"—is possible, however, only because the Word of God is a living Word. Its transforming power lies in the fact that it is a Word not of the past but of the present, a Word of today and for today.

This emphasis on actualization of the scriptural Word through the presence in our midst of the eternal Logos in fact goes back to Jesus himself. When Jesus reads from the prophet Isaiah in the synagogue at Nazareth, he proclaims to the people, "Today (*sêmeron*) this Scripture has been fulfilled in your hearing" (Lk 4:21). This does not mean simply that at that particular moment Isaiah's prophecy had become reality in the person of Christ. It means rather that in Christ every true reading of Scripture, every *lectio divina*, can become a reality for us "today."[14] As the Fathers insist, however, this actualization of the divine Word can occur only through the arduous struggle and the deep inner prayer that enable us to receive that Word and be transformed by it.

(v) This leads to further insight shared by representatives of the ascetic tradition. Scripture and prayer are *mutually illuminating*. Scripture directs and structures our prayer, providing it with content and preserving it in accordance with the norms or canons of faith. Yet any reading of Scripture that leads to revelation of "all the truth"—that opens before us "another aspect" of reality, in the words of Peter of Damascus—is itself the fruit of prayer. Scripture leads to prayer, yet prayer is essential for a "true" reading of Scripture.

However it may sound, this does not describe a closed circle. It is more like an ascending spiral. Increased knowledge of the biblical Word leads to

14 See E. Bianchi, *Prier la Parole*, 33.

deeper communion with God, a communion which naturally issues in supplication, adoration, thanksgiving and praise. At the same time, it is this
intense, intimate communion with God that provides ever deeper insight
into the true meaning of Scripture. "When you read Holy Scripture," St
Mark the Ascetic urges, "perceive its hidden meanings." To perceive those
hidden meanings—to "understand Scripture in a spiritual way" (St Maximus)
and to sound its inner depths and power—requires that our reading progress
from a rational *apprehension* of the text to *meditation* on its ultimate meaning—its meaning *for us*—and then to *contemplation* of the One who is "incarnate" within the text. Finally, in the experience of the more privileged of the
saints, that contemplation can lead, even in this life, to a *communion* with
God which is filled with such longing and such joy that, like the holy Elder,
we no longer know whether we are on earth or in heaven.

4. "Praying the Scriptures"

To this point we have attempted to describe certain intuitions common to the
Greek Fathers concerning the relationship between Scripture and prayer. Two
further questions require some exploration if we are to move toward a genuinely Orthodox *lectio divina*. First, what is the role of prayer in discerning the
higher, spiritual sense of a biblical passage? And second, how can prayer lead to
an internalizing of the biblical message, so as to create the conditions that will
foster an authentic communion with the eternal Word of God?

Returning to the hermeneutic presuppositions of the Church Fathers we
outlined earlier, we recall their emphasis on a christological, trinitarian and
ecclesial reading of the Bible. In a perfect world, this kind and quality of reading would occur naturally as a consequence of our participation in the Body
of Christ. In the fallen real world, on the other hand, we need constantly to
remind ourselves that God is Lord, that Christ is risen, and that the Holy
Spirit is "everywhere present, filling all things." From this perspective, we
come to appreciate once again that all of history is in God's hands, that every
event and every reality can serve the ends of his economy of salvation. It is
also from this perspective that we can sense a fundamental truth—perceived
today, it seems, more often by physicists than by theologians—that ultimate
reality and ultimate truth are situated both within and beyond the bounds of
history; they transcend the limits of time and space. While the physicist may
intuit this fact by observing the movement of elementary particles or the
effects of black holes, the theologian, in the Evagrian sense of the term, knows
it by virtue of prayer. Truth, and therefore meaning, are to be found ultimately in God. Yet our discernment of that truth depends on the work of the

Spirit of God within us, who "intercedes for us with sighs too deep for words" (Rom 8:26).

This implies that the *primary* sense of Scripture is not the literal or histori-cal sense, but rather what tradition calls the spiritual or transcendent sense, the *sensus plenior*. In making such an affirmation, it is important to stress the fact that we are not presupposing a radical dualism that totally separates time from eternity or the historical meaning from the transcendent meaning of Scripture. Eternity enfolds time, just as the fuller spiritual sense enfolds and gives meaning to historical realities.[15] Yet from our perspective, bound as it is by the limits of time and space, that spiritual sense is discerned precisely in and through historical reality. This is why Diodore of Tarsus asserted that the event contains a "double" sense, at once historical and transcendent.[16] And this is why we have insisted that the spiritual sense unfolds on the basis of the literal, historical sense. Otherwise we lose all grasp of reality, as events, per-sons and institutions of the biblical account are reduced to simple metaphors. This is the danger with excessive allegorizing. Nevertheless, as recent studies have so well demonstrated, appropriate use of allegorical method is indispens-able for leading the reader from the literal to the spiritual meaning of a given passage.[17]

Yet all allegory can do, as a method in and of itself, is point the reader to tran-scendent realities. Only the Holy Spirit can enable the reader actually to *partici-pate* in those realities. It is the Spirit who transforms an allegorical image from a mere sign into a symbol, a medium of participation. To quote St Maximus once again: "Though Holy Scripture, being restricted chronologically to the times of the events which it records, is limited where the letter is concerned, yet in spirit it

15 This insight is basic to Christian theology and needs very much to be developed. An im-portant contribution in this regard, from a non-theistic point of view, is provided by David Bohm, *Wholeness and the Implicate Order* (London/Boston: Ark Paperbacks, 1980). The author develops the theme of "the unbroken wholeness of the totality of existence as an un-divided flowing movement without borders" (p. 172); see esp. ch. 7, "The enfolding-un-folding universe and consciousness." In a theistic perspective, time and eternity, as well as the material world and human consciousness, can be properly conceived only holistically. This allows Plato, for example, at least in his later dialogues, to envisage the participation of transcendent "forms" within concrete realities, as it enables Diodore or even Theodore of Mopsuestia to perceive spiritual or eschatological meaning within historical events.

16 This theme is developed more fully in J. Breck, *The Power of the Word* (New York: St Vladimir's Seminary Press, 1986), 69-79.

17 See especially Andrew Louth, *Discerning the Mystery: An Essay on the Nature of Theology* (Oxford: the Clarendon Press, 1983), ch. 5, "Return to Allegory"; Frances Young, *Biblical Exegesis and the Formation of Christian Culture*, esp. Part III, "Language and Reference"; and John Behr, "Scripture, the Gospel, and Orthodoxy."

always remains unlimited as regards the contemplation of intelligible realities."[18] Limited regarding the letter; unlimited in the power of the Spirit (and surely in this passage the meaning is the Spirit of God).

It is the Spirit who provides the inspired vision that leads the reader beyond the literal, historical sense of a narrative to its deeper spiritual sense. It is the Spirit who unveils the fuller, eschatological meaning of a biblical account, in order that *through the reading of the text itself* the reader can achieve "the contemplation of intelligible realities." In the experience of the Church's doctors, saints and ascetics, *the Spirit guides the reader of Scripture from the literal to the spiritual sense by means of inner, contemplative prayer.* Such prayer is a gift, bestowed as an act of love by the Holy Spirit.

The two questions we have raised thus resolve into one. How can prayer, which enables discernment of the higher, spiritual sense of a biblical text, accomplish what is referred to as an "internalizing" of the gospel message and thereby lead to communion with God? Again, the answer concerns the work of the indwelling Spirit.[19]

The truth which the Spirit conveys is more than information. It is "knowledge," which implies participation, communion. The Spirit guides the reader along the pathway of *lectio*, from meditation on the meaning of a passage to contemplation of God *through* the biblical passage. God is known in and through the text of Scripture, just as he is known through the text of the liturgy and, we can add, through the "text" of the icon. This is not because God is in any way limited to those various forms of text, but because the text—particularly the text of Scripture, submitted to the laws of *lectio divina*—is a principal medium by which God reveals himself to us and enables us to participate in his own life. It is precisely through the text, in its multiple expressions, that we attain authentic knowledge of God. How, then, do we continue along the pathway of *lectio divina* so that knowledge *of* God leads to actual communion *with* God and *in* God?

Orthodox spiritual writers have usually been reluctant to speak of stages on the way to sanctification and deification, or of methods for reaching those

18 See above, pp. 74-75.
19 According to the evangelist John, Jesus promised his disciples that he would send upon them and upon the entire community of faith the divine gift of the Spirit of Truth. It is this Spirit, Jesus affirmed, who would lead the disciples into the fullness of truth, receiving from the risen Lord the message of life and declaring it to them (16:13-15). Repeatedly Johannine tradition makes the point that the Spirit—or Christ through the Spirit—"indwells" (*menein*) believers in order to accomplish this mission (Jn 14:17; 20:22; 1 Jn 2:20, 27; 3:9, 24; 4:13). This indwelling of the Spirit within us is the ground and precondition of our own indwelling in God.

stages. While the language of "purification, illumination, deification" is hardly unknown in ascetic writings, it has rarely been systematized into a program that might be construed as a technique for attaining a particular spiritual end. This is because the saints and other spiritual guides in Eastern tradition have always recognized and insisted that the work of sanctification and the blessing of *theôsis* are accomplished and bestowed by God alone, in response to a human commitment to wage warfare against demonic passions. If the interpreter of Scripture is to pass from a literal reading of the text to an understanding of its higher, spiritual sense, that too can be accomplished only by the presence and work of the indwelling Spirit. For once again, it is the Spirit who inspires, directs and fulfills not only the original *composition* of the biblical writings but also their *interpretation*, from apostolic times to the present. This includes their interpretation within the framework of a *lectio divina*.

Consequently, there is no formal technique, no systematic methodology, that will enable us to move from a literal to a genuinely spiritual reading of the text, or from knowledge of God to union with God. Nevertheless, there are many indications in the writings of the Church's spiritual guides that can help us in a very significant way as we attempt to hear God's voice in Scripture. Such indications can chart an inward journey from *meditatio* to *contemplatio*, from reflection on the text to a "praying of the text" which opens both mind and heart to actual communion with divine life.

Lectio divina requires certain conditions that can facilitate both reading and hearing the Word of God. The most important external conditions are silence, solitude and a rule of prayer.

The aim of *silence* is not merely to eliminate ambient noise. Silence leads to a new state of being, one that enables a person to focus upon "the one thing needful," (Lk 10:42), and to hear "the still small voice" of God (1 Kgs 19:12). Exterior silence is required for creating inner silence, the silence of the heart which St Isaac the Syrian calls the "mystery" or "sacrament of the world to come."[20] Once acquired, inner silence can overcome the "thoughts" (*logismoi*) that wreak such damage in the spiritual life by creating endless distractions and temptations. Silence brings peace; it facilitates concentration and attentiveness. Thereby it opens both mind and heart to the divine Presence, and enables one to "hear" the ineffable Word that God speaks through the passages of Scripture.

Solitude complements silence by creating a "sacred space," in which ordinary *lectio* can become *lectio divina*. It does not mean isolating ourselves from

20 *Letter* no. 3.

other people, not even necessarily distancing ourselves from them. The saints, after all, could enjoy both silence and solitude in the midst of a crowd. For the less experienced, solitude may well require that we separate ourselves for a while, go into our room, shut the door, and there pray to our Father, "who is in secret" and "who sees in secret" (Mt 6:6). To do so in a way that is faithful to the Gospel, however, we need to recall that we are members of the Body of Christ and members "one of another." The prayer and spiritual reading accomplished in solitude are essentially *ecclesial* acts. The desert Fathers went into the wilderness to confront the demons that urban dwellers no longer recognized. In their solitude they carried on spiritual warfare for the salvation of their own souls. Yet they took the sin and the anguish of the world with them, to offer them to God by means of intercessory prayer. The same properly occurs when we seek the solitude that allows for spiritual reading and contemplative prayer.

A *rule of prayer* is another indispensable element of the inward journey toward union with God. Human beings require nourishment, both physical and spiritual, and that nourishment needs to be received at regular intervals to maintain the health of body and soul. The basic liturgical unit is the twenty-four hour day, beginning with the evening (Gen 1:5). Each day is sanctified by the Church's daily offices, from Vespers, Compline and Nocturn, through Matins and the Hours, often culminating in the eucharistic Divine Liturgy. This liturgical cycle needs to be complemented by regularly set moments devoted to the reading of Scripture and to prayer. We need to acquire the habit of daily reading and prayer, since these complement liturgical worship by enabling us to concentrate for extended periods on a particular biblical Word and to bring to God particular "intentions" or subjects of intercession, thanksgiving and praise. Once acquired, a rhythm of daily personal prayer leavens and gives new meaning to our entire life. It provides a "sacred space" in the midst of our daily activity that nourishes and helps redirect our life away from "all earthly cares." Ideally, an effective rule of prayer will be self-transcending. It will lead us beyond every "rule" and every external form of worship, to unite us, with joy and with tears, to the Object of our deepest longing.

As for the content of our spiritual reading, there are various possibilities regarding both what we select and the method we choose. We can follow the daily lectionary, associating our personal reading with the cycle of the liturgical year. Or we can select an entire writing and read through it in small, easily digestible portions. Biblical commentaries, and particularly the homilies of the Church Fathers, can be of great help in this regard. Other critical tools can prove useful as well, such as introductions to the Old and New Testaments, a Bible atlas, and the notes that are included in many modern versions. Introductions and explanatory notes, however, need to be read with discernment, since they are often at variance with key elements of our ecclesial tradition.

An Orthodox *lectio* will take a particular approach to the reading of Psalms, the Gospels and Epistles. Here we can mention only the following points.

The Psalter has always been the principal "prayer-book" of the Church. In its words, Christians hear the voice of Jesus Christ, the Word of God, who speaks through the Old Testament as well as the New. And through the Psalms the Church, the "Israel of God" (Gal 6:16), addresses the Covenant-Lord with words of repentance, lamentation, adoration and thanksgiving. The Psalter, then, is both God's Word addressed to us and our response to God. This reciprocity is the basis of communion between God and ourselves. We take up the words of the Psalms and make them our own, as Jesus did ("My God, my God...", Ps 21[22]). The psalmist's cry of repentance becomes our own as we recite Psalm 50(51), "Have mercy on me, O God..." The Church celebrates the Paschal victory with the words of Psalm 67(68), "Let God arise!" And in the vesperal Liturgy of Holy Saturday the biblical verse following the Epistle reading, drawn from Psalm 81(82), is likewise given Paschal significance: "Arise, O God, and judge the earth, for to Thee belong all the nations!"

The Psalter thus offers us a model and provides precious content for our prayer, both personal and communal. Some of its imagery, of course, is difficult to incorporate into prayer, because it offends our sensibilities and seems to present an image of God that is basically incompatible with the merciful Father whom Jesus reveals. How can we use as prayer language that calls down wrath and destruction on Israel's enemies? Here allegory comes into play. The "enemy" is interpreted to be the devil and his minions, and God's victory over hostile forces is celebrated as a victory over demonic powers that hold the world in bondage (cf. 1 Jn 5:19).

The Gospels also offer themes of contemplation and models of prayer, both to the individual believer and to the gathered Church. Jesus' parables, for example, express divine judgment but also mercy in response to human sin and weakness. The parable of the two sons (Lk 15:11ff), presents an image of the Father who goes in search of the prodigal, embraces him with unqualified forgiveness, and welcomes him back home with joy and celebration. The Good Samaritan presents a similar image, particularly in the small but significant detail concerning the willingness of the benefactor to repay whatever costs the victim's care might incur. God's mercy is unbounded, his love is without measure. As the Orthodox penitential service declares, God desires not the death of the sinner, but that the sinner repent and live.

We should mention as well the apocalyptic parables: the Ten Virgins, for example, or the nuptial banquet. These are calls to vigilance, to *nepsis* or watchfulness, addressed to every follower of Christ, because we live in the "last days." Therefore the Markan "little apocalypse" (ch. 13) ends with the ringing command: "Watch!"

As much as any believer can relate to these themes and incorporate them into personal prayer, perhaps the Gospel stories that speak most forcefully to the greatest number are those that recount healings and exorcisms. Whether we invoke the image of the Gadarene demoniac, of the ten lepers, or of blind Bartimaeus, Jesus' healings of physical and spiritual diseases force us to come to terms with our own illness, our own weaknesses and vulnerabilities, as well as with the suffering they entail. Reading these accounts turns our attention to ourselves and to our own need for healing, just as it encourages us to pray for the sick and suffering world that surrounds us.

The passion narratives of the Gospels inspire a similar kind of reflection. A meditative reading of Jesus' suffering and death provokes on our part a response by which we can identify with his passion, grasp the enormity of it, and finally give heartfelt thanks for the victory over death and corruption that it achieved. The beautiful and tragic passion accounts convey a single basic message: by means of the sacrifice of his Son, God leads us through suffering and death to resurrection and eternal life.

As for the Acts of the Apostles, it is filled with themes that speak directly to our daily life and Christian vocation. Missionary ventures, proclamation of the apostolic gospel, healings, the planting and growth of new ecclesial communities, and even martyrdom, were all aspects of early Church life and experience, and they remain so throughout the world today. Consequently, the book of Acts illustrates as clearly as any other apostolic writing the way *lectio divina* can issue in mission, witness and service.

Finally, the occasional letters we call Epistles offer an inexhaustible number of theological and pastoral themes for our meditation. We can mention at random the mystery of Christian marriage (Eph 5; 1 Cor 7), the invitation to "justification by faith" (Rom, Gal), and the theme of personal and collective suffering (2 Cor; 1 Pet).

In each case, by the grace of the Holy Spirit, a prolonged, quiet and meditative reading of Scripture can lead beyond the original, literal sense of the passage to a "moral" or "mystical" sense which pertains to our own faith and life. And from there, also in the power of the Spirit, we can journey onward to what the tradition calls the "anagogical" sense. This is the higher, spiritual sense that enables us, in the most sublime moments, to perceive through the Spirit "what God has prepared for those who love him" (1 Cor 2:9).

Lectio divina is a kind and quality of Scripture reading that is made possible only by the Spirit of God at work within us. The movement from exegesis to *lectio*, like the movement from the literal sense of a passage to its spiritual sense, is accomplished less by our human effort than by the Holy Spirit. Therefore every genuinely spiritual reading of Scripture should begin with a trinitarian *epiklesis*: an invocation addressed to the Father, to send upon us the gift of the Spirit, in order for the Spirit to transform our reading into a deep and abiding communion with Jesus Christ, the eternal Word of God.

In the image of the Mother of God, we receive that eternal Word into ourselves precisely through the grace and power of the Spirit. We read it, we meditate upon it, and we interiorize it so that it comes to fruition within us, for our own spiritual growth. We take the words of Scripture and "ponder them in our heart" as the very source of knowledge, wisdom and life. And, like the Holy Virgin, we offer the Word to the world, "for the life of the world and its salvation." For *lectio* is fulfilled, it achieves its true purpose, insofar as it issues in loving service as well as in contemplation, in *diakonia* as well as in personal communion with God.

Yet even this element of service needs to be kept in perspective. The most important reason why Christians of all confessional traditions could benefit from a rediscovery of an appropriate *lectio divina* is not its effectiveness in promoting mission or service to the world. Nor is it to provide us with more extensive knowledge of the content of Scripture, nor even to help us discern what we have referred to as the "spiritual sense" of God's Word. It is, rather, to lead us on *an inner journey of the soul,* that we might attain in the fullest sense "knowledge of God." It is to create and nurture within us the vision and the longing expressed in a prayer of thanksgiving Orthodox Christians offer at the close of every eucharistic service:

"Thou art the true desire and the ineffable joy of those who love Thee, O Christ our God, and all creation sings Thy praise forever!"

Part Two

Rediscovering Biblical Chiasmus

5

Chiasmus as a Key to Biblical Interpretation

1. Chiasmus and the Literal Sense of Scripture

Any written text is dynamic. It possesses an inner movement which engages the reader in a process that in the best of circumstances leads to understanding. By virtue of that movement, the dynamic aspect of the text in question, the reader is drawn into the flow of the author's thought, to share the author's own perceptions, judgments and experiences. The text conveys meaning insofar as this process—this dialectic between author and reader—is successful.

Whether the text is trivial or profound, it is *meaningful* only insofar as it enables the reader to move from his or her own world into the world of the author, and to respond to the author's vision with understanding. That response can be sympathetic or critical; the reader can agree or disagree with the author's perceptions and elucidations. For a text to convey meaning, it does not have to convince. But it does have to elicit from the reader a *response*, one based on the way the text expands, modifies or confirms the reader's own life and experience.

This kind of reflection, however, raises an important question. Does the reader's response depend on his or her own understanding of the sense or meaning which the *author* wished to convey? Or can the text itself effectively elicit a response—and thus convey meaning—autonomously, independently of the author's purpose in writing and of his own understanding of the message he sought to communicate? A great deal of modern (or "post-modern") analysis of the way texts convey meaning concludes that the author's own intended meaning is irrelevant or at least secondary to the fundamental purpose of the text. That purpose, it is argued, is primarily to evoke an appropriate response from the reader: a response of enlightenment, understanding, enjoyment, and so forth. This implies, however, that the ultimate *authority* of the text lies with the reader rather than with the author and the author's "muse" or source of inspiration. Likewise from this perspective, *meaning* depends less on the author than on the reader. The ultimate meaning of a text and therefore its truth—its correspondence to reality and its value for understanding—is determined by the reader's own subjective response to the writing in question, rather than by the author's intention: the meaning the author personally understood and sought to convey.

Transposed to the reading of the Holy Scriptures, this implies that the ultimate authority behind the biblical texts is neither the author nor the source of the author's inspiration, understood by the Scriptures themselves to be God in the person of the Holy Spirit (for example, Jn 14:26; 16:13-15; 1 Tim 4:1; 2 Pet 1:20-21; 2 Tim 1:14; 3:16; cf. Lk 24:27). The ultimate authority regarding the meaning of Scripture is understood rather to be the reader himself. Whether the reader's understanding is thought to be inspired by the Holy Spirit, or to be the result of the literary dynamic between reader and text, the outcome is the same: the biblical writings in and of themselves possess no inherent authority and hence no real claim to truth. "Truth"— meaning an appropriate or relevant interpretation of a biblical passage— depends solely on the reader/interpreter and on the insight that person gains from the experience of engaging with the text.

Evidently, this kind of radical reader-response approach is unacceptable to those who identify themselves as orthodox-catholic Christians, that is, persons who adhere to the Church's Tradition regarding biblical inspiration and authority. That Tradition, however, allows for a more moderate reader-response approach that sees the inspirational work of the Spirit guiding *both the composition of sacred writings and their interpretation within the life of the Church.* The insights of modern literary criticism remain valid concerning, on the one hand, the dynamic character of the text and, on the other, the need for the reader's response; what specialists call the "artistic" (creative) pole and the "aesthetic" (interpretive) pole of a literary work.

In earlier chapters we defined the "literal sense" of a biblical passage as the meaning intended by the biblical author, whereas the "spiritual sense" refers to the message God seeks to transmit *through the biblical text* to the Church and world of today. We noted that the literal sense is usually taken to mean the biblical author's own understanding of the significance of an historical reality as such, whereas the spiritual sense refers to the higher, transcendent meaning discernible in that same reality by the later interpreter through the inspirational guidance of the Spirit. In other words, it is generally assumed that the biblical author provides the data that constitute the type, whereas the later interpreter discerns the fulfillment of that typological image in the antitype.

This is an oversimplification of the matter, since the biblical authors themselves seem on occasion to have perceived an ultimate sense beyond the historical references of their immediate experience. For example, the image of the *ebed Yahweh* or Servant of the Lord (Isa 52:13-53:12) was perceived by the prophet as in the first instance a future king of Israel, but also as a prefiguration of a vicariously suffering Savior to come. Within the historical or literal dimension of a biblical text there is often a hidden referent to some eschatological reality to be revealed in the future. Occasionally the biblical author was aware of that coming reality, albeit with less fullness than the later interpreter, to whom the Holy Spirit reveals "all the truth" *through the process of interpretation itself.* That later interpreter could be a New Testament writer who expounds an Old Testament passage, or a patristic writer who creates a homily around any biblical passage, Old Testament or New. And it includes interpreters of today: professional exegetes, preachers, and anyone who strives to grasp, under the guiding hand of the Holy Spirit, the full meaning of a scriptural passage. (See especially Jn 14:26; 16:12-15, passages that form the basis of any Orthodox hermeneutic.)

The work of biblical interpretation begins, then, with a quest for the *literal sense* of the text. Although they tended to be more interested in the spiritual than the literal sense, the Church Fathers recognized a fundamental truth: that *the spiritual sense unfolds only on the basis of the literal sense.*[1] It is imperative, therefore, that any attempt to *interpret* the sense of Scripture—and not simply impose upon it an arbitrary opinion, void of both meaning and authority—begin with an effort, using the best historical-critical and literary-critical tools and methods available, to discern within its own historical context the author's intended message. That is, to discern the literal sense of the text.

From the early nineteenth century through the middle of the twentieth, scholarly attention focused especially on the contributions and limits of historical-critical approaches to biblical interpretation. In recent years, interest among exegetes has shifted to various forms of literary analysis. Although the results have been mixed (much of the effort has been expended to correct false or one-sided conclusions drawn by other scholars), certain specific contributions have been especially helpful in clarifying the meaning of scriptural passages by locating the *center of the author's interest* and thereby pinpointing the literal sense of a given text.

---

1 This point, emphasized in ch. 4 above, has been well developed by Bertrand de Margerie, SJ, in his important study of the hermeneutics of St Augustine. For the "unipluralism" or multiplicity of literal senses in Scripture, see his *Introduction to the History of Exegesis. Vol. III, St Augustine* (Petersham, MA: St Bede's Publications, 1991), 47-88.

The most significant of these, to my mind, is the contribution made by a small number of biblical scholars, beginning in the mid-eighteenth century with the works of the Anglican hierarch Robert Lowth and continuing today with studies by scholars such as John Gerhard,[2] Charles H. Talbert,[3] and especially Peter F. Ellis.[4] These studies base their interpretation of biblical texts on a form of literary analysis that investigates the concentric parallelism or chiastic (also called "chiasmic") structures of biblical passages.

Without understanding the principles of concentric parallelism which governed the writing of the Gospel of John, for example, one is left with the impression, given by the vast majority of modern commentaries, that the Gospel is a hodgepodge of traditions, coming from a variety of sources, that were stitched together and interpreted by the evangelist, then reworked and edited by one or more disciples including a "final redactor" who delivered to us the end product. Thus, it is argued, the prologue (1:1-18) was originally a (quasi-gnostic?) hymn of independent origin; chapter 21 is a later appendix, the original Gospel having ended at 20:31; and passages such as 12:44-50 and 6:51-58 are to be understood as later additions, the former to correct a misunderstanding concerning the authority of Jesus' words, and the latter to provide a eucharistic interpretation to the Bread of Life discourse. In addition, the Gospel is purported to be based on several disparate blocks of tradition (e.g., a "signs" source, a "Son of Man" source) that were woven, more or less successfully, into the overall literary composition.

The studies of Gerhard, Ellis and others, however, go far toward proving that the Gospel was composed by a single author (using underlying oral and perhaps written tradition) and that the passages in question are in fact original and integral parts of the Gospel's message. In order to make that point, I would like to describe and briefly illustrate the nature of chiastic structures for those readers who are unfamiliar with them and with the centripetal flow they represent. My chief concern is to indicate how chiastic patterns focus the reader's attention on the literal sense of a text

2   *The Literary Unity and the Compositional Methods of the Gospel of John*, unpublished doctoral dissertation.

3   See esp. *Reading John. A Literary and Theological Commentary of the Fourth Gospel and the Johannine Epistles* (NY: Crossroads, 1994).

4   See *The Genius of John: A Composition-Critical Commentary on the Fourth Gospel* (Collegeville, MN: Liturgical Press, 1984; second edition forthcoming); also his "Inclusion, Chiasm, and the Division of the Fourth Gospel," *St Vladimir's Theological Quarterly* 42/3-4 (1999), 269-338. Here Ellis offers a complete analysis of the Gospel of John, showing that the author structured his work from beginning to end according to the principles of chiasmus. This is truly a groundbreaking achievement that greatly advances his work in the first edition of *The Genius of John* (1984).

and thereby serve as an indispensable key for proper interpretation of biblical passages.[5]

2. Examples of Chiastic Patterns

It seems obvious that any writing should be read according to its linear progression, from beginning to end, as we read a novel or newspaper article. In antiquity, however, a linear reading of a text was very often complemented by another kind of reading. This reading follows the laws of what is called "chiasm" or "chiasmus," a rhetorical form based on concentric parallelism. Parallelism normally involves two lines of prose or poetry in which the second line repeats and yet modifies words and themes of the first line. Take, for example, the couplet:

> Bless the Lord, O my soul /
> Let all that is within me bless His holy name! //

Here the first line is repeated by the second line, but with a certain modification that intensifies or completes the first line. From the basic admonition that one "bless" the Lord, the thought moves to the heightened command that "all within me"—that is, one's entire being—bless or adore the "Name" of the Lord which is proclaimed to be "holy." Since the "name" expresses the essence of a given reality, to bless God's "holy Name" is to offer the highest order of praise to his person and his purpose within creation.

Chiasmus is a rhetorical form developed on the basis of parallelism. But it takes parallelism an important step further by creating a movement that is in essence *concentric*. Although any passage reads in linear fashion, from beginning to end, it can also incorporate another movement: from the exterior to the interior, from the extremities toward the center. In this way, *meaning* is developed from the beginning and end of the passage toward the middle. Accordingly, the ultimate meaning of a chiastically structured passage is expressed not at the end, in what we understand to be the "conclusion." The real meaning or essential message of the text is to be found rather at its *center*.

This chiastic way of composing and reading a literary text, so that meaning develops from the extremities toward the center, seems to have originated in the Semitic world at least three thousand years before Jesus Christ. It is

---

5 For a more detailed account, demonstrating that virtually every apostolic author made extensive use of chiastic patterns in composing his work, see J. Breck, *The Shape of Biblical Language. Chiasmus in the Scriptures and Beyond* (New York: St Vladimir's Seminary Press, 1994). The following discussion of chiastic structures in Scripture and elsewhere is based largely on information found in that book.

found in ancient Akkadian and Sumerian texts, and it spread from there to the Greek world. The epics of Homer, for example, are chiastically structured, as, presumably, was much of the oral tradition that underlies them. Writers of both the Old and New Testaments used chiasmus extensively. Although it seems not to have been taught in rhetorical schools after the beginning of the Christian era, chiasmus nevertheless appears throughout the ages, down to the present day. It is a basic form of musical composition (e.g., the concentric movement of a Bach fugue); it characterizes many liturgical hymns and prayers (e.g., *Phos Hilaron* and many of the Kontakia of Romanos the Melode); and it is often found in modern essays such as newspaper columns and editorials.

Modern writers are unaware that they are composing their works both linearly and chiastically. This is because we are no longer familiar with the chiastic "flow" that is natural to the human mind as it attempts to express ideas. But consciously or unconsciously, writers use chiasmus to express their thoughts. (In antiquity, authors who employed chiasmus often reproduced it unintentionally. The evangelist Mark, for example, structured virtually every pericope of his Gospel according to the laws of chiasmus; yet the fact that he sometimes allows large chiasms to overlap one another indicates that he did not always use this rhetorical pattern consciously.)[6] The ubiquity of chiasmus suggests that the human mind itself "thinks" in terms of concentric parallelism. Chiasms may in fact be what structuralists call "deep structures." Like historical narrative and certain forms of myth, the literary form itself may be inscribed in the human brain. In other words, whether we realize it or not, we all tend to *think chiastically*. We express meaning from beginning to end, from A to Z; but we also express meaning in terms of the concentric parallelism that constitutes the particular rhetorical form known as chiasmus.

To illustrate what we mean by chiastic structures, we may begin with the phenomenon of Hebrew parallelism as it appears throughout the Old Testament.

Hebrew parallelism, once again, consists of two (or sometimes three) lines, in which a theme is repeated and developed. The second line of a Hebrew couplet, for example, can take up a word or theme of the first line. Then it amplifies, intensifies or completes the thought of the first line. Consequently, the couplet is structured as a first line that ends in a minor stop and a second line that ends in a major stop:

6   For a complete chiastic analysis of Mark's Gospel, see J. Breck, *The Shape of Biblical Language*, 144-176.

A: Blessed is the man who fears the Lord /
B: and who loves his commandments // (Ps 111/112:1)

A: I will bless the Lord at all times /
B: His praise will always be on my lips // (Ps 33/34:1)

Notice that the first line is not only repeated by the second line. In some important way, the second line (B) takes up and develops or sets forward the thought of the first line (A). The theme "Blessed is the man who fears the Lord" is repeated in the second line, "and who loves his commandments." But the second line (B) specifies just how fear of the Lord is to be expressed: namely, by loving the Lord's commandments. There is a progression, *a movement or development of meaning, through heightening or intensification, from A to B*, and not simply repetition.

Where two parallel lines express basically the same idea, the literary form is referred to as "synonymous parallelism." And yet, as we have seen, the two lines are never fully synonymous, since the second line develops the first in some significant way.

There are other forms of parallelism as well. One of the most common is "antithetical parallelism." In this case, the second line (B) expresses the antithesis or opposite of the first line (A). A good example is the passage 1 John 4:6.

A: He who knows God listens to us; /
B: He who is not *of God* (*ek theou*) does not listen to us. //

Here "B" specifies and intensifies "A" by transforming "to know God" into a statement concerning one's *origin*. In this epistle, the author's opponents are called "antichrists." They oppose members of the Johannine community and the author of the epistle (the apostle John or one of his disciples). They do not "listen" to the author's teachings about Jesus Christ and the need to love one another. Thereby they demonstrate that they are not "of God."

Now to move on to the phenomenon of chiasmus as such. Scholars often use the term "chiasmus" to designate any form of *inverted parallelism*. This is a rhetorical form in which the second line reverses the order of words or themes expressed in the first line. A classic example is Jesus' frequent saying, "The last shall be first / and the first shall be last."// If we set this out so that the first line is placed above the second, the inversion is apparent:

The *last* shall be *first*

and

the *first* shall be *last*.

The term "chiasmus" is taken from the Greek letter "chi" which is written like the Roman letter "X." If we connect the corresponding words in each line, this gives us the form of a "chi."

LAST   FIRST

X

FIRST   LAST

Authentic chiasmus, however, includes a *third line* or element. (In chiastic structures, in fact, there can be any number of lines. The crucial point is that they be structured in parallel around a central theme.) This central element is the *focus of meaning* about which the other parallel lines are constructed. This gives us the form A:B:A', in which A' repeats yet develops the theme of A, and both lines lead to and focus on the center of meaning expressed by B.

Entire writings can be structured according to this same model. For example, St Paul's Second Letter to the Corinthians begins with seven chapters describing the apostle's relations with the Corinthian Christians. Chapters eight and nine seem to change the subject by addressing the need to collect money for the mother church in Jerusalem. Then chapters ten through thirteen return to the theme of Paul's relations with the Corinthians. But in these last chapters, the tone is much more harsh and critical than in the first part of the letter. This apparent change in subject and mood has led scholars to conclude that 2 Corinthians is a collection of originally separate letters. They misunderstand the matter, however, because they are not aware that St Paul has written his letter *according to the laws of chiasmus*. The three parts of 2 Corinthians represent a chiastic movement A:B:A'. "A" states a theme that is taken up at the end of the letter as "A-prime." The original theme of "A" is intensified in "A-prime" as the apostle expresses sadness and anger over certain conditions in the Corinthian community. Yet his overall purpose is to stress the need for loving cooperation, and not only among themselves. He especially wants them to share with the church in Jerusalem, to ease that church's material burden, but also as a sign of unity between the mother church and communities of the diaspora. His main point, therefore, is expressed not at the end of the letter but *at the center*. That is, the principal message of 2 Corinthians is expressed in chapters 8 and 9, which speak of the collection for the Jerusalem church. Thus St Paul has written his letter according to the common literary form A:B:A', where

"A-prime" intensifies "A," and the primary meaning of the entire writing is expressed in "B."[7]

Chiasmus, then, contains a central element that represents the *focus of meaning* of the passage in question. Most chiastic structures are more complicated than A:B:A'. Some longer passages move incrementally from "A" all the way through "I," to arrive at the mid-point "J," which expresses the key theme; then they continue in reverse order from "I-prime" to "A-prime." (Such an example comprises nine parallel couplets [A-A', B-B', ... I-I'] that focus about the central theme [J]. Similarly, the entire Gospel of John constitutes a major chiasm of twenty-one "sequences": 1 through 10 [A-J] are paralleled, in reverse order, by 12 through 21; and the whole Gospel "turns" about the central element "K," which is sequence 11 [= 6:16-21], the motif of the New Exodus expressed by the episode of Jesus walking on the water).[8]

Then again, the center of a chiastically structured passage can consist of two lines (or an entire paragraph). An example is 1 John 4:7-8. This pericope begins with an introductory line that does not fit into the chiastic pattern (called "anacrusis," a Greek expression for "cast off"). This is a common phenomenon in chiasmus and can be found either at the beginning or at the end of a passage.

Beloved, let us love one another.

A : For love is of God
   B : and whoever loves is born of God and knows God.
   B': He who does not love has not known God,
A': for God is love.

Notice the parallelism between "A" and "A-prime" on the one hand, and between "B" and "B-prime" on the other. B:B' represent antithetical parallelism:

B : loves   born of God   knows God
B': does not love   has not known God.

"A" and "A-prime," represent inverted parallelism:

A : love is of God
A': for God is love.

Again the inversion (the "chi" or "X") is evident: Love-God // God-Love.

---

7   Similar analysis demonstrates as well the integrity of Paul's letter to the Philippians, often thought by scholars to be composite. On this entire question, see P.F. Ellis, *Seven Pauline Letters* (Collegeville, MN: Liturgical Press, 1984).

8   See P.F. Ellis, *The Genius of John*, 14-15; J. Breck, *The Shape of Biblical Language*, 193-197.

Throughout the entire Gospel of John, as in certain passages of 1 John, there is a fivefold structure (A:B:C:B':A'). Here there is parallelism between "A" and "A-prime," just as there is between "B" and "B-prime." Once again, "C" represents the *center of meaning*. And here again the movement from the extremities (A-A') toward the center (C) is one of increasing intensity or heightening. The concentric movement leads the reader progressively toward the central theme or focus.

This chiastic way of reading biblical writings has great importance for the work of exegesis or biblical interpretation. Written chiastically, biblical works must be read chiastically if they are to reveal the primary message the author wanted to convey. As the author wrote, his thought moved linearly, from his introduction to his conclusion. Yet it also moved *concentrically*, with increasing intensification or specification of meaning, from the extremities of the composition towards the center. With regard to the fivefold A:B:C:B':A' model, the result was a progression that moved from "A" to its parallel in "A-prime," constituting the first couplet; then to "B" and its parallel in "B-prime," constituting the second couplet; and concluded with the central affirmation "C." A good example is 1 John 3:9.

> A : Whoever is born of God
>> B : cannot commit sin
>>> C : because God's seed (*sperma*) dwells within him;
>> B': and he is not able to sin
> A': because he is born of God.

Notice again the development of meaning from the first half of the strophe (A-B) to the second half (B'-A'). The first two lines are heightened or intensified by the last two: "Whoever is born of God cannot sin... (precisely) because he is born of God." And the entire passage focuses around the central element "C": the person "born of God" is incapable of sin. Why? "Because God's seed dwells within him." "Seed" in this context is a symbol of the Holy Spirit. St John is telling his community that sin is impossible for them precisely because of the indwelling presence of God's Spirit. By virtue of the Spirit's presence (communicated at baptism?), they are simply unable to commit sin.[9]

---

9   The difficulty in reconciling this statement with 1 Jn 1:8—"If we say we have no sin, we deceive ourselves, and the truth is not in us"—is resolved if we understand that the author in 3:9 is speaking of the sin of apostasy, which is the specific sin of his antagonists, the antichrists. Members of the Johannine community are protected from the temptation to apostatize by the Spirit of God which dwells in them and preserves their communion with the Father and the Son; cf. 3:24 and 4:13.

A final example illustrates particularly well the usefulness of chiastic analysis for the work of interpretation. Two juxtaposed passages in the Gospel of John (5:19-24 and 5:25-30) have long perplexed scholars because they seem to represent incompatible perspectives concerning eschatology and the meaning of resurrection. The former, an example of "realized eschatology," stresses the present experience of believers who hear and believe Jesus' message. They do not come into judgment but, as v. 24 declares, they have (*already*, prior to their physical death) passed from death to life. The following passage, on the other hand, represents "future eschatology," insofar as it directs attention to the end-time, when the Son of God and Son of Man will return in his glory. In that final hour, the dead will hear the voice of the Son; they shall come forth from their graves, "those who have done good, to the resurrection of life, and those who have done evil, to the resurrection of judgment (*kriseôs*)."

In the first pericope, judgment has already occurred, in that those who obey Christ's word and believe the Father's testimony about his Son are no longer subject to a final judgment; they have already, in the sphere of their earthly existence, entered into eternal life. The second, on the other hand, lays emphasis on a future hour of judgment which will involve all the dead. Everyone will be judged according to his or her works, and—like the sheep and goats of Jesus' parable of the Last Judgment recorded in Matthew 25—the righteous shall rise to life while the unrighteous shall rise to judgment, implying condemnation.

The wording of these two passages is so similar as to suggest that they are doublets: parallel explanations of the way the Son exercises the authority, bestowed on him by the Father, that grants life to his followers and brings judgment or condemnation upon his opponents. Part of the difficulty we may have in reconciling these two perspectives lies in our rather artificial distinction between "future" and "realized" eschatology. From Albert Schweitzer to C.H. Dodd, debate in Protestant circles tended to become polarized over this issue, and biblical scholars of most traditions seem to have been carried along in the wake of that debate. If we attempt to grasp just how the evangelist himself understood the matter, however, it becomes clear that the two perspectives complement each other. A chiastic analysis of the two passages in fact demonstrates that they belong together as two panels of a diptych. As vv. 25-30 insist, there will indeed be a "last judgment," one in which righteousness and unrighteousness will be made manifest and will serve as the criterion by which final resurrection leads to eternal life or eternal condemnation (if indeed this is the implication of "judgment" in v. 30). On the other hand, v. 24 speaks of the passage from death to life that occurs in this age as a result of faith: the passage from unbelief and rejection of Christ to eternal communion in him.

Insofar as the Johannine Christians have already committed themselves to belief in Jesus as Son of God and Son of Man, to whom the Father has granted the authority to judge the living and the dead, they have already passed from "death" (unbelief) to "life" (belief). In the present age, the Son implicitly exercises judgment on the world through his teaching and healing mission (the "signs" of his ultimate, divine authority). Those who believe in him, and manifest that belief through their faithfulness to his word, participate *already* in "eternal life." Nevertheless, consistent with the traditional eschatological perspective of the early Church, the evangelist complements this affirmation concerning the present reality of eternal life by including the assurance that future judgment will occur at the parousia or return of Christ in glory. At the close of the present age the Son will come to call forth from the tomb all mankind, and to execute a judgment that will mean for some a final resurrection to life, and for others a final resurrection to condemnation. Yet in a distinctively Johannine perspective, even this end-time judgment occurs in the present, at least for those who now hear and now accept Jesus' testimony about himself. Thus v. 25: "Truly, truly, I say to you, the hour is coming, *and now is*, when the dead will hear the voice of the Son of God, *and those who hear will live*." Nothing is said of the "others." The focus in both v. 24 and v. 25 is upon the *faithful*: it is they who, in this present age, receive the gift of life, by virtue of their belief and their adherence to Jesus' "word" (the commandment to "love one another," 13:34). The passage from spiritual death to spiritual life occurs in the framework of the believer's present earthly existence. It will be confirmed at the final resurrection, however, when the faithful—who in this present life have already passed beyond judgment—will rise to eternal life, whereas the unfaithful and unrighteous will be subjected to a "resurrection of judgment" that will lead to condemnation. Once again, the two perspectives are complementary. They both emphasize the present experience of eternal life for those who believe in Jesus; they both declare that the Father has granted the Son his own authority to judge; and they both affirm that "judgment" is reserved for those who deny Jesus and thereby bring death upon themselves.

This complementary character of the two passages appears clearly once they are set out according to the chiastic flow that unites them in a single literary unit. Note that there occurs the typical intensification or completion from the first half to the last: from life beyond judgment in the present age, to life beyond judgment in the age to come. (*RSV* translation)

A : Jesus said to them, "Truly, truly, I say to you, *the Son can do nothing of his own accord* (*ou dynatai o huios poiein aph' heautou ouden*), but only *what he sees* the Father doing; for whatever he does, that *the Son does likewise.*

B : For the Father loves the Son, and shows him all that he himself is doing; and *greater works than these* will he show him, that you may *marvel.*

C : For as the Father raises the dead and gives them life, so also the *Son gives life* to whom he will. The *Father* judges no one, but *has given all judgment to the Son,* that all may honor the Son, even as they honor the Father. He who does not honor the Son does not honor the Father who sent him.

D : Truly, truly, I say to you, *he who hears* my word and believes him who sent me *has eternal life*; he does not come into judgment, but has passed from death to life.

D': Truly, truly, I say to you, the hour is coming, and *now is*, when *the dead will hear* the voice of the Son of God, and *those who hear will live.*

C': For as the *Father* has life in himself, so he has granted the *Son* also to *have life in himself, and has given him authority to execute judgment,* because he is the Son of Man.

B': Do not *marvel* at this; for the hour is coming when *all who are in the tombs will hear his voice and come forth,* those who have done good, to the resurrection of life, and those who have done evil, to the resurrection of judgment.

A': I *can do nothing on my own authority* (*ou dynamai egô poiein ap' emautou ouden*); *as I hear, I judge*; and my judgment is just, because I seek not my own will but the will of him who sent me.

The movement from the first strophe (A-D) to the second strophe (D'-A') can be indicated as follows:

A → A': The Son can do nothing by himself →
    I can do nothing by myself. //
    The Son does what the Father does →
    The Son wills what the Father wills.

B → B': The disciples will marvel at "greater things" →
    The disciples will marvel that the Son will call forth the dead from their tombs.

C → C': The Father and the Son give life to the dead →

The Father and the Son have life in themselves. //
The Father has given judgment to the Son →
    The Father has given judgment to the Son because he is the Son of Man
    (the apocalyptic Judge of Dan 7:13 and 1 Enoch).

D → D': He who hears and believes has eternal life now →
    The dead who hear will have life in the coming hour which is already
    present (*nun estin*). //
    Those among the living who hear and believe have passed from death
    to life →
    Those among the dead who hear the Son of God will pass from death
    to life.

The parallelism between these two strophes, 5:19-24 and 5:25-30, makes quite clear the evangelist's intended message: eternal life is a divine gift, presently accessible to those who believe in the Son of God and obey his commandment; and that gift will be confirmed at the last judgment, when the dead in Christ will come forth from the tombs to "the resurrection of life." Rather than opposing or even juxtaposing two different eschatological perspectives—"present" and "future"—the evangelist is in fact describing two complementary dimensions of eternal life: that lived in the present age through faith, and that lived in the age to come, following the "general resurrection."

The evangelist, then, has not juxtaposed two originally separate traditions representing diverse and irreconcilable eschatological perspectives. He has produced a single literary unit, structured according to the laws of chiasmus, which incorporates a unified and coherent theme concerning the role of the Father's Son in bestowing eternal life upon believers.

There is one additional point that this passage illustrates. It is the fact that chiastic patterns are governed by an inner dynamic that can be analyzed in various ways. In his study of John 6, for example, Charles Talbert lays out the parallel couplets of various sections in a way that is somewhat different from my own analysis.[10] This does not mean that one analysis is "right" and the other "wrong." It means, rather, that each of us has sensed the chiastic flow of the passages in question in somewhat different ways. Nevertheless, it can be easily demonstrated that both interpretations correspond to the movement intuited by the evangelist as he worked with and restructured his source material.

The reader will find that the same is true with regard to the analysis of John 5:19-30 offered above, as compared with the study by Peter Ellis.[11] Ellis'

10 Talbert, *Reading John*, 131-142; Breck, *The Shape of Biblical Language*, 204-213.
11 "Inclusion, Chiasm, and the Division of the Fourth Gospel," 295f.

concern is to demonstrate that the fivefold A:B:C:B':A' pattern is consistent throughout the Fourth Gospel and represents its most fundamental "shape." Consequently, he breaks down 5:19-30 as follows: A = 5:19-23; B = 5:24-25; C = 5:26-27; B' = 5:28-29; and A' = 5:30. His use of boldface type to indicate parallel words and themes makes it immediately clear that his analysis corresponds fully to the actual movement of the passage. The evangelist himself presumably had no set chiastic structure in mind as he composed this particular passage. He clearly wanted to structure the Gospel as a whole "from the extremities toward the middle," and he consciously composed the whole according to the twenty parallel sequences that focus upon sequence eleven, the New Exodus symbolized by the tradition of Christ walking on the water. Within this framework, he also consciously worked the Gospel into five major chiasms, each of which comprises other chiasms. The dominant flow or movement represented throughout thus takes shape as the fivefold pattern A:B:C:B':A'. This does not preclude other patterns, however, such as those that constitute the two strophes of the Bread of Life discourse in chapter 6. The first strophe, vv. 35-47, comprises seven parallel couplets (A-G and G'-A') that focus about v. 42a (H). The second strophe, vv. 48-58, contains eight couplets (A-H and H'-A') that have as their "center of meaning" v. 53 (I): "Truly, truly I say to you, unless you eat the flesh of the Son of Man and drink his blood, you have no life in you."[12] Yet as Ellis demonstrates, both of these strophes incorporate as well the fivefold movement typical of the Gospel as a whole.

With chiastic structures, in other words, we are dealing less with consciously crafted examples of literary artistry than with an *intuited movement*, a complex and flexible flow of thought, by which meaning is expressed through the use of parallel couplets that converge on the author's center of concern, and thereby reveal what we term the "literal sense" of the text.

3. Chiasmus, a Universal Structure

Where a biblical passage has been composed according to the laws of chiasmus, it is of the utmost importance that the reader recognize the chiastic structures and read the text accordingly. This recognition is vital if the reader is to follow the progression of the author's thought and discern his main point, his focus of meaning. Once again we may ask why an author would write this way. And again the answer seems to be that concentric parallelism represents a "deep structure" of the human mind. Without realizing it, we all

12 Breck, ibid., 209-212.

think this way; it is inscribed in our very nature. This rhetorical form represents a movement that can be described as spiral or, more accurately, helical. It constitutes a three-dimensional spiral or "rhetorical helix" consisting of *parallel lines that converge on a center of meaning.*

Elsewhere I have noted numerous examples that demonstrate the ubiquity of chiastic structures outside the biblical corpus.[13] To those examples we can add the Byzantine eucharistic liturgy (the "Divine Liturgy" of St John Chrysostom or St Basil), whose chiastic center is the offertory gesture which concludes the anaphora, "Thine own of Thine own, we offer unto Thee, on behalf of all and for all!" This is flanked by the Words of Institution and the epiklesis, then by various litanies and hymns that parallel one another as the text moves from the center toward the extremities. The Byzantine service of Great Vespers is loosely structured in similar fashion, focusing about the ancient hymn called *Phos Hilaron*, "O Joyful Light."[14]

These are not only literary texts; they are services of praise and supplication that incorporate vital liturgical gestures, the movement of corporate worship. The human mind perceives meaning in both linear and helical fashion, and it expresses that meaning accordingly, in graphic art, music and literature, as well as in the dance of sacred celebration.

Chiasmus thus represents an invaluable key to a proper understanding of Holy Scripture—and of much else in human experience. Because many biblical authors used this rhetorical method to produce their works, it is necessary for us to understand that method in order properly to interpret those works. To hear the Word of God and interpret it correctly and fully, we need to read the chiastic portions of the Bible according to the way they were written. We need to read them "chiastically."

13 *The Shape of Biblical Language*, 273ff.
14 This key element, which itself is arranged chiastically (see *The Shape of Biblical Language*, 287-289) is preceded immediately by the psalms of the *lucernarium* ("Lord I Call") and followed by the psalm verses of the prokeimenon with Old Testament readings. The remaining parallels, moving from the center toward the extremities, include the Great Litany which parallels the augmented and supplication litanies, Psalm 103/104 (Old Covenant creation) which parallels the Aposticha (New Covenant redemption), the repeated Trisagion prayers with their respective hymns ("O Heavenly King" and the Song of Simeon), and finally the opening and closing benedictions.

6

John 21: Appendix,
Epilogue or Conclusion?

1. Introduction

Was chapter 21 of the Gospel of St John composed by the evangelist as the conclusion to his work? Or, as most commentators today contend, does it represent a secondary addition to the Gospel, written by an editor or "final redactor" as an appendix or epilogue to the original writing that concluded with 20:31?[1] In this chapter I want to set forth reasons, based on chiastic analysis of the Fourth Gospel, for considering 21:1-25 to be an original and integral part of the Gospel's composition. These reasons, I believe, offer a strong and perhaps decisive argument for regarding this section not as a later addition to the work, but as the author's own conclusion.

To attribute to John 21 the status of a "conclusion," we need to demonstrate more than stylistic and thematic parallels between it and the preceding chapters. As numerous studies have noted, clever imitation of the evangelist's style and language on the part of a later writer could explain the close similarities between ch. 21 and chs. 1-20. The arguments set forth recently by a small number of scholars suggest rather that ch. 21 can be properly considered a conclusion only if it can be demonstrated that the material it contains actually *completes* or *fulfills* what precedes it in a way that is indispensable to the overall message of the Gospel.[2] My purpose in this chapter is simply to expand upon

1 An "appendix" adds supplemental information to a literary product, material that has no direct bearing on or consequences for the theme that work develops, whereas an "epilogue" *carries forward* some aspect of the theme by describing consequences resulting from its dénouement, its solution or outcome. The "conclusion" of a work, on the other hand, represents the dénouement itself; it presents the results or consequences of the actions or thoughts involved and is an integral part of the work as a whole. To be both complete and intelligible, a literary product must have a conclusion; it need not have an epilogue or an appendix.

2 See especially M. Franzmann and M. Klinger, "The Call Stories of John 1 and John 21," *St Vladimir's Theological Quarterly* 36/1-2 (1992), 7-15, and P.F. Ellis, "The Authenticity of John 21," same issue, 17-25.

certain arguments presented by Lachmann, Klinger, Ellis and others, to support the thesis that John 21 should be considered neither as an appendix[3] nor as an epilogue,[4] but as the actual conclusion to the entire Gospel.

2. Arguments Against the Authenticity of John 21[5]

Of the many arguments that have been advanced against the authenticity of this chapter, the following seem to many interpreters to be the most decisive. We shall consider them separately, together with reasons for rejecting them.

1. *The obvious conclusion to the Gospel of John is provided by 20:30-31, "Now Jesus did many other signs in the presence of the disciples which are not written in this book; but these are written that you may [continue to] believe that Jesus is the Christ, the Son of God, and that believing you may have life in his name." These two verses represent the theological and literary close of the work by declaring the author's purpose, together with his method of selecting among traditional materials available to him. Ch. 21 thus appears as a superfluous anticlimax, particularly in light of its weak ending in v. 25, obviously modeled after 20:30.*

In reply we should note the following:

(a) As Peter Ellis has pointed out, double endings are not unknown in Johannine literature (cf. 1 Jn 5:13, followed by vv. 14-21; and his remarks on ch. 12).[6] In fact, there seems to be a conscious pattern of imitation between the Gospel and the First Epistle: from the stylized prologue (Jn 1:1-18 // 1 Jn 1:1-4), through the body of the writings with their alternation of doctrinal and hortatory material, culminating in a common statement of purpose (eternal life through belief in the "name" of the Son of God: Jn 20:31 // 1 Jn 5:13), and ending with a section that develops the implications of the work's major themes for the life of faith within

---

3   R. Bultmann, *Das Evangelium des Johannes* (Göttingen: Vandenhoeck & Ruprecht, 1964), 542 [ch. 21 "ist ein Nachtrag"].

4   R.E. Brown, *The Gospel According to John* II (Garden City, NY: Doubleday [AB 29a], 1970), 1063ff; J. Zumstein, "La Rédaction finale de l'évangile selon Jean (à l'exemple du chapître 21)," in J.-D. Kaestli, J.-M. Poffet and J. Zumstein, eds., *La Communauté Johannique et Son Histoire* (Geneva: Labor et Fides, 1990), 207-230, esp. 219: "Le ch. 21 doit être considéré pour ce qu'il est, à savoir *un épilogue*, c'est-à-dire un regard retrospectif sur l'oeuvre, destiné à en dévoiler le sens et le statut." In fact, Z.'s arguments in favor of treating Jn 21 as an epilogue effectively confirm its function as an authentic conclusion to the entire Gospel (see below).

5   By "authenticity" we mean that the same author who produced chs. 1-20 also wrote ch. 21 as a conclusion to the entire work. It does not imply a value judgment regarding inspiration or authority. Even if it could be conclusively shown that Jn 21 was added by a disciple of the evangelist, that would in no way affect its canonical status.

6   "The Authenticity of John 21," 20-21.

the Christian community (Jn 21:15-23 // 1 Jn 5:14-21). Jn 20:30f, like 1 Jn 5:13, thus seems to represent a Johannine stylistic device that serves as a pivotal "definition of purpose" between the main body of the writing and the conclusion.

(b) Jn 20:30f and 21:25 form an "inclusion-conclusion" parallelism about the final chapter which, like the Gospel as a whole and each of its individual parts, is structured according to the laws of chiasmus or concentric parallelism, following a basic A:B:C:B':A' pattern:

A : (20:30f) Inclusion: many signs
  B : (21:1-14) The Beloved Disciple and Peter (the BD confesses Jesus)
    C : (21:15-19a): Peter's rehabilitation: "Feed my sheep"
  B': (21:19b-24) The Beloved Disciple and Peter (the BD witnesses to Jesus)
A': (21:25) Conclusion: an overwhelming number of signs.

It is unlikely that such a pattern, consistent as it is with the literary structure of the entire Gospel and of each of its parts, would appear if ch. 21 had been appended by a later and different hand.

(c) Jn 20:30f is a more fitting conclusion to ch. 20 than to the Gospel as a whole, with its mention of "signs" done by Jesus *in the presence of his disciples.* The final verse of ch. 21 refers to the "many other *things*" Jesus did, with no specification as to the audience. This is a general conclusion that concerns not only the disciples, but every believer to whom the entire Gospel is addressed.[7] Certainly 20:30f "sounds" like a conclusion. Consideration of overall Johannine style, however, shows that judgment to be quite subjective.

2. *It seems hardly likely that the original evangelist would depict appearances of the risen Christ in 20:19-29 that set the stage for the apostolic mission—including the commission (v. 21), communication of the Holy Spirit (v. 22), and bestowal of authority to forgive and retain sins (v. 23)—and then follow this with a scene that finds the disciples resuming their life as fishermen in Galilee.*

This objection can be most effectively met by considering the relation of 21:1-14 to the rest of the Gospel message (see below). For the present we can note that this passage depicts the "third time that Jesus was revealed to the disciples after he was raised from the dead" (21:14). R.E. Brown and others have argued that 21:1-14 is a composite of two original traditions,

---

7   See the arguments of Paul S. Minear, "The Original Functions of John 21," *Journal of Biblical Literature* 102/1 (1983), 85-98, at 87: "a strong case can be made for viewing the last two verses of chapter 20 as a conclusion of that chapter alone rather than of the whole book. Those verses are, in fact, very closely linked to verse 29, in which the central motif is that of seeing and believing." He supports his thesis with careful analysis of passages throughout the Gospel.

one a primitive story of Jesus' first appearance to Peter at a fishing scene, the other an account of the first Galilean appearance of Jesus to the disciples at a meal of bread and fish.[8] This is supported by the Lukan parallels, which separate the miraculous catch (5:1-11) from the post-resurrection meal of broiled fish (24:36-43). The chiastic structure of the former passage indicates that Luke received it intact, and that it was never associated, as John 21:9-13, with a post-resurrection meal.[9]

[Lk 5:1 is an example of "anacrusis," an introductory or concluding statement that falls out of the chiastic pattern.]

> A : (5:2) Boats—the fishermen are washing their nets
>> B : (5:3) Jesus teaches the people
>>> C : (5:4) Jesus' command
>>>> D : (5:5) No fish
>>>>> E : (5:6) The miraculous catch
>>>> D': (5:7) Abundant fish
>>> C': (5:8-10a) The disciples' reaction
>> B': (5:10b) Jesus commissions Peter
> A': (5:11) Boats—the fishermen leave all to follow Jesus.

As Ellis has shown, however, John 21:1-14 itself forms a chiastic unit,[10] indicating that the author either received the passage in its present (composite) form, or, more likely, merged the two traditions into a single composition that joins the appearance to Peter on the Lake of Galilee (Tiberias) with the meal of bread and fish shared by the risen Lord with his disciples.

> A : (21:1) Jesus revealed himself to the disciples
>> B : (2-6) The miracle: the disciples did not know that it was Jesus
>>> C : (7) The Beloved Disciple confesses, "It is the Lord!"
>> B': (8-13) The miracle: the disciples knew it was the Lord
> A': (14) Jesus was revealed to the disciples.

In the original call of the disciples (Jn 1:35ff) nothing is said to identify them as fishermen. The tradition lying behind 21:1-14 represents a primitive

---

8 *John* II, 1094.
9 The generally accepted view is that Luke has retrojected a post-resurrection appearance into the early ministry of Jesus, to serve as a setting for the original call of the disciples. While the tradition behind Lk 5 may have come from a resurrection appearance, Luke either received this passage as an independent unit or composed it himself on the basis of material drawn from Mark 1:16-20 and "L," his independent source. For a thorough discussion, see J. Fitzmyer, *The Gospel According to Luke I-IX* (Garden City, NY: Doubleday [AB 28], 1981), 559-564.
10 "Inclusion, Chiasm, and the Division of the Fourth Gospel," *St Vladimir's Theological Quarterly*, 42/3-4 (1999), 336f.

resurrection account that relocates the disciples in Galilee where they were to meet the Risen One (Mk 16:7). As the "third" appearance in the Fourth Gospel,[11] 21:1-14 is not a mere afterthought. In chapters 20 and 21 we are dealing with originally independent traditions. The first (20:19-29) concerns Jesus' appearance(s) to his disciples gathered in Jerusalem. The evangelist has shaped this tradition so as to address the question of apostolic ministry primarily *within the church community* ("Peace," the gift of the Spirit, the authority to forgive or retain sins). The disciples are "sent" (v. 21) even as the Father sent the Son, to call the world to faith. Yet as the Thomas episode and the statement of purpose in vv. 30-31 show, the evangelist's primary concern is with those who need to be strengthened in their belief, to preserve them from falling away, presumably under threat of persecution (cf. 16:2; 9:34-39).

The appearance story in ch. 21, on the other hand, serves to ground the apostles' *universal mission*, symbolized by the miraculous catch of 153 fish. The two elements, 20:19-29 and 21:1-14, complement each other and follow in natural sequence: the former in Jerusalem following the resurrection, the latter once the disciples had returned to Galilee, where they were to meet the Lord in preparation for their wider apostolic task. The modern reader may well be disturbed by the apparent anticlimax of ch. 21 following the crescendo effect of 20:19-29, with its bestowal of the Holy Spirit and Thomas' extraordinary confession. Nevertheless, the evangelist's concern is to interpret and convey his received tradition in such a way as to balance the double appearance in Jerusalem with the third and final appearance in Galilee. With its eucharistic overtones and the crucial element of Peter's profession of love (see below), the entire chapter serves as a fitting and, in fact, indispensable conclusion to the resurrection appearances and to the Gospel as a whole.

3. *Closely related to these first two arguments is the objection that 20:19-29 prepares for the period of the church after the resurrection, when belief rather than eyewitness verification will be required. Thus the "macarism" of v. 29, "Blessed are those who have not seen and yet believe." How, then, could the evangelist pass directly to 21:1-14, where the stress—and indeed, the concentric focus—is upon v. 7, the visual recognition of Jesus by the Beloved Disciple?*

To this we can reply simply that the very nature of an "appearance" or "manifestation" (*ephanerôsen, ephanerôthê*) necessitates visual perception. (Some commentators have tried to mitigate the problem by shifting 20:30f to the end of ch. 21; but in the light of 20:29, this hardly resolves the perceived *aporeia*.) Insofar as a final appearance in Galilee is called for according to the evangelist's plan, that

---

11 Since only males could serve as valid witnesses, Jesus' encounter with Mary Magdalene in the garden (20:11-18) does not qualify as a "manifestation."

too required eyewitnesses. More problematic is the fact that only the Beloved Disciple recognizes Jesus on the shore (vv. 4, 7), and he does so only after having heard and obeyed Jesus' command. This poses no problem, however, once we recall that those who first saw the risen Jesus regularly failed to recognize him (Mary Magdalene, Jn 20:14; Cleopas and his companion, Lk 24:16; cf. the "doubt" of some disciples in Mt 28:17). And as we shall see below, a theological motif lies behind the Beloved Disciple's witness in 21:7 and his interaction with Peter throughout the remainder of the chapter.

4. *The "we" of 21:24 reflects the Johannine community as a whole. Since 21:20-23 clearly implies that the Beloved Disciple is no longer alive at the time of writing, and v. 24 uses the third person ("we know that his witness is true"), the chapter must have been produced by someone other than either the Beloved Disciple or the evangelist.*

One of the peculiarities of Johannine composition is to pass from the singular to the plural in such a way as to incorporate the church community into the witness to Christ. Thus 1:14, "we have beheld his glory," and 3:11, "Truly, Truly I say to you, we speak of what we know, and bear witness to what we have seen..." Similarly, 1 John 1:1-5, where the author speaks in the first person plural regarding the apostolic witness, but shifts to the first person singular when he turns to exhortation (2:1, 7, 12-14, etc.).

In John 21:24, the author identifies the Beloved Disciple as the primary witness to the events recounted—not just in the resurrection scene of this chapter, but in the entire Gospel. His words reaffirm what was already claimed in 19:35, that the witness he bears is true and dependable. It is significant that in 19:35, as in 21:24a, the verb is in the present tense: he has borne witness, yet "he knows that he tells (*legei*) the truth"; "this is the disciple who *is bearing* witness (*ho martyrôn*) to these things." The author of the Gospel, in ch. 19 as in ch. 21, declares that he witnessed both Jesus' death and his resurrection, and that the written testimony itself comes from his hand. Moreover, he identifies himself as "the disciple whom Jesus loved" (21:23-24). Verse 23 does imply that this disciple is no longer alive; yet that is a supposition based on inference and is not clearly stated. In any event, the principle of affirming eyewitness tradition is consistent throughout the Gospel, from the first chapter to the last (1:14; 3:11; 19:35; 21:24). The statements in 21:24, then, simply because they reflect the collective "we" of the community's faith and witness, cannot be used to argue against the authenticity of the chapter.[12]

12 While some interpreters wish to eliminate 19:35 as a redactional gloss, to be consistent they would have to eliminate every other passage, from 1:14 on, that makes similar claims to direct witness or expresses the collective testimony of the community. Such excision would be wholly arbitrary.

5. *Chapter 21 must be considered an appendix, or at least an epilogue, to the Gospel because of its shift in perspective. Whereas the body of the work, chs. 1-20, is exclusively christological, focusing on the person of Jesus, the final chapter is essentially ecclesiological, setting forth the relationship and relative authority of Peter and the Beloved Disciple within the Johannine church.*[13]

While such a shift in perspective is evident in ch. 21, it does not warrant the conclusion that the unit stems from another hand. Ecclesiological concerns are evident throughout the Gospel, particularly in the Farewell Discourses (the Spirit-Paraclete sayings; warnings of persecution; the "vine" metaphor of ch. 15; affirmation that the disciples are "chosen" to "go and bear fruit," 15:16; the prayer for unity, 17:20-23) and in the appearances of the risen Lord in ch. 20. Taken with other passages that refer to the believing community and its mission (e.g., the parable of the sheepfold, ch. 10; the sacramental allusions in 3:5, 6:51-58; 13:10, etc.), it is clear that an "ecclesial" interest is present throughout the Gospel.

In addition, it should be pointed out that such a shift in perspective occurs only at the end of ch. 21, where the focus is on Peter and the Beloved Disciple. Surely the third appearance of the risen Lord in 21:1-14 is as thoroughly "christological" as the appearances in ch. 20; and even the dialogue between Peter and Jesus in 21:15-17, that serves to rehabilitate Peter after his threefold denial, focuses on Christ and Peter's commitment to him. Peter's love is an expression of the love of the church, and it is profoundly "christological."

It is misleading to draw a sharp distinction between christology and ecclesiology in the Fourth Gospel. The two are intimately interconnected. And as the central theme of the prologue demonstrates, both serve the primary interest of the evangelist, which is *soteriological*: that believing, "you may become children of God" and "have life in his name" (1:12f; 20:31).

6. *John 21 develops themes that appear only as secondary interpolations in the rest of the Gospel: vv. 12f reflect the eucharistic passage 6:51c-58; and vv. 22f recall the traditional expectation of the parousia as in 5:28f. These earlier verses, like chapter 21 itself, should be regarded as stemming from a final redactor, someone other than the evangelist.*

Once again, analysis of the chiastic structure of the Fourth Gospel shows that neither 6:51c-58 nor 5:28-29 is secondary. Both passages are thoroughly integrated into their respective contexts and therefore must have been composed by the evangelist himself. The so-called "eucharistic" passage that so

---

13 See in this regard Bultmann, *Johannesevangelium*, 543; and R.A. Culpepper, *Anatomy of the Fourth Gospel: A Study in Literary Design* (Philadelphia: Fortress Press, 1983), 101ff.

many critics want to remove from ch. 6 as an interpolation by an "ecclesial redactor" is actually an integral part of the unit 6:48-58.[14] And Ellis has shown that 5:28f is part of a chiastic unit that includes 5:19-30.[15] Chiastic structures are flexible, and although the basic Johannine pattern is the fivefold A:B:C:B':A', a somewhat different analysis, worked out in detail in our last chapter, preserves the proper tension between what appears to be "realized" and "future" eschatology reflected respectively in 5:24 and 5:25.[16] We can summarize that analysis as follows:

A : (19) The Son does nothing of his own accord
   B : (20) Greater works: that you may marvel
      C : (21-23) The Father has given the Son all judgment
         D : (24) "He who hears my voice and believes him who sent me has eternal life"
         D': (25) "The dead will hear the voice of the Son of God, and those who hear will live"
      C': (26-27) The Father has given the Son authority to execute judgment
   B': (28f) Resurrection and Judgment: the greater marvel
A': (30) The Son does nothing on his own authority.

These supposed interpolations into the text of the Gospel are not interpolations at all. Consequently they do nothing to support the argument that ch. 21 is a similar type of addition.

7. The vocabulary and stylistic expressions of ch. 21 are sufficiently different from the rest of the Gospel as to make it clear that they derive from a different author.

After evaluating the language and style of John 21, drawing from the work of his predecessors and applying his own remarkable analytical talents, Rudolf Bultmann concluded that neither the language nor the style of the chapter indisputably betrays the hand of a redactor.[17] He also noted that the passage includes many words that appear nowhere else in John. This can be

---

14 This is demonstrated, once again on the basis of chiastic analysis, in J. Breck, *The Shape of Biblical Language. Chiasmus in the Scriptures and Beyond* (New York: St Vladimir's Seminary Press, 1994), 204-213.

15 Peter F. Ellis, *The Genius of John: A Composition-Critical Commentary on the Fourth Gospel,* (Collegeville, MN: The Liturgical Press, 1984), 90f; "Inclusion, Chiasm, and the Division of the Fourth Gospel," 294-296; see also chapter 5 above.

16 In fact "the dead" of v. 25 refers most likely to those who in this world abide in spiritual death; when they hear (i.e., believe) the message proclaimed by (or about) the Son of God, they will live. The designation of v. 24 as "realized" eschatology and v. 25 as "future" eschatology, as we stressed earlier, is artificial and misleading. The latter, as much as the former, refers to the present: "The hour is coming *and now is...*"

17 *Johannesevangelium,* 542f. See as well Bishop Cassian (Besobrasoff), "John XXI," *New Testament Studies* 3 (1956-7), 132-136.

explained, however, by the fact that most are found in the narrative of the fishing expedition and represent technical expressions linked to the fishing trade (e.g., *halieuô*, to fish: v. 3; *piazô*, to catch: vv. 3, 10; *aigialos*, shore: v. 4; *prosphagion*, fish: v. 5; *diktuon*, net: vv. 6, 8; *syrô*, to drag: v: 8; *apobainô*, disembark: v. 9). There are other words in ch. 21 that appear nowhere else in the Gospel, but these too derive from their respective contexts (*prôïa*, before dawn: v. 4; *ependouomai*, to clothe, *gymnos*, naked: v. 7; *boskô*, to feed, *arnion*, lamb: v. 15; *poimainô*, tend / care for, *probation*, little sheep: v. 16f).

M.-E. Boismard has argued on the basis of parallels between John 21 and the Lukan writings that the third evangelist himself was the final editor of John's Gospel and the one who produced chapter 21.[18] As intriguing as the parallels are between Luke and John, they do not justify such a conclusion, and Boismard's thesis has been generally rejected.

3. The Structural Relationship of Sequences 1 and 21

There may be other, more decisive arguments against the authenticity of John 21 than those given above. Those, however, are the ones most frequently advanced, and they clearly fall short of proof. When this negative evidence is coupled with further consideration of the concentric structure of Johannine prose, the authenticity of ch. 21 seems virtually established.

Recalling that Ellis's analysis of John's Gospel balances sequence 1 (1:19-51) with sequence 21 (20:19-21:25), we can set out these passages in such a way as to demonstrate the inverted parallelism that exists between them.

A : (1:19-28) John the Baptist as witness.
   B : (1:29-34) John bears witness to Jesus.
      C : (1:35-39) Jesus to two disciples: "Come and see!" (theme: to follow Jesus).
         D : (1:40-42) Jesus calls Peter.
            E : (1:43-46) In Galilee: Jesus calls 5 disciples, including Nathanael.
               F : (1:47-49) Nathanael's confession (Son of God / King of Israel).
                  G : (1:50f) The disciples will *see* greater things: angels ascending and descending on the Son of Man.
                  G': (20:19-23) The disciples *see* the risen Lord who bestows the Holy Spirit.
               F': (20:24-31) Thomas' confession (Lord / God).[19]

18 "Le Chapitre xxi de S. Jean: Essai de critique littéraire," *Revue Biblique* 54 (1947), 473-501; "Saint Luc et la rédaction du IVe évangile," *RB* 69 (1962), 185-211.
19 Regarding the argument against the authenticity of Jn 21 based on the movement from Thomas' sublime confession in Jerusalem to the mundane fishing scene in Galilee: the

E': (21:1-14) In Galilee: Jesus appears to 5 (?) disciples, including Nathanael.[20]

D': (21:15-17) Jesus rehabilitates Peter.

C': (21:18f) Jesus to Peter: "Follow me!" (theme: to follow Jesus to death).

B': (21 20-23) Jesus bears witness to the Beloved Disciple.

A': (21:24) The Beloved Disciple as witness.

The parallels appear still more clearly in the following outline. With a careful reading, one can detect an important feature of much biblical poetry, including chiastic patterns: there is a "heightening" or "focusing" from the first parallel line to its prime complement, such that the movement of thought spirals from A:A' to B:B', to C:C', and on to G:G', which is the "conceptual center" or principal theme of the passage. This forward movement of thought can be indicated by an arrow.[21]

A : John the Baptist as witness →
A': The Beloved Disciple as witness

B: John the Baptist bears witness to Jesus →
B': Jesus bears witness to the Beloved Disciple

evangelist evidently felt that it was more important to establish a parallelism in his narrative between F and F' than to avoid the "problem" created by following 20:24-31 with 21:1-14. No other arrangement of his materials would have preserved the balance between the confession of Nathanael and the more exalted confession of Thomas.

20 In the entire NT, Nathanael appears only in these two passages, 1:47-50, and 21:2. In 21:2, seven disciples are named, including the sons of Zebedee (or rather, *hoi tou Zebedaiou*). The evangelist avoids mentioning these brothers throughout the rest of the Gospel, a striking fact, given their prominence in the Synoptic tradition. This seems intentional, presumably because one of the brothers, John, is himself the unnamed "other disciple," who is with Andrew in 1:35f, and in 18:15f is able to lead Peter into the court of the high priest where Jesus was tried, because he (John) "was known to the high priest" (perhaps implying that he, like his former mentor, John the Baptist, came from a priestly family). This "other disciple" is further identified as "the disciple whom Jesus loved" or the Beloved Disciple (13:23; 19:26; 20:2; 21:7, 20). If such care is taken to preserve his anonymity throughout the Gospel, why in 21:2 should the author—even a redactor—identify him as "a (son) of Zebedee"? M.-J. Lagrange, *Evangile selon Saint Jean* (Paris: Gabalda, 1936) made the interesting and plausible suggestion that 21:2 originally mentioned only five disciples: Simon Peter, Thomas, Nathanael, and "two others." A later scribe added a marginal gloss, identifying the two as *hoi tou Z.*, and the gloss was subsequently incorporated into the text. This would explain the abbreviated formula (the Synoptics read *hoi huioi tou Z.*). It would also leave the same number of disciples in 21:2 as in ch. 1. If Thomas is named in place of Philip or Andrew, it is to link the fishing scene of ch. 21 to the appearance of Jesus in Jerusalem, 20:19-29.

21 For the phenomenon of chiasmus and its focus upon a central theme, see ch. 5 above; also, J. Breck, *The Shape of Biblical Language*, 38-58; and P.F. Ellis, *The Genius of John*, 11-18. For the "heightening" characteristic of Hebrew poetry, see James Kugel, *The Idea of Biblical Poetry, Parallelism and Its History* (New Haven: Yale University Press, 1981).

C: Jesus summons two unnamed disciples: "Come and see!" →
C': Jesus summons Peter: "Follow me!"

D : Jesus calls Peter →
D': Jesus rehabilitates Peter

E : Jesus calls the disciples (Galilee, Nathanael) →
E': Jesus appears to the disciples (Galilee, Nathanael)

F : Nathanael's confession (Son of God / King of Israel) →
F': Thomas' confession (Lord / God)

G : The disciples shall see greater things →
G': The disciples see the risen Lord.

The sense of the passage unfolds in a progressive spiral, from the extremities (A:A') toward the center (G:G'). From the dual witness of John the Baptist and the Beloved Disciple, the flow of meaning develops the theme of witness, the command to discipleship, then the call and rehabilitation of the chief disciple. Progressing through the double confession, by Nathanael and by Thomas, its main focus is upon the disciples' direct experience of Jesus: seeing, they believe.

Yet within this spiraling movement, there is a heightening or increment from one line to the next: A is heightened or intensified by A', B by B', and so on, as the reader is drawn in a vortex toward the primary affirmation of the two sequences: the disciples' belief is ultimately grounded in their personal experience, their *vision*, of the Resurrected Lord.

No interpreter seriously questions that John 20:19-29 (30-31) is an original and integral part of the evangelist's composition. Analysis of the Gospel into sequences, however, demonstrates two key points: first, *that John 20:19-31 together with 21:1-25 constitutes a single literary unit;* and second, that *ch. 21, as much as 20:19ff, finds both verbal and thematic parallels in 1:19-51.* It is inconceivable that a redactor could have created such intricate parallelism beginning with 21:1, even if he had been aware of such parallelism throughout the rest of the Gospel. The structural correspondence between the two segments, sequence 1 and sequence 21, thus confirms that John 21 itself is an original and integral part of the composition, a genuine "conclusion" to themes introduced in chapter one.

4. Chapter 21 in the Overall Plan of the Gospel

As a final approach toward resolving the question of the authenticity of John 21, we may consider the way in which this chapter completes or fulfills themes developed earlier in the Gospel narrative. By examining individually the three main sections of the chapter, we can show that each one serves to conclude events, thoughts or actions that were left in some degree of suspension earlier on.

Most commentators find that the chapter divides into two main sections, vv. 1-14 and 15-23, followed by the "second conclusion," vv. 24-25.[22] Returning to the chiastic analysis of John 20:30-21:25, given above, we find a more likely division along the following lines, corresponding to the A:B:C:B':A' structure of the Gospel as a whole:

A : (20:30-31) Inclusion: many signs →
A': (21:25) Conclusion: an overwhelming number of signs

B : (21:1-14) The Beloved Disciple and Peter (the BD confesses Jesus) →
B': (21:20-24) The Beloved Disciple and Peter (the BD witnesses to Jesus)[23]

C : (21:15-19) Peter's rehabilitation: "Feed my sheep!"

The principal theme that serves as the focus of meaning for the whole of this passage is Peter's threefold rehabilitation, vv. 15-17. This is introduced by the third resurrection appearance at the Sea of Tiberias, which provides the setting for the entire chapter. It is followed by the dialogue between Jesus and Peter concerning the Beloved Disciple and his role in the ecclesial community relative to that of Peter. Taking these sections in order, we can suggest ways in which each serves as a necessary conclusion to themes that were introduced earlier in the Gospel.

The inclusion consists of a statement of purpose that appears to have been intentionally structured as a chiastic unit:

A : "Now Jesus also did many other signs
  B : in the presence of his disciples,
    C : which are not written
      D : in this book;
    C': but these are written
  B': so that you might believe that Jesus is the Christ, the Son of God,
A': and that believing you may have life in his name."

The parallels are more thematic than verbal; and again they evidence a tendency toward heightening, from the first line to its prime complement:

A : The signs →
A': The purpose of the signs

22 E.g., R.E. Brown, *John* II, 1123ff.
23 The witness referred to in 21:24 concerns all that Jesus did during his earthly ministry, and not merely his preceding dialogue with Peter.

B : The disciples →
B': The disciples' confession[24]

C : Signs not recorded →
C': Signs recorded

D : The written witness (the Gospel)

This is then balanced by the conclusion to ch. 21, which is possibly structured along similar lines:

A : "But there are also many other things
　B : which Jesus did,
　　C : which if every one were to be written,
　B': I think that the world itself could not contain
A': the books that would be written."

If there is in fact some intentional concentricity implied here, it would seem to be as follows:

A : Many other things (signs) →
A': Many written witnesses (to the signs)

B : Jesus' capacity (to work the signs) →
B': The world's incapacity (to contain the witness)

C : The written witness (gospels)

Within this envelope created by 20:30-31 and 21:25, there are three passages, the first and last of which focus on the relationship between Jesus, Peter and the Beloved Disciple. As we noted earlier, the first of these (21:1-14) follows a familiar chiastic pattern with heightening toward the central theme. With a minor modification of Ellis's analysis, we can set out the parallels as follows:

A : (1) Another appearance (Jesus revealed himself to the disciples) →
A': (14) The third appearance (Jesus was revealed to the disciples after he was raised from the dead)

B : (2-3a) The disciples embark to fish (sustenance) →
B': (9-13) The disciples land, they eat bread and fish (Eucharist)

24 Peter's confession, corresponding to Mk 8:29, occurs in Jn 6:69, "we have believed, and have come to know that you are the Holy One of God." With its stress on belief and knowledge, it represents the conviction of everyone who faithfully adheres to Jesus and his commandments. The closest parallel to the Synoptic confession of Jesus, however, is found in John's Gospel on the lips of Martha: "I believe that you are the Christ, the Son of God, he who is coming into the world" (11:27).

C : (3b-5) No fish →
C': (8) The net full of fish

D : (6) The disciples' response to Jesus (cast the net) →
D': (7b) Peter's response to Jesus (leaps into the water)

E : (7a) The Beloved Disciple's confession, "It is the Lord!"

The second and third sections of ch. 21 present Peter's threefold profession of love, and his questions concerning the Beloved Disciple. Peter Ellis has shown, however, that the two sections are woven into a single chiastic unit, 21:15-25.

A : (15-17) Peter's function as vicar-shepherd of Jesus. →
A': (24f) The Beloved Disciple's function as witness to Jesus.

B : (18f) John affirms that Jesus told Peter he would die. →
B': (21-23) John denies that Jesus told Peter the Beloved Disciple would not die.

C : (20) Peter and the Beloved Disciple.[25]

Note as well that B and B' contain Jesus' double command addressed to Peter, which again is heightened from v. 19b to 22b:

B : "Follow me" (*akolouthei moi*) →
B': "As for you, follow me!" (*su moi akolouthei*).

The theme of "following" is central to the Gospel and is a key to the relationship between Peter and the Beloved Disciple throughout the entire work. It is well known that St Luke, in both the Gospel and Acts, associates Peter and John in a particularly close way.[26] In the memory of the Johannine community, Peter and John exercise complementary roles both during and after Jesus' earthly ministry: Peter receives the call to "follow" to the point of martyrdom (21:19, 22), whereas the Beloved Disciple (John, son of Zebedee)[27]

25 P.F. Ellis, *The Genius of John*, 303; "Inclusion, Chiasm, and the Division of the Fourth Gospel," 337f.
26 The two apostles frequently appear working together; or when Peter appears with the sons of Zebedee, John rather than James is often named first: Luke 8:51, "Peter and John and James"; cf. 9:28; 22:8 where Jesus sends Peter and John to prepare the Passover; Acts 1:13; 3:1, 4, 11; 4:13, 19; and 8:14 where Peter and John are sent to the disciples in Samaria to bestow the Holy Spirit.
27 However the question of the authorship of the Fourth Gospel is to be decided, there can be little doubt that within the narrative itself the BD is to be recognized as the apostle John. This is the universal opinion of the ancient Church, and modern critics seem to be returning to it as the most likely hypothesis. R. Schnackenburg, *The Gospel According to St John*, vol. 1 (New York: Crossroad, 1987), 101-104, suggests that the Gospel "grew out of the preaching of John the son of Zebedee which was gradually committed to writing" by a

exercises the function of primary "witness" to the person and meaning of Jesus. A question that remains difficult to resolve is whether there is a conscious effort, reflected in chs. 1-20 as in ch. 21, to set the Beloved Disciple above Peter as the one who was and remains the faithful witness and disciple of the Lord.

If we pursue the theme of "following," we note that the description of the Beloved Disciple in 21:20 seems to support such a thesis: he is identified as "the disciple whom Jesus loved," "who had lain close to his breast at the supper," and had served as mediator between Peter and Jesus by raising the question of the identity of Jesus' betrayer. Moreover, although most critics deny the connection, there seems to be a conscious play on the word "following" in 21:19-22. Interposed between Jesus' double call to Peter to exercise faithful discipleship ("Follow me!"), the author notes that "Peter turned and saw *following* (*akolouthounta*)[28] the disciple whom Jesus loved." The Beloved Disciple, in other words, is already following Jesus, as he has throughout the Gospel (he is closest to Jesus at the Supper; he follows Jesus into the courtyard of the high priest; he alone among the male disciples is present at the foot of the Cross). Therefore he is and has been accomplishing what Peter, after his triple denial and triple affirmation of love, is now called to do: "Follow me!" Whereas Peter is called to lay down his life for Jesus, the Beloved Disciple "follows" his Lord by bearing faithful witness to him. The exchange between Peter and Jesus in 21:21-23, then, seems to reflect a deliberate intention on the part of the author to attribute priority, in both witness and authority, to the Beloved Disciple relative to Peter.

This opinion can be verified by examining the relation between the two men as it appears elsewhere in the Gospel. For the evangelist, as for the Christian tradition as a whole, there is no question that Peter was established by Jesus as the leader of the Twelve. Yet invariably there is some qualification that tends to diminish Peter's role or personal authority. In 1:42 Simon receives the new name Cephas/Peter, "the rock," but without any further explanation. Simon Peter confesses Jesus as "the Holy One of God" after the defection of many followers (6:69), yet the traditional confession of Jesus' messiahship and divine sonship is made rather by *Martha* (11:27). At the Supper, Jesus comes to Peter to wash his feet as a (baptismal) image of

Hellenistic Christian. The apostle's disciples, rather than he himself, substituted the expression "the disciple whom Jesus loved" for the original "I" in those places where he affirms eyewitness testimony.

28 The *Revised Standard Version* and *New Revised Standard Version* read "following them," whereas the pronoun object of the action is omitted in the Greek.

cleansing, but Peter misunderstands his intention and initially refuses the gesture (13:8). And again at the Supper, Peter does not address Jesus directly, but asks the Beloved Disciple to do so, since this Disciple was reclining close to Jesus' breast. After Peter's profession of faithfulness, Jesus replies with the prophecy of Peter's triple denial (13:38). In the Garden, Peter alone attempts to defend Jesus by the sword, and he is rebuked for his lack of comprehension of Jesus' true mission (18:10f). At Jesus' trial before the high priest, the Beloved Disciple enters while Peter remains outside; and once within, having been led inside by the Disciple, Peter proceeds to deny any association with Jesus (18:15ff).

Finally, in the account of the empty tomb (20:3-10), the Disciple outruns Peter and arrives first; and he is the first to witness the linen cloths, a sign of the resurrection.[29] Peter, as the undisputed "apostolic leader," enters the tomb ahead of the other. Yet although he beholds both the cloths and the napkin, he makes no apparent response. The Beloved Disciple, on the other hand, "saw and believed," even though "they did not [yet] know the scripture, that [Jesus] must rise from the dead." In each of these passages, the author clearly intends to affirm the priority, if not the superiority, of the Beloved Disciple relative to Peter.

Moreover, certain significant elements of the Gospel remain "hanging," suspended in the narrative as though awaiting further development. The most notable of these is Peter's call. Nothing is said in 1:40-42 about why Jesus renames Simon, or what Peter's role is to be within the Christian community. This is only provided in ch. 21, with Peter's threefold profession of love for Jesus[30] and the command, "follow me." As Lachmann and Klinger have argued,[31] Peter's call to discipleship, a basic and indispensable element of Gospel tradition, is only established in ch. 21. From a Johannine perspective, that call was contingent on Peter's rehabilitation, following his threefold denial of Jesus before the crucifixion (18:17, 25-27). That rehabilitation, however, includes not only the command "Feed my sheep." It also involves a commitment to "follow" Jesus on the pathway to martyrdom (vv. 19, 22). Thus 21:18f both continues and clarifies the prophecy uttered by Jesus to

29 In other ancient tradition, Peter is the first to witness the risen Christ: 1 Cor 15:5; and Lk 24:34, which is very likely an interpolation into the Emmaus story: note the awkward *legontas hoti;* the remainder of the phrase, "Truly the Lord is risen and has appeared to Simon," is a stereotyped, very early kerygmatic formula; and the entire verse can be lifted from its context, leaving a seamless narrative from v. 33 to v. 35.

30 Nothing can be made of the change in verb from *agapaô* to *phileô* in 21:15-17. In 20:2, the verb used to describe the BD is *ephilei,* whereas elsewhere the formula uses *ègapa.*

31 "The Call Stories of John 1 and John 21," note 2 above.

Peter in the Upper Room: "Where I am going, you cannot follow me now; but you shall follow afterward" (13:36).[32]

In ch. 21, then, Peter's initial call is given content and his rehabilitation is achieved, indicating once again that this chapter is an indispensable conclusion to the entire work.

Similarly, chapter 21 affirms the authority behind the witness of the Beloved Disciple, an authority that is only presupposed in earlier portions of the Gospel. Although Peter asks him to discover from Jesus the name of the betrayer, the Disciple says nothing. What is affirmed is the fact of his intimate proximity to Jesus and his capacity to receive privileged information. At the cross, he receives Jesus' mother in an extraordinary gesture of confidence, then he beholds evidence of Jesus' physical death in the outpouring of water and blood from the pierced side (19:34). At this he declares to the reader that what he has seen and proclaimed is true and the ground of Christian faith.

If the Gospel had been completed without chapter 21, then the final element in this Disciple's witness would be his "seeing and believing" the evidence of Jesus' resurrection in the empty tomb. That this was hardly the evangelist's intention, however, is clear from the statement in 20:9, that neither the Beloved Disciple nor Peter knew from the scriptures that Jesus must rise from the dead. The account cries out for a conclusion, one that is furnished precisely in the fishing scene of 21:1-14. As the chiastic analysis shows, the heart of that passage is the recognition—with the force of a confession—made by the Beloved Disciple, "It is the Lord!" (21:7). The disciple whom Jesus loved is again the first "to see and believe" the appearance of the Lord on the shore. (Significantly, Peter leaps into the water *only at the word of the Beloved Disciple*, and not because he has verified Jesus' presence for himself.) Here we find that Disciple's final and ultimate witness in the framework of the Gospel narrative: that the crucified Jesus is *alive*.

As the risen Lord, Jesus is present with his disciples, to guide and strengthen them in their apostolic mission and to nourish them with the "bread of life" which is his flesh, symbolized in the elements of bread and fish.[33] It is to this

---

32 Stress upon the verb "follow" is indicated in the Greek by inversion: *ou dynasai moi nun akolouthêsai, akolouthêseis de hysteron.* Cf. 21:19, 22: *akolouthei moi, su moi akolouthei.*

33 Cf. 6:51ff. That this passage has eucharistic overtones is suggested not only by Jesus' invitation to the disciples to share a post-resurrectional meal with him, but also by the fact that Jesus himself provides the bread and fish. An intentional link between 21:13 and 6:11 may be indicated by the use (unique to these passages) of the term *opsarion* for "fish." Is it merely coincidental that the resurrection appearances in Luke's Gospel also couple the presence of Christ in the Eucharist (symbolized in the independent accounts of Emmaus [24:30f] and the eating of broiled fish [24:41-43]) with the command to universal mission (24:45-48)?

that the Beloved Disciple bears witness in the conclusion of the Gospel, and it is for this that he is "to remain" until Jesus comes again. Peter, the shepherd of the flock, will go the way of his master, to crucifixion. The Beloved Disciple, on the other hand, is destined to *remain* (*menein*): that most significant of Johannine verbs, whose basic meaning is "to indwell."[34] Through his remaining or abiding within the community of faith, he serves to guarantee the truth of the witness which he bears to Jesus by means of his preaching, teaching and writing. Accordingly, he is the primary agent of the Paraclete, the Spirit of Truth, who receives from the risen Lord all that is his, and communicates it to the church through the written Gospel (Jn 16:13-15). Whether the Beloved Disciple died or not is immaterial. His witness will in any case endure (*menein*) throughout the present age, until the Lord comes again.

5. Conclusion

Evidence based on vocabulary and literary style alone offers very solid support for the authenticity of John 21. Much of that evidence has already appeared in commentaries on the Gospel and articles treating specifically the question of its literary integrity. Bishop Cassian advanced the discussion significantly by demonstrating the link between Jesus' role as Good Shepherd and Peter's call to assume responsibility for the Christian flock in the period following Jesus' glorification.[35] Paul Minear's study,[36] reinforced by Lachmann and Klinger,[37] demonstrated thematic parallels between ch. 21 and earlier passages in the Gospel that should settle the matter for all but the most skeptical minds. If further evidence were needed, it would seem to be provided by Peter Ellis's chiastic analysis of the Gospel and the links that analysis provides with other sections.[38] In each of these approaches the authors have attempted to show not only the similarities in language, style and theme between the so-called appendix (or epilogue) and the rest of the work, but to demonstrate as well that the final chapter in fact fulfills or completes elements of the Johannine witness that would otherwise be left in suspension.

We have attempted to do basically the same by extending the chiastic analysis to individual units, as well as to sequences 1 and 21 as Ellis defines them.

34 The Fourth Gospel alone declares that at Jesus' baptism the Spirit descended and *remained* on him (1:32f); the repetition reinforces the image of the Spirit dwelling within Jesus, to be first manifested and communicated at the "Johannine Pentecost" (cf. 7:39 with 20:22).

35 Note 18 above.

36 Note 8 above.

37 Note 2 above.

38 Notes 2, 11, 16 above.

The first and last sequences of the Fourth Gospel were intentionally composed by the evangelist according to the pattern of inverted parallelism: the opening section of seq. 1 (the Baptist's witness) corresponds to the closing section of seq. 21 (the Beloved Disciple's witness), etc., moving through the initial call and rehabilitation-call of Peter, and the complementary confessions of Nathanael and Thomas, to focus upon the central theme of "seeing and believing" the Son of Man to be the Risen Lord (1:51 // 20:19ff). Given the overall chiastic structure of the Gospel, the parallelism between 1:19-51 and 20:19-21:25 can hardly be coincidental. It is a deliberate literary technique used by the evangelist to draw the reader's attention toward *a central point of focus*. The Gospel and its component parts, in other words, must be read from two complementary perspectives: according to the linear development of narrative prose; and "concentrically," from the extremities toward the middle, following the flow of meaning that unfolds through use of inverted parallelism.

Once this principle is accepted, then the function of ch. 21 as a genuine *conclusion* becomes all the more evident. As Lachmann and Klinger detected (on other grounds), there is an intentional parallelism between the call stories of ch. 1 and those of ch. 21. The latter, moreover, not only complement the former, they actually "fulfill" them. The disciples are initially called by Jesus to "come and see." This invitation only achieves its purpose, however, with the apostolic commissions of ch. 21, implied in the miraculous catch of fish and made explicit in the dialogue between Jesus and Peter. It is only in this final chapter that the disciples are truly qualified to serve as "fishers of men," a designation the Synoptic tradition attributes to them from the outset of their travels with Jesus during his public ministry. And it is only here as well that the relation between Peter and the Beloved Disciple is clearly delineated. What is hinted at in earlier portions of the Gospel becomes explicit both with Peter's establishment as "vicar-shepherd," and with the Beloved Disciple's (or his community's) claim to authoritative witness. Without chapter 21, the disciples' call, together with the roles of Peter and the Beloved Disciple, are left hanging, begging for resolution.

Returning to the inclusion-conclusion envelope created by the witness to Jesus on the part of John the Baptist and the Beloved Disciple: it is perhaps significant that in each case that witness is heightened and given prominence through repetition. In 1:31-33, the Baptist twice declares, "I did not know him," yet affirms that he saw the Spirit descend like a dove and remain upon him. It is for this witness that he came, baptizing in water, to prepare the way for that one who will baptize with the Holy Spirit. That baptism is accomplished in the Upper Room on the night of the resurrection (20:22).

The Baptist's witness, however, is fulfilled only through the ministry of the Disciple whom Jesus loved, about whom Jesus twice affirms that "he will remain until I come" (21:22-23). The "we" of v. 24 should not be regarded as "editorial." Rather, like the "we" of 1:14-16, 3:11 and 1 John 1:1-5, it expresses the solidarity of the author with the community he represents. The Gospel which enshrines his witness, then, most appropriately closes with the recollection that the truth of that witness, together with its authority, are guaranteed by the risen Lord himself.

7

The Function of Πᾶς in
1 John 2:20

Καὶ ὑμεῖς χρῖσμα ἔχετε ἀπὸ τοῦ ἁγίου
καὶ οἴδατε πάντες / καὶ οἴδατε πάντα

"But you have an anointing from the Holy One
and you all know / and you know all things."

Since the publication of several influential commentaries on the Johannine Epistles early in the twentieth century,[1] most scholars have considered the question of the correct reading for πᾶς in 1 John 2:20 to be closed. The *Textus Receptus* (TR) has been set aside at this point in favor of older witnesses. Recent discoveries of gnostic documents and the light they shed on the type of heresy believed to be opposed in the First Epistle have to most minds weighed conclusively in favor of the reading πάντες ("you all know" / "all of you have knowledge") rather than πάντα ("you know all things"). The aim of this chapter is threefold. It is first to illustrate certain textual problems involved with ascertaining the dependability of variant readings in a given witness; then to indicate the special, characteristically Johannine usage of πᾶς in 1 John 2:18-28. In addition, we want to demonstrate the importance of chiastic analysis of the passage for settling the question of the variant reading for πᾶς in 2:20.

1. The Textual Witnesses

Primary witnesses for the πάντα reading are A, C, M (Majority text), latt (it vg), sy[h], aeth, and L.

---

1 E.g., B. Weiss, *Die drei Briefe des Apostel Johannes* (Göttingen, 1899-1900); Holtzmann-Bauer, *Johannesbriefe* (Tübingen, 1908); A.E. Brooke, *Johannine Epistles*, (Edinburgh, 1912).

A—Codex Alexandrinus, fifth century, Alexandria;[2] Gospels are α (Byzantine) text type; Acts, Epistles, Revelation are β type. The A text of 1 John contains several noteworthy variants. In 1:7, A M vg sy[h] insert Χριστου after Ιησου. In 2:15, A C read Θεου for πατρος. In 4:7, A inserts τον Θεον after αγαπων. In 4:19, A, vg read ο Θεος for αυτος. In 4:21, A, vg[cl] read απο του Θεου for απ᾽ αυτου. In 5:6, A inserts (with Sinaiticus) πνευματος after αιματος. In 5:10, A inserts του Θεου after the first μαρτυριαν and reads τω υιω for τω Θεω. In 5:14, A reads ονομα for Θελημα. And in 5:20, A inserts Θεον after αληθινον.

C—Codex Ephraemi (palimpsest), fifth century, Syria; text type γ, a revision of β (Alexandrian) according to Westcott-Hort. Nestle groups C with B and Sinaiticus as representing the so-called Hesychian Egyptian text type—a designation now discarded. The manuscript preserves a few insignificant variants, usually in common with A and/or M.

M—Majority text, corresponding roughly to the "Koinê" (Nestle's K), "Byzantine" (von Soden) or "Syrian" (Westcott-Hort) text. The earliest form of the Koinê text goes back to Lucian of Antioch (late 3rd or early 4th cent.); its latest version constitutes the *Textus Receptus*. This Byzantine witness is considered "secondary" by most scholars because of its many revisions, including a marked tendency to harmonize the Gospel tradition. In 1 Jn 4:3, M reads Ιησουν Χριστον for τον Ιησουν, and with Sinaiticus repeats from 4:2 εν σαρκι εληλυθοτα.

it—Old Latin version, ca. 200; North Africa, Rome, Gaul; of δ or Western text type.

vg—Vulgate version (Jerome's revision of *it*), 385 A.D.[3] Text type δ. In 5:6, vg reads Χριστος for το πνευμα.

sy[h]—Harklean Syriac version, 616 A.D., Alexandria; δ text type.

aeth—Ethiopic version, fifth to sixth centuries, with extant mss. from the thirteenth century.

L—Codex Regius, eighth century; of β text type.

2 Or, as Souter contends, Constantinople: A. Souter, *Text and Canon of the New Testament* 2nd ed., London 1954, 22. See B. Metzger, *The Text of the New Testament* (New York: Oxford, 1964), 46f.
3 The best extant Vulgate ms. is probably Codex Amiatinus, which dates from the eighth century. See B. Metzger, *Text*, 77. Dates given here are those of the original manuscript; most extant copies are much later.

Primary witnesses for the πάντες reading are B, Aleph.

B—Codex Vaticanus, fourth century, Egypt; β text type. This Neutral (Westcott-Hort) or Alexandrian (Streeter) uncial manuscript may be regarded as the best overall authority.[4] In B the only significant variant from the Nestle-Aland text of 1 John 2:18-27 occurs in v. 27, where χαρισμα is read for the first χρισμα. The variant can be safely attributed to the common scribal error of substituting a more familiar for a less familiar term. The second χρισμα is retained. As in virtually all manuscripts, B includes certain insignificant spelling variations (e.g., -ει for -ι in 2:18; -α for -ο in 2:25; and -α for -ε in 2:27).

Aleph—Codex Sinaiticus, fourth century, Egypt; β text type. In their discussion of the *Scribes and Correctors of the Codex Sinaiticus*,[5] Milne and Skeat distinguish important characteristics of the hands which transcribed this mid-fourth century manuscript. Of the three scribes who contributed to the original text (A, B and D; a revision of Tischendorf's hypothesis which included scribe C), they note that scribe A "is markedly inferior to D."[6] Scribe A, they hold, is responsible for most of the New Testament portions of the Codex, including all of 1 John. It will be useful, therefore, to examine in detail the various readings of this portion of Sinaiticus, in order to evaluate its dependability as a witness to the πάντες reading in 1 John 2:20. Apart from countless spelling differences, which reflect both local preference and ignorance, the following are the most significant variants in the Aleph witness to 1 John, having little or no other manuscript support.

1:3, inverts to read ο ακηκοαμεν και εωρακαμεν; interpolates και after εωρακαμεν, and υμων after ημετερα.

1:9, omits εστιν (corrected); interpolates ημων after the second αμαρτιας, probably by simple duplication of the first αμαρτιας ημων.

2:3, reads φυλαξωμεν for τηρωμεν (corrected). Φυλασσω appears elsewhere in the Epistle only in 5:21. The reading, therefore, is not the result of a simple sight-error. The sense of the passage is preserved, and the reading indicates that the scribe may have inadvertently paraphrased from his exemplar by

4 Metzger, *Text*, 39-41 and appendix, cites P[66] and P[72] (ca. 200 A.D.) as evidence for second century dating of portions of this manuscript. Neither of these papyri, however, includes 1 John.
5 British Museum, 1938. The facsimile of Aleph used here is by K. Lake, *Codex Sinaiticus* (NT), Oxford, 1911.
6 *Scribes and Correctors*, p. 54.

depending upon his memory to reproduce what he had just read. This common error is especially significant for the variant reading in 2:20.

2:4, omits εν τουτω. The interpolation of του θεου after αληθεια is repeated in 4:10, η αγαπη του θεου. In 4:19 the simple ημεις αγαπωμεν is changed in meaning by the interpolation of τον θεον: "we love God." Each of these additions represents a theological concern to "improve" the text.

2:9, interpolates ψευστης εστιν και after μισων. This can hardly be a simple sight-error. Either these words appeared in his exemplar, or the scribe remembered the identical construction from 2:4 (antithetical parallelism beginning with ο λεγων) and added this descriptive phrase himself.

2:18-3:1. In this passage spelling variants include -ι for -ει in 2:19b, 20, 21, 25, 27; and -αι for -ε, the second person plural verb ending, in 2:20f (οιδαται; but οιδατε also appears in 2:21). Inversion occurs in 2:19b and 2:14. In 2:24 the scribe has twice substituted the formula ο ακηκοατε απ᾽ αρχης, once for ο απ᾽ αρχης ηκουσατε, and once for ο ηκουσατε απ᾽ αρχης. There is no other textual support for this reading. Apparently he reproduced the formula which appears in the prologue of the Epistle as ο ην απ᾽ αρχης ο ακηκοαμεν. Again, one has the impression that the scribe often wrote from memory rather than from meticulous reference to his exemplar. On the other hand, in 4:3 he has written οτι ακηκοαμεν for ο ακηκοατε.

The most significant variant preserved by Sinaiticus in this section appears in 2:27b, where πνευμα is read for χρισμα. Unlike the B variant in this verse, the Aleph reading cannot be lightly attributed to unintentional scribal error. This manuscript clearly preserves a tradition which taught "his Spirit (πνευμα) teaches you about all things..." At one point in the transmission of the witness, a corrector probably substituted the more familiar πνευμα, understanding it to be a synonym for χρισμα.[7] Yet why was a similar substitution not made in 2:20 and 2:27a? Note that a corrector has inserted χρισμα in the margin of 2:27b. In 5:6, Aleph, together with the probably independent witness A, interpolates και πνευματος after αιματος. This theologically motivated variant teaches that "Jesus is he who has come through water and blood and Spirit."

Other variants in this portion of Aleph deserve mention. In 2:24 the second εν has been inserted above the line to correct its original omission.

7   Recall that the term χρισμα occurs in the NT only in 1 Jn 2:20, 27.

The particle δε is interpolated in 2:26. The close of 2:27 is followed by ινα εαν φανερωθη..., an example of haplography due to homoeoteleuton: the words και νυν αυτω are omitted.[8] In 2:28, haplography is erroneously corrected by interpolation after παρουσια αυτου. The scribe omits απ᾽ αυτου εν, and at the end of the verse he adds απ᾽ αυτου (actually αυτου απ᾽ αυτου, transposed from its proper place following αισχυνθωμεν). This is followed by illegible erasures. The scribe at this point has become tired and has stopped to rest. His lines are uneven, letters are poorly formed, and mistakes abound. The first variant reading then appears in 3:1, ειδετε for ιδετε, an error which is the reverse of his tendency to substitute -ι for -ει.

3:4, interpolates και after εστιν (corrected).

3:5, reads οιδαμεν for οιδατε; interpolates ημων after αμαρτιας (with C, Mpm, vg, sy^p, a variant which may have appeared in the exemplar); inversion produces ουκ εστιν εν αυτω.

3:11, reads επαγγελια (with C) for αγγελια. This variant changes the sense of the reading from "message," to "this is the promise which you heard."[9] The similarity between the two nouns makes it impossible to determine whether at some point in transmission the change was made intentionally.

3:13, interpolates και (with C*al, sy^p) before μη.

3:14, reads μεταβεβηκεν for μεταβεβηκαμεν. The interpolation of ημων (with sy^p, to read "we love our brethren") is perhaps an intentional addition which emphasizes the difference between our brethren and the false teachers (2:18ff). It reflects an exclusivism that accords with the tone of the Epistle in some parts but not in others.

3:18, substitutes και for μηδε τη.

3:19, interpolates (with C, M, sy^p) και before εν τουτω. The meaningless εκπροσθεν stands for εμπροσθεν and may indicate that the scribe was unaware of the meaning of the text. The words εκ της appear in the preceding clause and might account for his error. With C, M, latt and sy^h (supported

8 Note the similar omission in the M text of 2:23. "Haplography" refers to the error of omitting portions of text; "homoeoteleuton" means a similar ending of lines. The scribe's eye jumped from the first "abide in him" to the second, leading him to omit the beginning of v. 28.

9 ηκουσαται απ᾽ αρχης: here the scribe has not substituted the perfect for the aorist tense. See notes on 2:18-3:1.

by Tischendorf), Sinaiticus reads τας καρδιας for την καρδιαν. This represents the attempt of scribe A or a predecessor to improve the text.

3:21, reads αδελφοι for αγαπητοι.

3:22, reads αιτωμεθα for αιτωμεν. This substitution of the middle subjunctive stresses personal request: "if we ask for ourselves," and may be an intentional refinement.

4:2, reads γινωσκομεν for γινωσκετε. This may perhaps be explained by the occurrence of the same formula in 3:24. Nevertheless, eleven lines of text separate the two phrases and make mental retention of a particular form unlikely. The phrase εν τουτω γινωσκομεν occurs elsewhere in the Epistle at 2:5; 3:24; 4:13; and 5:2; but since the scribe writes γεινωσκομεν in 5:2 and reproduces εν τουτω γνωσομεθα accurately in 3:19, the error in 4:2 remains a puzzle.

4:3, reads Ιησουν κυριον for τον Ιησουν; interpolates (with Y, M, sy) εν σαρκι εληλυθοτα; substitutes οτι ακηκοαμεν for ο ακηκοατε. Why the scribe should have added κυριον, rather than simply repeat Ι. Χριστον, is unclear. The addition of the second "having come in the flesh" is almost certainly doctrinally motivated. If the scribe had mistakenly recopied it, he would not have substituted "Lord" for "Christ." The verses 4:2-3 are usually understood by commentators to be part of an antidocetic polemic which stresses confession of Jesus Christ's true incarnation, his real presence in the flesh. If such a polemic were in fact the author's intention, however, then he would most naturally have repeated the formula "having come in the flesh" in 4:3, as did the scribes of Sinaiticus and the Majority text. In any case, the witnesses Aleph and M appear to preserve an antidocetic polemic with their interpolations in this verse.[10] Once again doctrinal interests have produced an alteration of the original text, one which was probably intended to combat gnostic teachings. A similar interest may explain the Sinaiticus reading of παντες in 2:20, as we shall see further on.

4:8, haplography again due to homoeoteleuton: omits ο μη...τον θεον (corrected).

10 Cf. Polycarp, Phil. 7.1, a direct parallel to 1 Jn 4:2f and 2 Jn 7, although there is no clear dependence of Polycarp on the Johannine Epistles (but see C.H. Dodd, *The Johannine Epistles*, London 1946, p. xi-xii; R.E. Brown, *The Epistles of John* (Garden City, NY: Doubleday, 1982), 492. The confessional formula was probably a device preserved and used by Christian groups against the gnosticizing heresy which was prevalent in Asia Minor at the time. Note also the variant reading λυει for μη ομολογει in 1 Jn 4:3, discussed below.

4:10, interpolates του θεου after αγαπη (see notes on 2:4 above); reads απεσταλκεν for απεστειλεν.

4:17, interpolates εν ημιν after μεθ᾽ ημων and may represent a doctrinal improvement. Whether the reading originated with scribe A cannot be determined. Here, too, Sinaiticus reads εχομεν for εχωμεν and εσομεθα for εσμεν The substitution of αγαπη for ημερα is to be noted in the formula "in the day of judgment." This illustrates two significant tendencies of this scribe: to retain words and phrases mentally and to reproduce what he had written earlier (αγαπη occurs three times in the preceding one and a half verses); and to transcribe words while being oblivious to the context. No other explanation can account for such a distortion within a familiar formula.

4:19, interpolates (with 33al, vg^d, sy) τον θεον after αγαπωμεν (see notes on 2:4).

4:20, haplography: omits ειπη οτι (partially corrected).

5:2, the reading (with M) τηρωμεν for ποιωμεν is due to intentional or unintentional assimilation to the following line.

5:6, interpolates (with A, sy^h) και πνευματος after αιματος (see notes on 2:18-3:1).

5:9, reads του θεου for των ανθρωπων (corrected). This substitution may have been due to a simple error in transcription, as it empties the following independent clause of its meaning. The variant provides further evidence that the scribe was not always aware of the sense of his text.

5:15, haplography again due to homoeoteleuton: omits και εαν...ημων (corrected, but reads ιδωμεν for οιδαμεν); interpolates εαν between οτι and εχωμεν (corrected).

Several conclusions can be drawn from this evidence. The types of variants indicate that the scribe copied from an exemplar rather than wrote from dictation. Homoeoteleuton and similar sight-errors account for a large number of probable deviations from that exemplar. He has frequently altered verb forms[11] and made significant interpolations and alterations in the text,[12] at times unintentionally, but occasionally to serve doctrinal interests. We have shown

11 These alterations affect roots, tenses, spelling of endings, person: 2:3, 20f, 24; 3:5, 22; 4:2f, 10, 17; 5:2, 15 (corrector's error?).
12 Thus 1:3 (corrected); 1:9; 2:4 (cf. 4:10, 19; 5:9); 2:9, 27; 3:5, 11, 18, 21; 4:3, 10, 17, 19; 5:6, 9.

that the scribe transcribed isolated words and phrases while often being unaware of the context or meaning of what he reproduced. Words which appear frequently in proximity, together with an occasional formula typical of the Epistle, were at times mentally retained and erroneously repeated (see especially 4:17).

This evidence taken as a whole casts serious doubt on the Sinaiticus Codex as a reliable witness to the correct reading of πᾶς in 1 John 2:20.[13] It also illustrates a general principle which should govern all textual study: the value of a given witness can not be judged merely by the criteria of date, text type, and geographical distribution. Within each manuscript the *reliability of different scribes* must be ascertained as well, in order to resolve accurately questions of variant readings.

On the basis of these findings we can suggest possible reasons for the reading οἴδατε πάντες in the Sinaiticus witness to 1 John 2:20.

1. The phrase appeared in the exemplar and was accurately reproduced by Aleph, scribe A. It was original with the author of the Epistle and had been faithfully transmitted by successive witnesses.

2. Either this scribe or a predecessor substituted πάντες for πάντα because of the common error of repeating frequently occurring or similar words. In this case, having just written οὐκ εἰσὶν πάντες, the scribe repeated the nominative form to produce οἴδατε πάντες.

3. The scribe or a predecessor may have substituted πάντες for πάντα because of the thrust against gnostic exclusivism which the word provides ("you *all* know"). In Sinaiticus such a substitution would be consistent with the antidocetic interpolation of the second ἐν σαρκὶ ἐληλυθότα in 4:3.

For our present purposes, we can note that both the Alexandrinus and Sinaiticus witnesses to 1 John contain significant and highly questionable variants. Vaticanus (B) remains primary and overall the most reliable. As for the relative weight of B, Aleph on the one hand and, on the other, A, C, **M**, latt, sy[h], aeth, and L, we can conclude: obviously the latter group, which supports the πάντα reading, contains the largest number of witnesses. This,

---

13 A similar study of Codex Alexandrinus reveals many such errors, some of which are clearly the result of doctrinal considerations, e.g., the tendency to interpolate the noun θεός. The effect of many of these variants is to smooth out the text. Similar tendencies to improve readings are observable in C, M, vg and sy. Since these witnesses read πάντα in 2:20, it is of course possible that this represents still another "improvement" of the text by providing an object to the otherwise objectless οἴδατε.

however, is a criterion of slim dependability when taken by itself apart from other considerations. Regarding age and text type, Aleph and B (fourth century, β type) are primary. With respect to geographical distribution, though, the πάντα group is definitely preferable, representing traditions from Syria to North Africa and from East to West. This latter group also comprises all text types. On the basis of external evidence, the testimony of B and Aleph cannot be accepted as conclusive. Because of geographical distribution, text types and the relative weakness of the Sinaiticus witness at this point, manuscript evidence for the πάντα reading may be considered to be at least as strong as for πάντες, indeed even stronger. Nevertheless, to determine probability for one reading against the other it is necessary to examine the internal evidence of the Epistle.

2. Knowledge of "the Truth"

In their discussions of 1 John 2:20, A.E. Brooke[14] and R. Schnackenburg[15] hold that the emphasis of the clause καὶ οἴδατε πάντες is upon the act of "knowing," i.e., upon the verb οἴδατε.[16] The force of the reading thus lies in the omission of the object. As it stands (B omits καί, thus throwing its witness into some question), the clause may be rendered: "(and, or adversatively, but) all of you know" or "you all know." Note the syntactical structure: the independent clause is formed simply of the active verb followed by a pronominal subject. Apart from this suggested reading in 2:20, the object is never omitted with a transitive verb in the Epistle. The construction οἴδατε πάντες, an independent clause consisting of an active verb followed by the subject without object or predicate modifier, occurs nowhere else in this writing or, apparently, in the entire New Testament.[17] It is an awkward as well as

14 *Epistles*, 57.

15 *Die Johannesbriefe* (Freiburg im B., 1965).

16 Cf. R.E. Brown, *Epistles*, 349, who likewise opts for the nominative plural reading: "...the fact of their knowledge (*pantes*), not the extent of its object (*panta*), seems best to fit the reassurance [against the antichrists' claims]." Similarly, F.F. Bruce, *The Epistles of John* (Grand Rapids, MI: Eerdmans, 1970/79), 72; and D. W. Burdick, *The Letters of John the Apostle* (Chicago: Moody, 1985), 198.

17 B. Weiss, *Briefe*, 65ff, maintains that οἴδατε is objectless as are ἴστε in Jas 1:19 and εἰδότας in 2 Pet 1:12. The use of these as parallels, however, must be questioned. In Jas 1:19, ἴστε is usually understood by commentators and translators to be the first word of a new paragraph. A better reading would be to take the entire phrase ἴστε,...ἀγαπητοί as a closing parallel to the phrase μὴ...ἀγαπητοί in 2:16 which opens the paragraph. By reading vv. 16-19a as a unit, the object of ἴστε is seen to be the assurance given in vv. 17f. Nor

unique expression, whereas οἴδατε πάντα is in complete accord with the writer's style (cf. 3:20b, καὶ γινώσκει πάντα).[18]

The pronominal use of πᾶς in 1 John occurs most frequently in constructions with ὁ and the participle (2:23, 29; 3:3, 4, 6, 9f, 15; 4:7; 5:1, 4, 18; cf. 2 Jn 1, 9). In absolute usage πᾶς occurs in 2:19, 20, 27 and 3:20. In the first two instances it stands as the subject of a clause; in the latter two it serves as the object of a verb. That is, only in 2:19 and 2:20 is πᾶς used by the writer of 1 John in an absolute, subjective construction (i.e., as neither adjective, subject of a participial phrase, nor as direct object). The nominative plural form of πᾶς occurs nowhere else in the Epistle. Thus the syntactical structure of 2:20 as described above, when correlated with evidence concerning the writer's use of πᾶς, shows that the phrase οἴδατε πάντες is stylistically unique in the Epistle, both in its form and in its content.[19]

Commentators disagree as to the force and meaning of οἴδατε in 2:20. B. Weiss[20] believes it to be objectless, and he discounts as arbitrary any attempt to read in as an object τὴν ἀλήθειαν. Emphasis, he maintains, is upon the possession of knowledge, not upon its content. Brooke[21] puts it somewhat differently: "The possession by all of them (πάντες) of the knowledge which enables them to discern, and not the extent of their knowledge, is the ground of the writer's appeal." The great majority of exegetes continue to follow this line of reasoning.[22]

is εἰδότας in 2 Pet 1:12 objectless. The subject is you (pl., ὑμᾶς), and the verb forms are the participles εἰδότας and ἐστηριγμένους, of which the common object is τῇ παρούσῃ ἀληθείᾳ. These two verbs are not objectless as οἴδατε in 1 Jn 2:20 would be if read with πάντες.

18 This does not mean that one should ignore the rule of thumb for textual criticism which holds that of two (intelligible) variants, all other factors being equal, the most difficult reading is to be preferred. It is our purpose to show that "all other factors" tip the balance in favor of the πάντα reading. And we might add that πάντα has also been regarded as the more difficult reading, since knowledge of "all things" is at best improbable. As we shall see, the expression is comprehensible only in light of the specifically Johannine usage of πᾶς.

19 The form πάντες occurs in Jn 1:7, 16; 3:26; 5:23, 28; 6:45; 7:21; 10:8; 11:48; 13:10f, 35; 17:21; 18:20; and 2 Jn 1. The construction that most closely parallels the πάντες reading of 1 Jn 2:20 appears in Jn 7:21. Here, however, πάντες precedes an intransitive verb, whereas in 1 Jn 2:20 it would follow a transitive verb. D has substituted ὑμεῖς for πάντες to produce a smoother reading in Jn 7:21.

20 *Briefe*, 65f.

21 *Epistles*, 56ff.

22 Judith Lieu, *The Theology of the Johannine Epistles* (Cambridge, England: Cambridge University Press, 1991), makes a curious attempt to split the difference. Noting that "there is some textual uncertainty" regarding the reading in 2:20 (p. 26, n. 6), she states: "Believers

Against it, F. Büchsel,[23] A. Wilder[24] and others insist that τὴν ἀλήθειαν is indeed the object of οἴδατε, and consequently they read οἴδατε πάντα with stress upon the object. Where, then, does the emphasis in this clause lie? What in fact is the object of οἴδατε?

Leaving 2:20 aside for a moment, we read in v. 21, "I did not write to you because you do not know the truth, but because you do know it." Emphasis here is not upon "knowing" per se, but upon "knowing the truth." When Brooke says that knowledge, and not the extent of that knowledge, is the ground of the writer's appeal, he is only partially right. The focus, as we shall see, is not upon the extent of that knowledge, but upon its *content*; that is, they possess *knowledge of the truth*. Given this emphasis in 2:21, we have to disagree with R. Schnackenburg's view that the object of οἴδατε in 2:20, "otherwise than in 2:27," is not obvious.[25] That object is clearly "the truth" as distinguished from "every lie" (2:21), a conclusion which is confirmed by the following examination of the objects of verbs "to know" in the Epistle.

The verbs εἰδέναι (οἶδα) and γινώσκειν as they are used in the Epistle have several objects in common: Christ,[26] born of God,[27] truth,[28] and others. In his valuable study of these two verbs, I. de la Potterie has illustrated their distinctive usages in the Fourth Gospel.[29] The implicit contrast is between realized or intuitive possession of the truth (οἶδα) which provides certitude that is not contingent upon experience, and the progressive, gradual acquisition of knowledge (γινώσκω) through the relationship of subject to object, e.g., of the disciples to their Lord. This distinction, which is characteristic of John's Gospel, is preserved in the First Epistle.[30] There γινώσκω expresses shades of meaning which can be described as progressive "recognition" based upon prior experience, or as "acknowledgment" of what is demonstrated to be true. Such

also simply 'know'—they know the truth, they are taught concerning all things and so they all 'know' (2:21, 27, 20) [*sic*]," (p. 28). This is a typical example of the difficulty interpreters have had with this verse.
23 *Die Johannesbriefe*, Leipzig, 1933, 40.
24 "The Letters of John," *Interpreter's Bible* XII, 1957, ad loc.
25 *Johannesbriefe*, 154.
26 In 2:4f, 29; 3:2, 5f; 5:20.
27 In 2:29; 5:18.
28 In 2:20f; 3:19.
29 "Οἶδα et γινώσκω: Les deux modes de la connaissance dans le Quatrième Evangile," *Biblica* 40 (1959), 709-725.
30 Fr. de la Potterie makes only passing, and somewhat misleading reference to the First Epistle's usage in a footnote, p. 716, n. 1.

acknowledgment is always based on the experiential or existential relationship of the subject to the object, of the knower to the truth which is known.[31] Where the two verbs are used together in the same sentence (2:29; 5:20), the distinction between them is clearly discernible. The writer first states what is known absolutely or intuitively (οἶδα): "he is just," "the Son of God has come." From this absolute knowledge (the content of faith's confession) follow its consequences expressed by γινώσκω in 2:29b and 5:20b respectively (cf. Jn 8:55, καὶ οὐκ ἐγνώκατε αὐτόν, ἐγὼ δὲ οἶδα αὐτόν).[32]

Significant is the fact that of its fifteen usages in the Epistle, οἶδα is followed by a ὅτι clause in all but four instances, 2:11, 20, 21bis. In 2:11 its usage is negative and denotes "radical ignorance."[33] In the other three instances the objects of οἶδα (viz. πάντα, τὴν ἀλήθειαν, αὐτήν) serve as substitutes for the ὅτι clause. Where the ὅτι clause is employed, it describes the absolute, intuitive knowledge which the believer possesses.[34] In each case this knowledge is the Christian's self-knowledge in relation to God or Christ (or to God through Christ). In a characteristically Johannine sense, objects of the verb οἶδα may be defined by their close relationship to that truth which is Christ. In 2:20, "knowledge of the truth" is expressed by the synonymous formulas οἴδατε πάντα and οἴδατε ἀλήθειαν.

Οἶδα is the appropriate verb for such formulas because it denotes the absolute, intuitive character of the knowledge possessed. Γινώσκω, on the other hand, denotes knowledge of that same truth, but as acquired by experience with it.[35] The difference between οἶδα and γινώσκω lies in their designation of differing modes of apprehension: by intuition or by experiential

---

31 Thus, for example, 1 Jn 2:3 might be paraphrased: "By this we acknowledge (γινώσκομεν) that we have recognized (ἐγνώκαμεν) him, if we keep his commandments."

32 One may question this example from Jn 8. C.C. Tarelli, "Johannine Synonyms," *Journal of Theological Studies* 47 (1946), 175-177, has shown that differences of tense or mood rather than nuances of meaning can determine which of two synonyms was selected by the Evangelist. Nevertheless, Tarelli does not consider the pair οἶδα / γινώσκω, and Fr. de la Potterie has made a good case for distinguishing between them as he does.

33 de la Potterie, ibid. 724f.

34 As in 2:29; 3:2, 5, 14f; 5:13, 15, 18ff.

35 Thus, as de la Potterie notes, it is the verb used most frequently in the Fourth Gospel to express the disciples' progressive awareness of the reality of truth in Christ; cf. 1 Jn 5:20. See also the discussion of knowledge of God in 1 John in U.C. von Wahlde, *The Johannine Commandments: 1 John and the Struggle for the Johannine Tradition* (New York: Paulist Press, 1990), 140-143.

relationship of the knower to what is known. The nuance pertains to the subject rather than to the object, which in each case may be summarized as "the truth," ἀλήθεια.

3. Πάντα: a Synonym for "the Truth"

Thus far we have seen that the object of οἴδατε in 2:20, irrespective of the reading for πᾶς, is ἀλήθεια. It remains to be demonstrated that πάντα in fact does stand for ἀλήθεια and is therefore the original reading.

The question resolves into three possibilities: the writer's meaning is either

1. πάντες, in the sense of universal knowledge possessed by all Christians, including gnostics ("you *all* know"), over against gnostic exclusivism;

2. πάντες, read in parallel to 2:19 to express exclusivism of a different sort: the faithful and not the antichrists are those who possess the truth ("*you* all know"); or

3. πάντα, implying knowledge of all the truth ("you know *all things*").

The first reading, supported by Brooke and many others,[36] is virtually excluded by the context. Here, as in the Epistle as a whole, the writer expresses himself in terms of antithetical categories. In 2:15-19 he sharply distinguishes between those who "love the world" and those who "do the will of God," between the antichrists and those to whom the Epistle is written, who "know the truth" as opposed to every lie.[37] Emphasis here is not upon the universality of knowing among all Christians, including "you" who are not of the gnostic elite. It is rather upon the difference between "loving the world" and doing God's will, between the "lie" and the "truth." The reading πάντες to express Christian inclusivism (both the faithful and the antichrists) is simply out of place. It is not merely irrelevant to the context, it is clearly contrary to it.

This is not the case, however, if with R. Schnackenburg and others we read πάντες in such a way as to emphasize true knowledge of those to whom the Epistle is addressed as opposed to the false knowledge of the antichrists. This reading is consistent with the context insofar as it preserves the antithesis between Truth and Lie. The antichrists claim to know the Truth, but in fact

---

36 Cf. R. Bultmann, *Die drei Johannesbriefe*, Göttingen, 1967, 42, who draws a comparison with 1 Cor 8:1, οἴδαμεν ὅτι πάντες γνῶσιν ἔχομεν.

37 See J. Bonsirven, *Epîtres de Saint Jean* (Paris: Beauchesne, 1954), 128ff, and his references to Augustine's commentary on the First Epistle (critical edition: *Sources chrétiennes* 75, Paris [Cerf], 1961).

they do not know it. Their denial of Christ, who is the Truth, coupled with their immoral behavior, makes them liars (1:6, 8; 2:4, 22; etc.).

Nevertheless, two objections can be brought against this reading. On the one hand, the verse would have to be translated, "But (adversative καί) you (in contrast to the antichrists) have an anointing from the Holy One, and you know." This, however, is inconsistent with the hortatory mood of the passage. The immediate context begins with an eschatological motif ("it is the last hour") which is clearly both summons and warning. Schism has already rent the local congregation (2:18f), and the author addresses his flock to warn them against succumbing to the deception of the false teachers (2:26f). The emphasis in 2:20 is not upon the fact that they know, whereas the antichrists do not; it is rather upon *what* they know, namely the Truth which alone can preserve them from deception (2:27; cf. 4:6; 2 Jn 9). On the other hand, it seems most unlikely that the author would have employed the construction οἴδατε πάντες if his purpose had been to stress the fact that "you" know, whereas the antichrists do not. In this case, emphasis would necessarily be upon the subject "you." The most natural way to express this emphasis would be by using the familiar construction πᾶς with a pronoun[38] to bring the clause into parallel with the preceding ὑμεῖς χρῖσμα ἔχετε. Whereas ὑμεῖς πάντες οἴδατε (cf. Jn 1:16), for example, clearly expresses the subject, οἴδατε πάντες does not. As we have already demonstrated, this construction is unique, it is contrary to the writer's style, and it refuses to rest easily in context. On the other hand, πάντα, supported by the parallel in 2:27 ("just as his unction teaches you περὶ πάντων"), is appropriate to the context and accords fully with the writer's style.

If we can thus ascertain with reasonable certainty that the correct reading for this clause is οἴδατε πάντα, what then can we say about the specific function of the term πάντα?

The adjectival use of πᾶς with ἀλήθεια occurs in ancient Greek[39] as well as in Koinê literature to denote "the whole truth." As shown by the coupling of πᾶς with other nouns, both concrete and abstract, this adjectival usage expresses not so much quantity as "totality" or "completeness."[40] The Fourth Gospel illustrates this nuance quite clearly (e.g., 1:3; 3:31; cf. Rom 9:5; 1 Cor

---

38 There are nearly thirty such usages in the NT. See esp. Mt 26:31; Acts 4:10a; 20:25; Gal 3:28; Jn 1:16; 2 Cor 3:18; Eph 2:3.

39 For example, *Odyssey* 11:507; *Iliad* 24:407. Other references are given in Liddell & Scott, *Greek-English Lexicon.*

40 B. Reicke, art. πᾶς, Kittel, *TWNT* V, 885-895, notes that the word appears in the NT some 1228 times: "Es zeigt sich darin eine Vorliebe für den Begriff der Totalität."

8:6). There is in the Gospel and First Epistle, however, a somewhat different use of πᾶς, one which is characteristically Johannine. In 1 John 4:1 we read, μὴ παντὶ πνεύματι πιστεύετε, which may be translated, "do not believe just any spirit."[41] The contrast here, as spelled out in 4:6 and maintained throughout the Epistle, is between the Spirit of Truth and the Spirit of Deceit, between the truth and the lie. This is an absolute distinction which in 2:20f, 27 is based on the Johannine conception of the teaching function of the Spirit expressed most fully in John 16:13, "When that one comes, the Spirit of Truth, he will guide you into all the truth (τὴν ἀλήθειαν πᾶσαν)," i.e., into the absolute Truth which is Christ himself and which the Spirit imparts to the Christian community. Similarly, John 14:26, "The Paraclete, the Holy Spirit, whom the Father will send in my name, he will teach you all things (πάντα) and recall to you all things (πάντα) that I said to you." Compare 1 John 2:27, "His Spirit teaches you about all things (περὶ πάντων)."

This teaching function of the Spirit-Paraclete depicted in the Gospel of John, is fulfilled in the First Epistle by the χρῖσμα, the "anointing" that refers to the work of that same Spirit, received in baptism (the "unction" of chrismation), and through which believers abide in God and he in them (1 Jn 3:24; 4:13). It is this anointing by and with the Spirit that "teaches you about all things" (1 Jn 2:27; Jn 14:26). In 1 Corinthians 8:6, the apostle Paul employs πᾶς (τὰ πάντα) as a nominal synonym for the whole of creation in a polemic against the gnostic conception of the Creator as a "demiourgos."[42] The author of 1 John, also engaged in a struggle against false teaching, uses a nominal form of πᾶς in 2:20 as a synonym for Truth, taking as his model the traditional Johannine teaching which is given fullest expression in John 16:13 and 14:26. In these contexts, πᾶς functions as a quasi-technical term: to know "all things" (πάντα) is to know that eternal Truth which is embodied by the Son of God (Jn 14:6) and imparted to the Church by the *Chrisma* or Spirit of Truth.

4. The Chiastic Shape of 1 John 2:18-28

One further consideration lends important support to the πάντα reading in 1 John 2:20, namely, the literary structure of the passage. As we discussed in

41 See Arndt & Gingrich, *A Greek-English Lexicon of the New Testament* (Chicago-Cambridge, 1957/60), 636.
42 This use of πᾶς reflects Stoic influence (cf. Col 1:15-20; Rom 11:33ff). Cf. also Marcus Aurelius, Bk. IV.23, "...O Nature, ἐκ σοῦ πάντα, ἐν σοὶ πάντα, εἰς σὲ πάντα" (quoted by W.D. Davies, *Paul and Rabbinic Judaism*, London 1962, 181).

detail in chapter 5, recent study of Johannine and other New Testament witnesses has shown that the biblical authors relied largely on the form of inverted, concentric parallelism known as *chiasmus* to compose individual
units of tradition as well as entire writings.[43] The passage 1 John 2:18-28,
translated literally, reveals the following structure. Verse 18 is an example of
"anacrusis," an introductory element with its own independent structure.
A-A' constitutes an "inclusion," with other elements developed incrementally
toward the central propositions E-E', with the focus on the message "heard
from the beginning," (cf. 1:1). Parallel themes in the main section, 2:19-28,
are indicated by italics.

(2:18) Little children, [anacrusis]

A: It is the last hour,
   B: and just as you have heard
      C: that antichrist is coming,
      C': so now many antichrists have come;
   B': whereby we know
A': that it is the last hour.

A: (v. 19) They [the antichrists] went out from us,/ but they were not of us;/ for if
they were of us/they would have *abided* with us.// But [they went out from us]
that it be *manifest* that none of them is of us.[44]

   B: (v. 20f) But *you have* an *anointing* from the *Holy One* and you know *all things*
(πάντα). I did not *write* to you because you do not know the truth, but because you do know it, and [know] that no *lie* is of the *truth*.

      C: (v. 22) Who is the liar if not the one denying that Jesus is the Christ?
This is the antichrist: the one denying the Father and the Son.

         D: (v. 23) No one who denies the *Son* has the *Father;*/whoever con-
fesses the *Son* also has the *Father.*//

            E: (v. 24a) Let what you heard/ from the beginning/abide in you.//

            E': (v. 24b) If in you abides/ what from the beginning/you heard,//

         D': (v. 24c) then you will abide both in the *Son* and in the *Father*.

      C': (v. 25) And *this is the promise* which he promised to us: eternal life.

---

43 See chs. 5 and 6 above.
44 This is the correct reading, and not (as RSV, etc.) "they all are not of us," implying that
some indeed (still) are. See R. Brown, *The Epistles of John*, 340f.

B': (v. 26-27d) These things I *wrote* to you about the ones deceiving you. But [as for] you, the *anointing* which *you received from him abides* in you; and you have no need that anyone should teach you, but as *his anointing* teaches you about *all things* (πάντων) and is *true* and is not *false,*

A': (v. 27e-28) so just as he taught you, *abide* in him. Now, little children,[45] *abide* in him, so that when he is *manifested* [in his parousia]...[46]

In the entire New Testament, the term χρῖσμα occurs only in the parallel phrases 1 Jn 2:20 and 27. With the balance established between "anointing from the Holy One" and "anointing from him," between knowledge and teaching, between truth and lie, it is clear that the writer intended to reflect and develop in v. 27 the affirmation made in v. 20. It is therefore virtually certain—on the basis of chiastic analysis alone, apart from the other external and internal considerations we have noted—that the author also intentionally paralleled the object of that knowledge and teaching. Anointed by God (or the risen Christ), faithful members of the Johannine community are able to distinguish absolutely between the lie and the truth, because they have been taught the fullness of that truth by the unction of the Spirit. Therefore, they "know all things."[47]

5. Conclusions

1. A comparison of manuscripts with regard to dates, text types and geographical distribution produces inconclusive evidence by which to judge the correct reading for πᾶς in 1 John 2:20. External support for πάντα is at least as strong as it is for the widely accepted πάντες. Internal evidence alone can determine the preferred reading. An investigation of scribal errors due to carelessness, illegible portions of the exemplar, ignorance of context and word-meaning, and doctrinal interests, illustrates the precariousness of

---

45 Verse 18 reads παιδία, and v. 28, the close of the inclusion, τεκνία.

46 J. Breck, *The Shape of Biblical Language,* 346f.

47 Throughout the Fourth Gospel πᾶς also denotes the absolute knowledge or authority of Jesus, 1:3; 3:31, 35; 4:29, 39; 5:20, 22; 6:37, 39f; 13:3; 16:15, 30; 17:2, 7, 10; 18:4; 19:28; 21:17; cf. 1 Cor 15:27; Eph 1:22; Rev 21:5. Note also the so-called "Johannine verse" in the Synoptics, Mt 11:27 // Lk 10:22, where πάντα probably stands for "teaching" or "knowing" rather than "power." See Arndt & Gingrich, p. 638 and 842 for important literature on this question. In 1 John it is God himself who knows πάντα (3:20). The use of πᾶς in Jn 10:41 is similar to that in 16:13; 14:26; and 1 Jn 2:20, 27, although its meaning hovers between "totality" or "completeness" and the designation of quantity: "all things that John said about this (man) were true." Here it is the Baptist rather than the Spirit who bears witness to him who is the Truth.

assessing the worth of a manuscript merely on the basis of date, text type and place of origin. A fourth criterion is equally important: the *reliability of different scribes* who contributed to the manuscript should be determined if questions of variant readings are to be resolved accurately.

2. On many counts—christology, pneumatology, atonement—the First Epistle reflects a theology that is decidedly "primitive" when compared with the Gospel. The same must be affirmed of the tradition concerning the (baptismal?) anointing with its corresponding communication of "truth." Compared with John 14:26 and 16:13, the affirmations of 1 John 2:20, 27 appear to represent a less developed stage of reflection on the role of Spirit in the life of the Christian community. If this is the case (and the suggestion needs to be judged on the basis of a detailed and comprehensive exegesis of the two writings), it would tend to counter the usual scholarly opinion, which holds that the Gospel is older than the Epistle, and that the latter was written in part to correct an erroneous (gnosticizing) interpretation of Gospel tradition. Equally plausible is the hypothesis that the Epistle represents an *intermediary stage* in the growth of Johannine theology, between the oral preaching of the apostolic leader(s) and the written witness of the Gospel.

3. Syntactical evidence and the use of $πᾶς$ in 1 John clearly demonstrate that the clause $οἴδατε\ πάντες$ is unique and stylistically anomalous, whereas $πάντα$ reads in complete accord with the author's style and with his thought. The object of $οἴδατε$ in 2:20 is $τὴν\ ἀλήθειαν$ of 2:21. Emphasis in 2:20 is upon "knowing the truth," or, in terms of its expressed object, "knowing all things." Here as in 2:27 (Jn 16:13; 14:26) $πᾶς$ functions as a quasi-technical synonym for $ἡ\ ἀλήθεια$. As analysis of the *chiastic structure* of the passage shows, it is used in the context of a polemic against false teaching, and denotes the absolute quality of the Truth which is imparted.

8

Mary in the New Testament

1. Mary in the Faith of the Church

The mystery of the Holy Virgin Mary belongs, as much as any other in Christian experience, to the *disciplina arcani*: the secret, inner life of the Church. In his letter to the Ephesians, St Ignatius of Antioch declared that there are "three mysteries hidden from the Prince of this age: the virginity of Mary and her birth-giving, together with the death of the Lord" (*Eph* 19:1). Only the Holy Spirit can fathom the depths of the mind of God, to perceive the full truth surrounding Christ's sacrifice upon the Cross (cf. 1 Cor 1:10-12). And it is only the Spirit, within the life and experience of the community of faith, who can reveal the central place of the Holy Virgin in the divine economy. This is because the mystery of Mary is preeminently a mystery of Christ and the Church. She can only be truly known and venerated in relation to her Son and the Body of believers of which he is the Head.

This implies that the proper context for investigating the person of Mary and her place within God's work of salvation is in the broadest sense ecclesial, and not merely scriptural. If this perspective is lost, then it is impossible to grasp and to share the Church's knowledge and experience of her. We are all aware that there exists a significant hiatus between the biblical witness to Mary and the orthodox/catholic tradition that speaks about her. A great many Marian dogmas and festal celebrations in her honor simply have no direct or obvious grounding in the New Testament. Feasts honoring her conception and birth, her presentation in the Temple, her protection (*Pakrov*), and her dormition, for example, are grounded in noncanonical witnesses such as the mid-second-century Protoevangelium of James and the much later (4th to 5th century) legends of the Assumption or Dormition of the Virgin. Dogmas concerning her perpetual virginity or her role as intercessor are similarly derived from ecclesial experience and piety, rather than from the Scriptures themselves. From a perspective of *sola scriptura*, we could never beseech Mary to "save us." Yet that is precisely what Orthodox Christians do at the close of nearly every liturgical service.

Orthodoxy knows and venerates Mary as Theotokos (Θεοτόκος), "God-bearer" or "Mother of God," a title formally endorsed by the Third Ecumenical Council held at Ephesus in 432. It also attributes to her the title "Ever-Virgin" (ἀειπάρθενος), confirmed at the Fifth Ecumenical Council of Constantinople, in 553. Just as the original Nicene Council of 325 accepted the nonbiblical term "homoousios" ("of one substance / essence / nature") to describe the relation of the divine Son to God the Father, so the Church adopts non-biblical language in its efforts to articulate the mystery of the Virgin. Thus she is known as the παρθενομήτηρ, the "Virgin-Mother," and lauded as the "Unwedded Bride." The Akathist Hymn in her honor invests her with titles such as "the Morning Star" and "Dawn of the Mystic Day." And increasingly throughout the history of the Church she has received titles "borrowed," as it were, from her Son, so that in Western piety especially she is proclaimed "Mediatrix" or even "Co-redemptress."

If Orthodoxy has never been able to accept the Roman Catholic dogma of the Immaculate Conception, it is because Eastern Christendom has always affirmed that Mary is fully human and subject to temptation, even if she is assumed to be "passionless" and free from actual sin. Yet in her uncompromised humanity, she is glorified as "the type of the Church" (Ambrose of Milan), the first in the communion of saints, exalted into heaven with her Son as the most perfect of human creatures who already, prior to the general resurrection and the last judgment, knows the joy and perfection of *theôsis* or "deification." As such, she is praised in the Byzantine liturgy as "our most holy, pure, blessed and glorious Lady, the Theotokos and Ever-Virgin Mary, more honorable than the cherubim and beyond compare more glorious than the seraphim."

Language of this kind, and the accompanying piety it reflects, are clearly not to be found in the New Testament. Nevertheless, Orthodox Christians have always been convinced that their Marian piety is thoroughly grounded in the apostolic writings. Our task here is to look briefly at the New Testament evidence concerning the Mother of Jesus, in an effort to show how, on the basis of that witness, together with the Church's living experience, an authentic Mariology came to be articulated.

2. Mariology, a Function of Christology

Surveying the Old Testament, early Christians found a variety of images that served as types or prophetic prefigurations of the Virgin. She was seen to be foreshadowed by Eve of the "proto-gospel," Gen 3:15; by the Daughter of Zion of the Psalms and prophetic writings; and by the personified Sophia or

Wisdom figure of Proverbs and Ecclesiasticus. St Matthew found her prefigured by the virgin mother in Isaiah 7:14; and recent scholars have maintained that St Luke modeled his image of Mary after the portrait of King David as builder of a "house of the Lord" (2 Sam 7).

In addition to these personifications, the Hebrew Scriptures also contain images that metaphorically, through the allegorical eye of the Church, came to be associated with the Virgin. She is likened to Jacob's Ladder, stretching between earth and heaven (Gen 28; Jn 1:51). She is the Burning Bush, filled with divinity and yet not consumed (Ex 3). She is the Red Sea, the way of liberation for the people of God, whose womb was opened and then closed again, signifying her perpetual virginity (Ex 14). She is the Ark of the Covenant that bears divine life and healing power, or the cloud that fills the house of the Lord with divine glory (Num 9; 1 Kgs 8). Thus she is the Eschatological Temple, the sacred space in which God dwells, to make himself known and accessible to his people for their salvation (Ezek 44).

Each of these images made its way into the mind and heart of the Church, providing material for liturgical celebration and nourishment for popular piety. This kind of imagery is possible, however, only when it is grounded in a deeper truth: that *Mariology is first and last a function of Christology*. Mary can only be properly understood, her mystery can only be faithfully celebrated, insofar as she is revealed by the person and saving work of her Son. But the converse is true as well. The mystery of Christ's redemptive suffering, the secret of his saving work hidden from the Prince of this age, is only fully revealed to eyes of faith through the person of his Holy Mother.

From the writings of the apostle Paul, we can cite just two passages that allude to Mary, and those only questionably. In Galatians 4:4f, Paul declares: "When the fullness of time had come, God sent forth his Son, born of woman, born under the law, to redeem those who were under the law, so that we might receive adoption as sons [children] of God." Here the woman from whom the divine Son is born is not named. The focus is not upon her person but upon the one born of her. Like the hymnic passages Philippians 2:5-11 and Colossians 1:12-20 (cf. Jn 1:1ff), it stresses a double christological motif: the preexistence of the incarnate Lord and his consubstantiality with humankind. It proclaims that the Son of God, by virtue of his appropriation of human nature through birth from a woman, is truly the God-man. On the basis of this witness, however, no conclusion can be drawn regarding Paul's knowledge of the virginal conception.

The second passage, Romans 1:3-4, likewise makes no mention of Mary. It affirms that the Son of God was "descended from David according to the flesh and designated Son of God in power according to the Spirit of holiness by his resurrection from the dead." Once again, this ancient confessional formula stresses the true incarnation of the preexistent divine Son. He is born into history, born of the lineage of David, and therefore he stands in total solidarity, even ontological identity, with the whole of fallen humanity. Yet this one, born in the flesh, is exalted through his victory over death and acknowledged to be "Lord," *Kyrios*, which is the very name of God (cf. Phil 2:10f).

Although Mary is not mentioned by name, she is nevertheless alluded to in these two passages as the one who brought forth in the flesh the preexistent Son of God. It is through this woman that "the Lord from heaven" (1 Cor 15:47) receives his human nature and, in the words of St Ignatius and later patristic tradition, "becomes what we are, to make us what he is" from all eternity: the New Adam, the archetype of humanity, who embodies the plenitude (*plêrôma*) of divine life.

3. Mary in the Gospels of Matthew and Mark

Among the Synoptics, Mark shows no knowledge of the birth and infancy narratives with which Matthew and Luke begin their gospel proclamations. In fact, Mark's allusions to Mary appear at first reading to be demeaning rather than laudatory. In 3:31-35, Jesus is informed that his mother and brothers are outside asking for him. He replies with a rhetorical question, "Who are my mother and my brothers?" The answer is, "whoever does the will of God." The purpose of this exchange, however, is not to diminish the importance of those closest to Jesus. Rather, it is to reply to an obviously burning issue within St Mark's own community: just who constitutes Jesus' true "family"? Recalling Jesus' insistence on doing the will of God, Mark distinguishes Jesus' physical family from his eschatological family, which can, of course, incorporate his own family members. As he did so often, Jesus here takes an earthly question and transforms it into an eternal truth: only those are genuine members of his family or Body, who hear, receive, internalize and act upon the Word that he, Jesus, embodies and proclaims.

A similar theme appears in Mark 6:3, where Jesus' own countrymen and perhaps his own kinfolk take offense at him, failing to understand either his person or his mission. Here, as in 3:31ff, it is important to consider the Gospel context. Both passages reflect what is known as the "messianic secret" that plays such an important role in the second Gospel. Throughout the narrative, the disciples and Jesus' own family members fail to perceive the full truth about him, and at times they are embarrassed by his words and actions. This element is toned down by Matthew and Luke in their parallel passages.

But the irony of the matter—and its true purpose—is made clear by Mark, who concludes, "And he could do no mighty work there, except that he laid his hands on a few sick people and healed them..." The reader or hearer of the Gospel can only conclude with the Centurion, "truly this man was the Son of God!"[1]

Whereas St Mark begins his proclamation with Jesus' baptism, Matthew and Luke locate the origin of the gospel message at Jesus' conception in the womb of the Virgin Mary. Their birth and infancy narratives, however, differ in a number of important details. Matthew focuses on the person of Joseph and includes bestowal of the name Emmanuel, the visit of the Magi, the flight into Egypt, and the massacre of the innocent children. Luke, on the other hand, focuses on Mary and the angelic annunciation addressed to her rather than to Joseph. He includes the infancy cycle concerning John the Baptist, and he adds the accounts of Jesus' presentation in the Temple and his return at twelve years of age, when the child astounds the elders of Israel with the depths of his wisdom.

More important, however, are the elements common to Matthew and Luke: the Davidic descent of Joseph, the virginal conception by Mary through the power of the Holy Spirit, and Jesus' birth at Bethlehem. Throughout his narrative, Matthew takes pains to demonstrate his major theological theme, the fulfillment of prophecy. Thus he harks back to Isaiah 7:14, to identify the child Jesus as the coming Emmanuel, the one who actualizes in his incarnate being the promise, "God is with us!" In his genealogy, reaching from Abraham through Joseph, the ostensible father of Jesus, Matthew includes four women: Tamar, Rahab, Ruth and Bathsheba. All four were of foreign, Gentile origin, and all were involved in irregular marital unions. Together with the Magi, they serve the evangelist's interest in the universal outreach of Jesus' saving mission (cf. 28:16-20). But they also presage Mary's unusual marriage to Joseph, and her still more remarkable virginal conception of the Messiah. Each of these women of the genealogy plays a special role in Israel's salvation-history. They are typological images that point forward to the Holy Virgin, and Mary fulfills their various roles by giving birth to the Savior himself.

1 That this is the proper reading, and not "a son of God," is shown by the fact that the Centurion's confession parallels the opening statement of the Gospel that identifies Jesus as "Christ, the Son of God" (1:1). And although the Nestle 26th ed. of the Greek text brackets *huiou theou* in 1:1, it is well attested by the text tradition. Mark's purpose from beginning to end is to announce Jesus of Nazareth and to proclaim him as Messiah and "Son of God."

The Virgin Birth is in fact a virginal conception. No sexuality is involved in Mary's bringing forth of the Son of God. The Holy Spirit is not a divine consort, but the creative, generative power of God who works in the womb of the Virgin the miracle "without seed." "That which is conceived in her," the angel tells Joseph in a dream, "is of the Holy Spirit." Her miraculous conception constitutes an anticipatory Pentecost, an outpouring of the Spirit in view of a New Creation. Yet neither this affirmation, nor the reality of the conception itself, is susceptible of exegetical proof. The dogma of the Virgin Birth, an ancient and universal article of Christian tradition, can be neither proved nor disproved by reasoned argument. It is a matter of faith, affirmed and confirmed by the living experience of Christian people.

The same must be said, *a fortiori*, about the dogma of Mary's perpetual virginity. Passages such as Ezekiel 44:2 may be seen as etiological: "This gate shall remain shut; it shall not be opened, and no one shall enter by it; for the Lord, the God of Israel, has entered by it." It is clear, nevertheless, that St Matthew first received the ancient tradition of the virginal conception of Jesus and only later applied to it the prophecy of Isaiah 7:14. Similarly, it seems most likely that the Church first received or perceived the truth of Mary's perpetual virginity, and only then sought in the Old Testament typological images that would relate promise to fulfillment. Prophecies of this kind from the Hebrew Scriptures did not provoke the creation or invention of miracle stories concerning the Messiah; for these prophecies had no relevance for the people's expectation of a coming Savior. They were discovered only after the fact, in the course of the Church's reflection on the miracle and the significance of God incarnate. For our purposes, their value lies especially in their affirmation that Mary is the chosen "Bride of God," the "holy, pure and blameless one," destined from all eternity, yet preserved in total freedom, to devote herself uniquely to God and to his work of salvation.

4. Mary in the Gospel of Luke

In his own birth and infancy sequence, St Luke presents five interconnected narratives: the annunciation scene, Mary with Elizabeth, the birth of Jesus and the shepherds' veneration, the presentation of the child to the elder Simeon, and Jesus in the Temple at twelve years of age. The entire account, once again, is written from the perspective of Mary rather than Joseph (some have argued that Mary was the evangelist's primary source for this information). The narrative focuses particularly on her acceptance of the ineffable mystery of her Son, a mystery she treasured and pondered "in her heart" (2:19, 51).

The Annunciation scene (Lk 1:26-38) offers another example of the ancient rhetorical form known as *chiasmus* or concentric parallelism. Its structure can be set out in the following way.

[Verses 26-27 constitute the introduction (*anacrusis*)]

A (28): The angel comes to Mary and greets her.
  B (29): Mary is troubled and questions the angel.
    C (30f): The angel prophesies Jesus' birth.
      D (32f): He will be great, Son of the Most High and Messianic King.
        E (34): Mary's question: "How can this be, since I have no husband?"
        E' (35ab): Gabriel's reply: "The Holy Spirit will come upon you,
          and the power of the Most High will overshadow you."
      D' (35cd): He will be called holy, the Son of God.
    C' (36f): The angel prophesies John's birth.
  B' (38a): Mary accepts the angel's word (her "fiat").
A' (38b): The angel departs from Mary.

The parallel or chiastic structure of this passage, focusing on the question and answer of v. 34f, shows that these verses are not later interpolations, as some interpreters have proposed, but are integral to the narrative and form central elements of Luke's message.

The chiasm shows the central elements of the passage to be Mary's perplexed question, "How can this be...?" and the Angel's revelatory response, "The Holy Spirit will come upon you / and the power of the Most High will overshadow you." Mary's child will be conceived by "power from on high," the power of the Holy Spirit, who descends upon the Virgin in anticipation of his descent upon the Messiah at his baptism (Lk 3:22; 4:1) and upon the gathered Church at Pentecost (cf. Lk 24:49; Acts 2:1-4). Filled with the Spirit from his conception, the child will be called "Great," *Megas*, the name the psalmists attribute to God (Pss 48:1-2; 135:5; etc.). A "Son of the Most High," he will reign forever over the house of Jacob as the Davidic Messiah. His true identity, however, is expressed by the still more exalted title of v. 35: "He will be called holy, the Son of God."

The passage preserves an extraordinary tension between humility and exaltation in the person of Mary, as well as in the God-man she will bear. This simple, formally uninstructed Jewish peasant girl, who is probably still in her teens, is declared *kecharitōmenē*: "she who has been granted favor or grace." The object of God's election, she embodies in her unique vocation the people of ancient Israel together with the new Israel of the Church. She is eternally destined for her role, yet she pronounces her *fiat* in total freedom. The decision to accept the joyous burden of virginal motherhood remains her own. She willingly embraces the vocation to be the handmaiden of the Lord, to bring forth through her own flesh him who receives from her the fallen human nature he "enhypostasizes" (Leontius of Byzantium) in order to deify it, to transfigure it by uniting it with his own divine nature. By her emphatic "Yes" to the Angel's invitation, Mary becomes the ideal Disciple, following her Son in faithful, loving obedience from his conception until his crucifixion. But more than this, she becomes the eschatological Sinai, Ark of the Covenant, and Temple of the Lord, the locus of divine Presence. In response to her humble obedience, the Holy Spirit "overshadows" her, to produce a new creation, the ultimate theophany, by which God appears on earth as the New and Last Adam.

The second section of Luke's narrative depicts Mary's visit to her kinswoman Elizabeth (1:39-56). The entire pericope is set off by a typical "inclusion": an A-A' balancing of themes that indicates the beginning and end of a literary unit:

A (39f): Mary goes to Elizabeth's house and greets her /
A' (56): Mary remains with Elizabeth about three months and returns to her home. //

As the Mother of his Lord appears, the child in Elizabeth's womb leaps for joy. The gesture signals John's recognition of the Messiah and also presages his role as Forerunner, who will prepare the way of the Lord in fulfillment of Isaiah's prophecy (40:3-5; Lk 3:4-6). Elizabeth blesses both Mary and her child, the "fruit of her womb." In response, Mary utters the hymn known as the Magnificat. Only the first portion, vss. 46-48, apply directly to Mary: two couplets that glorify God for the "great things" he has done for her.

My soul magnifies the Lord /
and my spirit exults in God my Savior. //
For he has regarded the humility of his handmaiden /
for behold, henceforth all generations will call me blessed. //

It has been remarked that in fact only v. 48 refers clearly to Mary.[2] The remainder of the hymn is considered by many commentators to be a reworking of a composition of Jewish-Christian origin that originally referred to Israel. It is evidently structured on the model of the Song of Hannah (1 Sam 2:1-10) and of Psalms such as 134/135 and 135/136. Beginning with a magnification of God, who has transformed Mary's humility into a state of

---

2   See J.A. Fitzmyer's discussion, *The Gospel According to Luke I-IX* (New York: Doubleday, 1981), 356-369. Three manuscripts of the Old Latin version, together with Irenaeus and Origen, read "Elizabeth" for "Mary," attributing the canticle to the former. This is probably secondary, since the great majority of Greek texts attribute it to the Mother of Jesus.

blessedness, the canticle continues by praising God for what are in effect victories over the enemies—internal or external—of the true Israel, the *'anawim* or "poor ones." Whatever the source of the underlying tradition, Luke has adapted it in such a way that it constitutes an introduction (vv. 46b-48), a body composed of five couplets (vv. 49-53), and a conclusion that recapitulates the whole and links God's saving deeds with his covenant promise to "Abraham and his posterity," that is, the people of Israel. The final portion of the Magnificat (49-55), then, is spoken not by the Virgin, but by God's "servant Israel," understood collectively (v. 54).

There seems to be as well a loosely defined chiastic movement to at least the last part of the hymn, vv. 49-55. This is not to say that it was consciously structured after some predetermined chiastic pattern. Rather, the themes find expression according to a parallelism that seems intuited, moving from fulfillment of God's promises to Israel (A: 49), to the covenantal promise made to Abraham (A': 55), then from a display of divine mercy (B: 50—B': 54) to a display of divine power (C: 51-52a—C': 53), and culminating in exaltation of the lowly (D: 52b).

In somewhat more detail, this can be set out in the following way:

A (49) He has done great things for me (*Israel*) / the Mighty One / and holy is his name
  B (50) And his *mercy* / from generation to generation / is to those who fear him
    C (51a) He has *shown strength* with his arm
      D (51b) He has *scattered* the proud in the imagination of their hearts
        E (52a) He has *put down* the mighty from their thrones
          F (52b) *And exalted the humble*
        E' (53a) He has *filled* the hungry with good things
      D' (53b) And the rich he has *sent empty away*
    C' (54a) He has *helped* his servant Israel
  B' (54b) in remembrance of his *mercy*
A' (55) As he spoke to our fathers, to Abraham and to his seed (*Israel*) forever.

The concentric parallelism, with intensification from the original line to its prime, can be indicated using summary statements and arrows:

A → A': God's saving acts toward Israel → God's promise of salvation to Israel *forever*.

B → B': God's mercy on all who fear him → God's mercy on *Israel*

C → C': God has shown his strength → God has helped his servant *Israel*

D → D': God has scattered the proud → God has banished the rich

E → E': God has humbled the mighty → God has fed the hungry with *good things*

F: God has *exalted* his people Israel.

Although the parallels are less clear than in other chiastic patterns we have examined, it seems likely that the author of the composition, consciously or unconsciously, relied on the familiar movement of concentric parallelism in producing this work. It is characterized by the common features of *anacrusis* (the introduction, vv. 46-48), *intensification* of the second element of the parallel relative to the first (from A to A', from B to B', etc., indicated above by italics: *forever, Israel, good things*), and a *focus* on the central theme: God's exaltation of his formerly humbled people.

In its original form, then, this second part of the Magnificat was very likely a liturgical hymn, uttered by "Israel" as a song of thanksgiving and praise to the God who has exalted his people by casting down and destroying their enemies (the proud, the mighty, the well-fed, the wealthy; compare Jesus' woes addressed to the wealthy, the well-fed, the contented and the praised, Lk 6:24-26). The interweaving of these originally independent elements, allows the evangelist to identify Mary with the true Israel, the object of God's saving mercy. Thereby her hymn of magnification becomes a song of victory for the Church as the true Israel. And therefore all generations will henceforth call Mary blessed, for through her person, as the Mother of the incarnate Lord, salvation has come into the world.

The account of Jesus' birth (Lk 2:1-20) fulfills the heavenly promise of 1:35, the child will be called Holy, the Son of God. Whereas Matthew depicts the Magi visiting the Christ-child as a sign of the universality of Jesus' saving mission, Luke contrasts the presence of the angels with the visit by the lowly shepherds. All creation, from the angelic host to the humblest of human creatures, attends the miraculous birth, to proclaim and praise this "Savior, who is Christ the Lord."

It has often been argued that the statement, "Mary gave birth to her first-born son," implies that she bore other children as well. The Greek, however, does not support this interpretation, any more than does Matthew's statement, "[Joseph] knew her not until she had borne a son" (1:25). The expression "first-born" is frequently used of children without siblings; and the preposition "until" (*heôs*) signifies "up to," or in the negative, "not prior to" the time indicated. It implies nothing about subsequent events or circumstances. Its purpose here is to stress the point that Mary's conception is miraculous, and not the result of sexual relations with Joseph. On the other hand, neither Matthew nor Luke shows a concern to proclaim Mary's perpetual virginity; but neither one can be used to refute that understanding, which the later Church accepted as dogma.

The moving narrative of Jesus' presentation in the Temple (Lk 2:21-40) illustrates the obedience of Mary and Joseph to Jewish Law: they dedicate their first-born child to the Lord. The child Jesus is received into the Temple by the Spirit-filled elder Simeon. His hymn of blessing, the *Nunc Dimittis*, further declares the universal scope of the salvation God is to accomplish through his Son. But in the midst of this thanksgiving, Simeon utters to Mary what can be properly considered St Luke's first prediction of the Passion. "Behold, this child is set for the fall and rising of many in Israel, and for a sign that is spoken against." And he adds in an aside to the Holy Mother, "a sword will pierce through your own soul also" (2:35).

The traditional interpretation of this verse holds that the "sword" to pierce Mary's soul is her suffering at the death of her Son on the Cross. Commentators today tend to reject this view, pointing out that St Luke does not explicitly place Mary at Golgotha as, for example, the evangelist John does (19:25). Accordingly, they tend to hold that the "sword" refers rather to divisions in Mary's human family concerning Jesus' actual identity and the significance of his work. Christian tradition, however, clearly knew of Mary's presence near the cross with the other women of Galilee, and there can be little doubt that Luke's community shared that knowledge. The image of the Pieta, the *Mater Dolorosa*, is not just a product of medieval Roman Catholic piety. It is a profoundly "evangelical" truth, firmly rooted in the biblical witness.

St Luke concludes his infancy narrative with the story, unique to his Gospel, of Jesus at twelve years of age with the teachers in the Temple. Here we find Jesus' first pronouncement, addressed to Mary and Joseph: "Why are you seeking me? Did you not know that I had to be about the affairs of my Father?"[3] Luke's admission that "they did not understand him" (2:50) creates a link with passages such as Mark 6:3 and John 7:5, "even Jesus' brothers did not believe in him." As Mary needed to ponder in her heart the ineffable mystery of Incarnation, so she, Joseph and others in Jesus' family, together with his disciples, needed to grow in their comprehension of both his person and his mission. The boy Jesus is found in the house of God, being taught by the elders of Israel, but also astonishing them with his words and wisdom. The passage thereby foreshadows Jesus' future role as Teacher, the one who embodies the very Truth he comes to proclaim.[4]

The final Lukan allusion to Mary appears in Acts 1:14. Here the disciples, "together with the women and Mary the mother of Jesus," are gathered in the Upper Room, united in prayer and awaiting the outpouring of the Holy

---

3 The plural expression *en tois tou patros mou* most likely signifies "affairs of my Father" rather than (with Fitzmyer et al.) "my Father's house."

4 For the chiastic structure of this passage, see J. Breck, *The Shape of Biblical Language: Chiasmus in the Scriptures and Beyond* (New York: St Vladimir's Seminary Press, 1998), 121-122.

Spirit. Extrapolating on this scene, Orthodox iconographic tradition sees here the *Orante*, the Mother of the Lord who stands before him to make ceaseless intercession on behalf of the faithful. The disciples, together with Mary, constitute the Church: One, Holy, Catholic, Apostolic. In the center of that gathering she images the true and faithful Disciple. Beyond that, however, she is the Virgin Mother of the "Deisis" icon: a flame of living prayer before the throne of her exalted Son.

5. Mary in the Gospel of John

The last biblical images of Mary we should consider are found in two related scenes in the Gospel of John: the wedding feast at Cana (2:1-11), and the crucifixion of Jesus (19:25-27). Some interpreters have found allusions to Mary and the virginal conception in 1:13; 7:41-43; and 8:41; but these are based on unacceptable variant readings or pure misunderstandings. The Evangelist John knows the tradition of Jesus' preexistence as the Logos of God, but his incarnational theology (1:14) seems to be independent of the traditions reflected in the birth-narratives of Matthew and Luke.

At the wedding in Cana, Jesus' mother warns him that the wine has run out, suggesting that he both can and should remedy the situation. Jesus answers her with an apparent rebuke, rendered by most versions as "Woman, what have you to do with me?" (*RSV*; cf. *NAB*, "woman, how does your concern affect me?"). The Greek phrase, *ti emoi kai soi, gynai?*, in fact carries nothing of a rebuke. "Woman" is a polite form of address, even if otherwise unattested in reference to one's mother. The meaning is clearer with a literal translation: "What is that to you and me?" Why, in other words, should you or I be concerned about such a mundane matter, since "my Hour has not yet come?" The coming Hour is the moment of Jesus' passion, and the question thus involves priorities. But since the marriage feast is an image of the heavenly banquet, it is appropriate that Jesus respond. And he does so with a miraculous gesture that transforms the water of the Old Covenant into the wine of the New.

Most significant here, though, is Mary's own attitude. She serves once again as intercessor, advocate or mediator with her Son. Pointing out the situation to him in full confidence that he can provide, she instructs the servants: "Do whatever he tells you." From a patristic perspective she thereby heals the sinful rebellion of Eve, calling for faithful obedience rather than proffering an object of temptation. She accomplishes the *Eva-Ave* reversal (a play on words possible only in Latin), becoming the New Eve, just as her Son has become the New Adam.

In his chiastic analysis of the Gospel of John, Peter F. Ellis has demonstrated that the central element of this passage focuses on the jars used for Jewish rites of purification:

A (2:1): Jesus present at the wedding in Cana →
A' (2:11): Jesus manifests his glory at the wedding in Cana.

B (2:3-5): The old wine fails →
B' (2:7-10): Abundant new wine.

C (2:6): The jars for Jewish rites of purification.[5]

This emphasis serves to make the point that in the person and mission of Jesus the Old Covenant has been replaced by the New. In Ellis' words, "the water of purification is related to the old dispensation, and the miracle to the new dispensation, which replaces the old."[6] This is a typical example of the recurring Johannine theme of "replacement." Here the old wine is exhausted by the guests (Israel) and is replaced by the "good wine" (v. 10) which only Jesus can provide. Notice once more the features of the chiastic pattern: heightening or intensification from A to A' and from B to B', with a central focus on C. This focus signifies that to the evangelist's mind the miracle not only provides new and better wine for the guests. It also transforms water of Israel's ritual purification into wine that symbolizes the Christian Eucharist. At his Mother's behest, Jesus works a miracle that foreshadows both the coming "Hour" of his death and resurrection, and the possibility for his followers to participate in the victory of that Hour by partaking of the "good wine" of eucharistic communion.

Finally, at the foot of the cross Mary appears again as the ideal disciple. At the moment of crucifixion, all of Jesus' followers flee, except his Mother and the Beloved Disciple, the primary witness behind John's Gospel. Jesus commends them to one another: "Woman, behold your son!...Behold your mother!" Thus Mary becomes the mother of the disciple closest to Jesus, so that henceforth their mutual discipleship might be grounded in familial love. It may be, as some have suggested, that Mary represents Jewish Christianity while the disciple represents Gentile Christianity (Bultmann). More likely, the evangelist sees in Mary the true Israel, received in a covenantal bond of love by the one who represents the Church. In the vision of the Fathers, in any event, the Mother of Jesus has become through this gesture the Mother of all Christians.

5   P.F. Ellis, "Inclusion, Chiasm, and the Division of the Fourth Gospel," *St Vladimir's Theological Quarterly*, vol. 42/3-4 (1999), 269-338, at 287. This is slightly different from his analysis given in *The Genius of John* (Collegeville, MN: The Liturgical Press, 1984), 40.
6   *The Genius of John*, 42.

At the moment of Jesus' death, according to St John, he bowed his head toward Mary and the Beloved Disciple, and "gave up his spirit." This is an unambiguous declaration that the incarnate Logos, the eternal Son of God, died a tragic human death. His was no docetic appearance in the flesh; his death was real and undeniable.

Yet in this account there may also be a secondary message that the evangelist is attempting to convey. On Easter night the risen Lord will visit his disciples behind closed doors and breathe upon them his life-giving Breath, which is the Holy Spirit (20:22). This marks the so-called "Johannine Pentecost." Given the prominence of the Spirit in the Farewell Discourses (Jn 14-16) and his role in spiritual regeneration throughout the Gospel (3:5; 6:63; 7:37ff), it seems likely that the evangelist's account of Jesus' death was intended to suggest a preliminary effusion of the Spirit, not upon the Church as a whole, represented later by the gathered disciples, but upon those who remained faithful to him during his trial and crucifixion. In their mutual commitment to one another, Mary and the Beloved Disciple become "pneumatophores," bearers of the indwelling Spirit, as Jesus was from the moment of his baptism (1:32f). And thereby their reciprocal covenantal bond, established by Christ himself, becomes an archetype of the bond of mutual love that should characterize the Christian community in its very essence (15:12).

6. Veneration of Mary in the Scriptures

To do justice to the biblical witness regarding the Virgin Mother, it would be necessary to include the image of the Woman clothed with the sun, who appears in Revelation 12, and similar figures, such as Sophia or Holy Wisdom. These are at best secondary allusions, however, and had only indirect bearing on the growth of the Church's christology or its Marian piety.

From what we have seen, it is clear that all Marian theology—like all Christian doctrine—must be grounded in and controlled by the canon or norm of Scripture. The cult of the veneration of Mary has been exaggerated at certain periods in the Church's history, and her image has been distorted by a dogmatic confusion between her own vocation and the mission of her Son. Nevertheless, Scripture itself provides us with the foundation of an authentic Marian piety. If Elizabeth blesses Mary for her faithful obedience to the word and will of God (Lk 1:41-45), Mary can declare, "henceforth all nations will call me blessed" (1:48). In Luke 11:27, a woman in the crowd cries out to Jesus, "Blessed is the womb that bore you..." Although Jesus turns the benediction to include all those "who hear the word of God and do it," early Christian readers (and hearers) of the Gospel would confirm the woman's intuition: given the grace and authority with which Jesus speaks and heals, his mother can only be "blessed." This is confirmed as Jesus entrusts his mother to the Beloved Disciple at the foot of the cross, and in effect entrusts her to the Church as a whole while making of her the *Mêtêr Ekklêsias,* "Mother of the Church."

Veneration of Mary is also supported by Old Testament tradition, such as Isa 7:14 on the virginal conception of the Messiah; or Isa 66:7-13 and Ezek 44:2, which in the later Church grounded belief respectively in Mary's painless birth-giving and her perpetual virginity. Such veneration grew very quickly in the post-apostolic period. The most ancient icon we possess is, significantly, a catacomb fresco of the *Orante,* Mary at prayer.

If this veneration has persisted and intensified over the centuries, it is because its truth, its validity and even its necessity, are confirmed through ecclesial experience. This returns us to our initial point: the mystery of the Mother of God is ultimately fathomable only within the life of the worshiping Church. To be known, Mary must be *celebrated.* Liturgical language used of her is often poetically expansive, as in her dialogue with the Angel Gabriel at the Feast of the Annunciation. Expressions of piety addressed to her may at times seem effusive. Doctrines concerning her may occasionally sound almost blasphemous, attributing to her attributes and characteristics that are appropriate rather to her Son Jesus. If the Church allows and even encourages such expression, however, it is for two basic reasons.

On the one hand, Mariology is and must remain a function of Christology. By praising her, we are in fact praising her Son, acknowledging and proclaiming that he is indeed the Son of God incarnate, the Second Person of the Holy Trinity, who has taken his human nature from the Virgin in order to deify both her and us. An authentic Mariology, then, points beyond the person of Mary herself to the God-man born of her. By celebrating the Mother of God, we in reality celebrate her Son, and the salvation he has accomplished on behalf of us all.

On the other hand, the Church allows and encourages an intense Marian piety because it recognizes that no human words can adequately convey the beauty and depth of the mystery that surrounds the Holy Virgin. Hidden from the Prince of this age, the mystery of Mary is in many respects hidden from believers as well. The Church's language concerning her must conform to biblical revelation, since that remains normative for every expression of faith. Liturgical language, however, functions in many respects like poetry. It uses verbal symbols to grasp inexpressible truths and to depict ineffable beauty. One day, for each of us, the truth and the beauty of Mary will be known fully, as it is revealed in the Kingdom of God. For the present, we are left with our inadequate images and our liturgical stammerings, attempting however modestly to offer the praise and glorification that are due to the Mother of God.

Yet repeatedly, in our personal and corporate experience, Mary manifests to us her compassion, her protection, and her undying love. Therefore we exalt her and proclaim her to be the Most Holy, Ever-Virgin Bride of God, the Handmaiden of the Lord, through whom Life has entered into the world. And we turn to her in total confidence, "now and at the hour of our death," beseeching her to intercede for us before the Son whom she bore. It is from this perspective, and with this conviction, that we can address her with the supplication, "Most Holy Theotokos, save us!"

> "You, O most holy Theotokos, are the hope, the defense and the refuge of Christians, the unassailable wall, the peaceful haven for the weary. But *as one who saves the world with your unceasing prayer*, remember us also, O most praised Virgin!"

> (Troparion of the Third Hour)

Part Three

Christ and the Spirit in Scripture and Tradition

9

Christ and the Spirit in
Nicene Tradition

1. The "Relevance" of the Nicene Creed

From the time of the fourth Ecumenical Council (451), the so-called "Nicene Creed" has been universally accepted by Churches of both East and West as an authoritative expression of Christian truth.[1] In Kelly's apt words, the Nicene-Constantinopolitan formula (C) "is one of the few threads by which the tattered fragments of the divided robe of Christendom are held together."[2] The matter of its relevance for our contemporary ecumenical situation, then, is of undeniable importance.

If the relevance of "C" can be called into question today, it is largely because of new approaches to christology that have emerged under the influence of factors as diverse as historical-critical exegesis and American popular psychology. These approaches pose two interrelated questions. First, can a creedal statement that omits all reference to Jesus' earthly ministry speak pertinently and with authority to an age whose social and religious consciousness focuses especially upon the 'historical Jesus,' together with his teachings on the meaning of the human person and application of his commandment to love? And second, does the language of "C"—that uses ontological rather than existential categories to spell out the relationship between Jesus and God the Father—give us a true and adequate picture of what that relation in fact is?

These questions rightly imply that "C" can be of value in our contemporary situation only insofar as it expresses the truth about God and his relationship to

---

1   Based on an ancient baptismal formula of Syro-Palestinian origin, the confessional statement formulated at Nicaea in 324 (N) is popularly thought to have been modified (including the last five articles) and promulgated by the Council of Constantinople in 381, to give us the "Nicene-Constantinopolitan Creed" (C) used in baptismal and eucharistic liturgies to the present day. While the history behind "C" remains obscure, the Creed has survived unchanged since its official reading at Chalcedon, with the exception of the *filioque* clause, discussed further on.
2   J.N.D. Kelly, *Early Christian Creeds*, London 1969, 296.

human life. Are affirmations such as "*homoousios* with the Father," "begotten before all ages," and "came down from heaven," simply relics of an outmoded, mythical worldview? Or can they still be understood and proclaimed in a way that corresponds to the theological and pastoral needs of our day? In other words, does the Nicene Creed convey the essence of God's self-revelation, or doesn't it? If it does, then its continuing relevance for modern Western societies, as for any others, follows from that very fact. If it does not, then it should be relegated to the department of Church archives, along with canon laws concerning the menstrual cycle and the biblical attitude towards slavery.

From an Orthodox point of view, the problem of the relevance of the Nicene Creed is well illustrated by John Cobb's reply to Jürgen Moltmann's paper on "The Unity of the Triune God," published back in 1984:[3]

> "My difficulty with Moltmann's thesis arises from my inability to follow the way in which Moltmann connects, or almost identifies, the history of salvation events to which the New Testament witnesses with an everlasting tri-unity in God. In my pedestrian imagination the proper name Jesus refers to a human being who came into being as such at a particular time and place in human history. He cannot be simply identical with the lamb slain from eternity. It is because of Jesus' crucifixion that we Christians have become aware of the everlasting suffering in the heart of God, but that is not quite the same thing... As I read Moltmann I receive the impression that for him Jesus is, as such and without any ambiguity, one of the persons of the Trinity. I find that startling, even shocking..."

This statement illustrates three closely related tendencies common to a great deal of contemporary reflection in the realm of christology. In the first place, it betrays a failure to grasp the traditional trinitarian doctrine of the Church, which affirms that the eternal Son of God (the "lamb slain from eternity") *assumed without change* (*atreptôs*) the fullness of human nature through his incarnation in the womb of Mary. While Jesus of Nazareth "came into being as such at a particular time and place in human history," he did so in total ontological unity with the uncreated, eternally begotten Son of God. Therefore the *person* of Jesus is one with and inseparable from the *person* of the divine Word: humanity and divinity united, without confusion and without separation, in the hypostasis or personal being of the God-man. There is and can only be complete hypostatic unity between Jesus and the Son; otherwise it could hardly be affirmed that "the Word became (*egeneto*) flesh" (Jn 1:14).

The second tendency flows from the first and amounts to a rejection of the biblical witness to the incarnation: a witness by no means confined to the

3   In *St Vladimir's Theological Quarterly*, 28/3 (1984), 157-177; quote, 174.

birth narratives of Matthew and Luke, but constitutive of both Pauline and Johannine christologies, which are rooted in the unambiguous conviction that the historical Jesus is hypostatically one with and inseparable from the eternal Son of God.

The third tendency is a consequence of the first two: in practice, if not in intention, to separate christology from trinitarian theology by separating the person (*hypostasis*) of Jesus from the person (*hypostasis*) of the Son of God, and thereby to represent a view of Jesus not unlike that of Cerinthus or Nestorius: a "hypostatic dualism." Or perhaps it would be more accurate to speak of the separation of Jesus from christology, if we mean by 'christology' reflection on the nature and activity of the second Person of the Trinity, the eternal Word of God. Yet stated in this way, it becomes immediately evident that there can be no meaningful reflection about the inner life of the Trinity that is not grounded both in the teaching *and in the person* of Jesus himself. To sever Jesus from the Son is to vitiate not only trinitarian reflection, but theology as a whole.

While Arianism as such is not at issue here, it seems clear that the Nicene Creed was formulated to refute just the sort of technically 'heretical' views that Prof. Cobb and many other contemporary theologians put forth in the name of theology. This of itself demonstrates the continuing relevance of the Creed. While Orthodox Christians would accept that conclusion as self-evident, however, it is far from clear that others would do so. The question nevertheless comes down to this: which christology, that of the Creed or that of 'differing opinions' (*haireseis*), most adequately expresses the truth about God and his saving work in the person of Jesus of Nazareth? It is this question, rather than lack of witness to Jesus' historical ministry, that will determine whether or not the Nicene Creed continues even in our own day to be a true and indispensable witness to divine reality.

2. The Pattern of Revelation

Ever since Athanasius wrote *De Decretis*, theologians have defended one or another term or phrase in "C" by demonstrating that it is directly scriptural or else faithfully reflects the "scriptural mind." To explain and attempt to justify the conviction that the Creed remains relevant to the needs of the Church today, however, it might prove more useful to examine it holistically. We should ask how the Creed functions *as a whole*, as a unified, global witness to divine life and activity. Rather than viewing it as merely a compilation of disparate dogmatic statements, devoid of internal cohesion, we can perhaps best understand it—and appreciate its abiding worth for both didactic and liturgical use—as a coherent depiction of the *movement of God*, who reaches out

from the unapproachable mystery of his inner being in order to render himself knowable and accessible to mankind.

Since our concern is primarily christological, we can begin by asking
whether the overall vision of the Nicene Creed actually corresponds to the
vision of Scripture concerning the nature and mission of the Son of God. To
what extent does the pattern of biblical revelation shape the content of "C"?
Does the Creed faithfully reproduce the kerygma of the early Church, or does
it represent an unwarranted extrapolation that in effect distorts the image of
Jesus and undermines his message? Then we should ask if the trinitarian focus
of "C" is itself a true and legitimate reflection of biblical revelation concerning the relationship between God the Father, Jesus and the Spirit. The final
criterion has to be the one formulated by the early Church, that no creedal
statement can be accepted as orthodox that does not rest upon "demonstrable
harmony with Scripture."[4]

The christological articles of "C" follow a particular pattern which is
shaped by biblical narrative. Following affirmation of the creative activity of
the one God and Father, it uses Johannine language to speak of the relationship between the Father and the Son ("Lord," "the only-begotten Son of God
[*monogenês*], "begotten of the Father," "Light," "true God"; Jn 20:18, 28;
1:14, 18; 3:16, 18; 1:4, 5; 8:12; 1 Jn 4:9; 5:20; etc.). It is noteworthy that the
expression "born of God / of the Father" is never used of Jesus / the Son, but
only of believers. The Nicene formula *ton ek tou patros gennêthenta*, then,
does not appear as such in the New Testament. Its justification is found rather
in the corresponding expression, *monogenês* or "(only) begotten Son." The
affirmation that Christ is the author of creation (*di' hou ta panta egeneto*) is
also Johannine (1:3), but like the title "Lord" (*kyrios*), it is equally proper to
Pauline thought (1 Cor 8:6; Col 1:16f; Phil 2:11; etc.).

Perhaps more important than these verbal and conceptual parallels
between the Creed and the New Testament, however, is the overall *pattern*
that expresses the movement of the eternal divine Son toward the world. The
primary pattern or conceptual model is that of "descent/ascent" through
incarnation, crucifixion and ascension." As such, it might also be taken as
specifically Johannine (cf. Jn 3:13, "No one has ascended into heaven but he
who descended from heaven, the Son of Man"). But in fact this pattern is
common to a multitude of NT "forms," from the most primitive kerygmatic
statements to early liturgical hymns, as the following examples illustrate.

4   The late Lutheran theologian Carl A. Voltz developed this theme in his important study,
     "A Lutheran View of the Council of Nicea 325 AD," presented in the context of the Lu-
     theran-Orthodox bilateral dialogues, on Dec. 10, 1984, esp. pp. 16-17.

The early Church saw in the Servant Song of Isaiah 53 a typological image of Christ's own incarnation, death and exaltation. Although it begins with assurance that the Servant will be "exalted and lifted up" (Isa 52:13), this prophetic promise is followed by an itinerary that parallels the "kenotic" movement of Philippians 2:7ff. "Despised and rejected by men," the Servant bears the "griefs and sorrows" of the people. Whereas they imagine him "stricken by God," in reality he is revealed as the one who is "wounded for (their) transgressions." Because he voluntarily makes of himself "an offering for sin," the Lord will cause him to prosper and "divide him a portion with the great."

This pattern of descent/ascent, humiliation/exaltation, provides the basic structure for the Christ-hymn of Philippians 2:5-11. The vast majority of interpreters excise v. 8c ("even death on a cross," *thanatou de staurou*) as a Pauline interpolation into the original text of the hymn. A rhetorical (chiastic) analysis of the passage, however, reveals that the very center of the hymn is the inverted parallelism represented by v. 8bc: *mechri thanatou / thanatou de staurou*. This is the pivotal affirmation about which the entire movement occurs: from eternal divine existence (*en morphê theou, isa theô*), through the kenotic act of incarnation (*heauton ekenôsen*) and the absolute humiliation of crucifixion (*etapeinôsen heauton)*, to exaltation (*hyperypsôsen*) and universal acclamation with bestowal of the divine name *Kyrios* or Lord.[5]

This descending-ascending movement, however, is by no means limited to Isaiah 53 and Philippians 2. It appears as well in the primitive kerygmatic statements recorded in Acts 2-3 (2:22-24; 3:13-15), as it does in related fragments scattered throughout the Pauline letters (1 Cor 15:3f; Gal 1:3-4; Rom 1:3-4; 8:32-34; etc.), and in the passion predictions of Christ (Mk 8:31; 9:31; 10:33f and parallels). In these Synoptic predictions there is, of course, no allusion to preexistence and post-resurrectional exaltation. The "katabatic/anabatic" or descending/ascending pattern is expressed rather as humiliation and vindication, on the model of the Isaiah Servant Song.

The point here is that revelation of the divine economy itself follows a specific pattern: one of descent and ascent, the movement of God toward the world in the person of Jesus Christ, followed by the exaltation and acclamation of Christ by the cosmic powers. The purpose of that revelation is essentially *soteriological.* By affirming that God, in the person of the preexistent divine Son, accepts total identification with humanity to the point of death upon a cross, followed by exaltation into heaven, the apostolic witnesses declare what later Church Fathers would formulate by use of the term *theôsis*:

5   For a graphic presentation of the chiastic structure of these passages (Isa, Phil), see J. Breck, *The Shape of Biblical Language,* 256-266.

"He became what we are, so that we might become what he is" (Ignatius, Irenaeus); "God became man so that we might become god" (or "deified"—Athanasius); or, in St Basil's bold expression, salvation consists in "becoming god," meaning participation in the fullness of trinitarian life (*theon genesthai*, "Treatise on the Holy Spirit" IX 109C).

Because it describes the way in which God accomplishes his work of salvation, this pattern itself is an essential element of divine revelation. Jesus can save mankind only insofar as he is personally identical with the eternal Son of God, who "descends" to earth, assumes "flesh" (total human existence) in the womb of Mary (the *Theotokos* or "Mother of God"), goes down into death and rises again, to break the bonds of sin and death (Rom 5:12ff). The resurrection of Jesus, however, would have no existential meaning for anyone but himself if it were not completed and fulfilled by his ascension or exaltation. For it is by this final act that God in Christ raises fallen humanity from the abyss of death, and *exalts it together with him*. If Ignatius overstates the matter by declaring that Jesus rose "in the flesh" (*Smyrn* 3.1), his point is nevertheless consistent with Scripture, as it is with later patristic teaching: through baptism our humanity is united to Christ so fully that we actually participate with him in his own resurrection and glorification.

The pattern of descent/ascent must remain intact in order to affirm that the Son of God "came down from heaven." Ultimately there can be no christology *von unten*. If God did not become man, if the Savior is not the eternal Son of the Father, "begotten before all ages and of one essence with the Father," then Jesus died in vain and Christian people are indeed "the most to be pitied" (1 Cor 15:19). But conversely, this *Christologie von oben* centers precisely upon the *death* of the Son of God. That death, however, is vindicated through resurrection, and achieves its purpose through the exaltation and glorification of human nature.

With regard to the overall structure of the Nicene Creed, therefore, we can state the following. Its pattern of revelation is identical to that of the Church's earliest kerygmatic hymns and statements. This is necessarily so, for the pattern itself—the movement of descent and ascension, "from heaven to earth to heaven"—is an integral part of revelation because it describes the very way in which God accomplishes his work of salvation within human experience. If we dismiss this pattern as a mere literary device or as the product of a mythical worldview, we inevitably, if unwittingly, deny the content of revelation itself.

From the point of view of this pattern of revelation, then, the Nicene Creed is as relevant as the apostolic kerygma itself. Structure and content, form and meaning, are inseparable in confessional statements, just as they are in kerygmatic elements. To proclaim the Word, as kerygma or as the scripturally based Creed, is to "actualize" the Word by communicating its meaning through a universally accepted and authoritative form. Consequently, by its baptismal and eucharistic recitations of the Creed, the Church is able *to affirm and to reactualize* in its midst God's work for the salvation of mankind.

3. The Trinitarian Focus

The final article of the original Nicene Creed (N) stated simply, "And in the Holy Spirit" (*Kai eis to hagion pneuma*). The anathemas which followed were directed against those who distorted the affirmations concerning Christ, and they made no reference to the Spirit. This cursory allusion to the Spirit in "N" is explained by the polemical cast of the Creed: its concern was with Arianism and its threat to orthodox christology. In the half-century between the first and second Ecumenical Councils, however, several other creedal formulations included expanded statements on the Spirit. These were drawn almost exclusively from Scripture, especially the Johannine farewell discourses and the "great commission" of Matthew 28.[6]

The received form of "C" includes a number of significant additions concerning the Spirit. In the christological articles, it declares that the Son was "incarnate from the Holy Spirit (*sarkôthenta ek pneumatos hagiou*) and the Virgin Mary." Then in the final series of articles it attributes the divine name *Kyrios* to the Spirit (while avoiding explicit use of *homoousios*) and specifies both his origin and his activity within salvation history: he "proceeds from the Father" (*to ek tou patros ekporeuomenon*); he is accorded the same worship and glorification as are due to the Son and the Father; he "spoke by the prophets." As many commentators have shown, the following three articles, on the Church, baptism and resurrection, are properly understood to be fruits of the work of the Spirit. The Creed, therefore, is composed of three major articles devoted respectively to God the Father, the Lord Jesus Christ, and the Holy Spirit.

The problem of the abiding significance of "C" in today's theological climate cannot be resolved simply by pointing out the parallel between its structural flow and the descent/ascent movement of the divine economy. The question remains as to whether the underlying trinitarian vision of "C" is in

6 The most important of these are connected with the Dedication Council held at Antioch in 341. Texts in Kelly, *op. cit.*, ch. 9; see also J. Stevenson, *Creeds, Councils and Controversies* (London: SPCK, 1966), 11-15.

harmony with the witness to God contained in Scripture. Is trinitarian dogma simply a product of the later Church? Or is it a faithful expression of the inner life of the Godhead as revealed in the apostolic writings? It would be fruitless, of course, to attempt to discern a full-blown trinitarian theology in the New Testament. Romans 8:9-11, where Paul speaks in the same breath of the Spirit [of God] and the Spirit of Christ—and apparently identifies the Spirit with both the Father and the Son—is enough to illustrate that any attempt to force his thought into a trinitarian "system" would be anachronistic. That does not mean, however, that the foundation of trinitarian theology is not fully laid, both in Paul's letters and in the Gospels. This is evident not only from Christ's statements in the Fourth Gospel concerning the Father, Son and Spirit. It is also clear from the trinitarian liturgical fragments that appear in Paul's writings and throughout the New Testament.

It is not possible here to present the biblical evidence for a trinitarian conception of God.[7] Let me simply state my conviction, based on exegesis of liturgical formulas in the New Testament,[8] that the continuity between the biblical image of God and the Church's traditional Orthodox-Catholic teaching about the tri-unity of Persons within the Godhead, is such that in this regard patristic tradition stands in complete harmony with Scripture. Liturgical formulas such as 2 Corinthians 13:13/14—"The grace of the Lord Jesus Christ, and the love of God, and the communion of the Holy Spirit be with you all"—may not be "trinitarian" in the technical sense. If the Byzantine eucharistic Liturgy has expanded this formula by rendering it more personal ("The grace of *our* Lord Jesus Christ") and making explicit the relationship of God to Jesus and believers ("and the love of God *the Father*"), this is nevertheless a thoroughly legitimate step in the light of those Pauline and other passages that speak of the Fatherhood of God.[9] The same can be said of the Church's baptismal use of the "great commission" in Matthew 28, and of a multitude of other formulas that present the work of salvation as an *economia* of Father, Son and Spirit.[10] These should be read in conjunction with the two Gospel pericopes, of Christ's baptism and his transfiguration, that constitute theophanies of the Father, the Son and the Spirit during the period of the incarnation. Further evidence is

7   See esp. J. Lebreton, *Les Origines du Dogme de la Trinité*, vol. I (Paris: Beauchesne, 1910); A. W. Wainwright, *The Trinity in the New Testament* (London: SPCK, 1962/69); and B. de Margerie, *La Trinité chrétienne dans l'histoire* (Paris: Beauchesne, 1975).
8   J. Breck, "Trinitarian Liturgical Formulas in the New Testament," in *The Power of the Word* (Crestwood, NY: St Vladimir's Seminary Press, 1986), 141-184.
9   Rom 1:7; 8:15f; 2 Cor 1:2-3; cf. Jn 1:14 and passim.
10 See 1 Cor 6:9-20; 12:4-6; Rom 5:1-5; 8:2-11; Eph 2:18-22; Phil 2:1; Col 1:6-8; Heb 2:3-4; 1 Pet 1:2; 3:18-22; 1 Jn 2:18-27; etc.

provided by the multitude of references that point, albeit indirectly, to the divinity of Christ: from affirmations such as John 10:30 ("I and the Father are one") and 20:28 ("My Lord and my God"), to the significant if curious syntax of formulas such as 1 Thessalonians 3:11 ("Now may our God and Father himself and our Lord Jesus Christ direct [*kateuthunai*] our way to you") and 2 Thessalonians 2:16f ("Now may our Lord Jesus Christ himself and God our Father...comfort [*parakalesai*] and establish [*stêriksai*] your hearts..."), where the aorist optative verb in each case is in the singular.

While examples such as these do not offer grounds for reading back into the New Testament traditional trinitarian dogma, they do make it clear that to the apostolic mind (1) Father, Son and Spirit are inseparable, both in their divine origin and in their common work of salvation; and (2) that christology is inseparable from trinitarian theology, just as the person of Jesus is inseparable from christology. Any confessional statement that denies or obscures that twofold conviction inevitably distorts revealed truth itself.

The enduring value of the Nicene Creed lies precisely in its authoritative reflection, grounded in the apostolic witness, of the hypostatic relationships within the Godhead that reveal themselves in the economy of salvation. The significance of the Creed, in other words, lies in its capacity to reveal and proclaim—and thereby to reactualize within the confessing community—not only "what God does" within human history, but also "who God is" in his innermost being. For what God does in granting salvation to the world is to communicate his own personal, divine life to those who receive him in faith. Therefore Jesus of Nazareth is both revealer and savior insofar as through his ministry as the incarnate yet eternal Son of God, he communicates through Word and Sacrament the life of the triune Godhead itself: *ek tou patros, dia tou huiou, en tô pneumati hagiô*. It follows, then, that any attempt to sunder Jesus from christology, or to propose a "christology" that posits a Christ who is other than the eternal Son of God, is to preach "another Gospel" which neither Paul nor any other apostolic witness would acknowledge or proclaim.

4. The (Intractable) Problem of the Filioque

The question of the importance of Nicene christology is inextricably linked to a critical theological issue that for centuries has divided the Orthodox from Roman Catholics and Protestants: the issue of the *filioque* clause interpolated into the third article of the Creed.

Vast numbers of publications in recent years have focused on the question of the Spirit and his relation to the Father and the Son. Some of the most interesting of these date from the early 1980s.[11] Further useful contributions, dealing particularly with the *filioque* question, were presented at the NCCC-USA Holy Spirit Consultation held in Boston on Oct. 24-25, 1985. These and similar studies have relied heavily on the writings of the eminent Catholic theologian André de Halleux.[12] Since that time, serious and informed debate between Orthodox and Catholic scholars has continued, particularly following the "clarification" on the *filioque* published in *Osservatore Romano* on September 13, 1995.[13] It is not possible here to review this material. My purpose is rather to summarize certain aspects of Orthodox thought on the matter and draw a few conclusions concerning the Nicene witness to Christ and the Spirit.

Again we must begin with the biblical writings. The key passage on which the Nicene formula concerning the "procession" of the Spirit was based is John 15:26, a confessional element structured in chiastic parallelism, that stands at the heart of the farewell discourses (Jn 14-16).

A: "When the Paraclete comes
　　B: whom I shall send to you from the Father,
　　　　C: the Spirit of Truth,
　　B': who proceeds from the Father,
A' he will bear witness concerning me."

Of the five Spirit-Paraclete passages in the discourses, the first two affirm that the Father will "give" (*dôsei*, 14:16) or "send" (*pempsei*, 14:26) the Spirit, whereas in 15:26 and 16:7 it is said that Jesus himself will "send" (*pempsô*) the Spirit. In the central passage, 15:26, a clear distinction is made in B-B' between two actions: "sending" and "proceeding." To the Greek Fathers, this indicates a distinction between the inner life of the Trinity and its temporal, "economic" manifestation within human history, referred to respectively in contemporary theological language as the "immanent Trinity" (*ad intra*) and the "economic Trinity" (*ad extra*). Whereas the "sending" of the Spirit, by the Father or the Son, concerns the earthly mission or *economia*, the "procession" has been understood in Eastern patristic thought to refer to an eternal act by which the Father, as the unique principle (*archê*), source (*pêgê*) and cause

---

11　See especially the World Council of Churches volume, *Spirit of God, Spirit of Christ* (ed. Lukas Vischer; Geneva, 1981); *Credo in Spiritum Sanctum* (2 vols.) (Vatican City: Vatican Publications, 1983); and the article by J. Meyendorff, "The Holy Spirit, as God," in *The Byzantine Legacy in the Orthodox Church* (Crestwood, NY: St Vladimir's Seminary Press, 1982), 153-165.

12　See his collected works in *Patrologie et œcuménisme* (Leuven: University Press, 1990).

13　For an Orthodox critique of this document, see especially Jean-Cl. Larchet, "La Question du 'Filioque'," in *Le Messager orthodoxe* 129 (1997), 3-58.

(*aitia*) of all divine life, brings forth the hypostatic being of the Spirit and communicates to him his own divine essence. The question is whether we can affirm, in the "filioquist" perspective of the Latin tradition, that the Son plays an active role in that eternal bringing forth of the Spirit.

The classical Orthodox answer to the question has been an unambiguous "no," expressed most adamantly by Patriarch Photius († c. 895), who insisted that the Spirit proceeds "from the Father *alone*" (*ek monou tou patros*). Recent Orthodox studies based on the teachings of the Greek Fathers, however, have qualified that reply in ways that offer a degree of hope for bringing into alignment, if not into total agreement, Eastern and Western positions on the subject. A brief sketch of the historical background will help put those studies in perspective.

The doctrine of the "double procession" of the Spirit, from the Father and from the Son (*a patre filioque procedit*), has characterized Western trinitarian thought since the time of Augustine. In his *De Trinitate* Augustine took as his starting point the unity and simplicity of the divine substance or essence, rather than the personal or hypostatic differentiation of three persons (*prosôpa*). Drawing an analogy between human self-knowledge and self-love on the one hand and the generation of the Son and procession of the Spirit on the other, he was led to posit the double procession of the Spirit from the Father *and from the Son* (*filioque*) by conceiving of the Spirit as the "bond of mutual love" (*nexus amoris*) that unites the other two hypostases.[14]

The original Western position, represented by Tertullian, held that the Spirit proceeded "from the Father through the Son" (*a patre per filium*).[15] Augustine continued to defend the threefoldness and the consubstantiality of the Godhead (a point too often overlooked by Orthodox critics who charge him with subordination of the Spirit). Yet his view that the Spirit proceeds from the Father and the Son *as from a single source* (*a patre filioque, tamquam ab uno principio*)[16] came to supplant the older formulation and set the stage for the inevitable clash between East and West.

The *filioque* appears to have been first formulated ca. 380 in Spain by the synod of Saragossa, to combat the modalistic and docetic teachings of Priscillian († 386) and his followers. It surfaced temporarily at the first council of Toledo in the year 400 and was officially promulgated by the third council of Toledo in 589.[17] Its insertion into Latin confessional statements

---

14 *De Trin* XV.17
15 *Adv. Praxean* 4.1.
16 See *de Trin*. V.14f; XV.26-27.
17 This chronology concerning the early development of the *filioque*, however, has recently

was intended to combat lingering Arianism by attributing to the Son a role equal to that of the Father in "processing" the Holy Spirit. Interestingly, a number of Roman popes opposed its use until the early eleventh century (1014), when Benedict VII formally inserted it into the Roman rite. It was officially promulgated as Roman dogma at the so-called "unionist" Council of Lyons in 1274, a council rejected by the Orthodox. Already in the early ninth century, Charlemagne had vigorously defended the *filioque*, claiming in total ignorance of history that it was part of the original confession and that it had subsequently been suppressed by the Eastern Churches!

Eastern reaction began with Maximus the Confessor († 662), who affirmed that from the self-revelation of the Trinity we can infer the common nature of the three Persons, but not a causal role of the Son in the Spirit's procession. Such procession can only be properly conceived as being "from" the Father and "through" the Son,[18] a position that received classical formulation in John of Damascus' *Exposition of the Orthodox Faith*: "The Spirit is the Spirit of the Father as proceeding from the Father..., but he is also the Spirit of the Son, not as proceeding from him, but as proceeding through him from the Father, for the Father alone is the cause."[19]

Well before Western promulgation of the *filioque*, Eastern theologians had excluded on principle the possibility of two "causes" within the Godhead. There can be no speculation regarding the immanent Trinity that is not grounded in the self-revelation of the economic Trinity. We encounter three distinct hypostases or personal expressions of divine life in Scripture and in our ecclesial experience, and from that we infer their essential unity or consubstantiality. The oneness of nature, however, does not exclude

been called into question. Several manuscripts of the acts of the ancient councils involved are lacking the *filioque*, leading some scholars to conclude that the clause first surfaced only at Toledo IV (633). In earlier conciliar decrees it would then appear as an interpolation. See M. Stavrou, "Filioque et théologie trinitaire," *Communio* XXIV, 5-6, no. 145-146 (Sept.-Dec. 1999), 152 and note 1.

18 See in this regard J. Meyendorff, *Byzantine Theology*, (New York: Fordham University Press, 1974), 93; M. Orphanos, "The Procession of the Holy Spirit according to certain later Greek Fathers," in *Spirit of God, Spirit of Christ*, 38; and Jean-Cl. Larchet's extensive analysis in "La Question du 'Filioque'," (note 13 above).

19 "*...ouch ôs ex autou, all' ôs di' autou ek tou Patros ekporeuomenon monos gar aitios ho Patêr*," *de Fide Orthodoxa* I.12. See Th. Stylianopoulos, "The Filioque: Dogma, Theologoumenon or Error?", in Th. Stylianopoulos and S.M. Heim, *Spirit of Truth*, (Brookline, MA: Holy Cross Orthodox Press, 1986), 25-58; and B. Bobrinskoy, "Le 'Filioque' Hier et Aujourd'hui," *Contacts* 34, no. 117 (1982), 7-27; original English version: "The Filioque Yesterday and Today," *Spirit of God, Spirit of Christ* (London: SPCK, Geneva: World Council of Churches, 1981), 133-148.

hierarchical ordering within the Godhead. Thus we encounter Father, Son and Spirit respectively as first, second and third Persons. Based on scriptural passages such as John 15:26 and 1 Corinthians 15:28, Eastern tradition insisted that the Father alone is the principle (*archê*) and end (*telos*) of all life, both divine and created. Athanasius declared that the unity of the Word and the Spirit is in "the divinity and perfection of the Father."[20] And the Cappadocians, with their distinction between *ousia* and *hypostasis*, posited the Father as the sole cause of deity: from his essence, the unoriginate Father brings forth the Son through generation and the Spirit through procession (*ekporeusis*, a term coined by Gregory of Nazianzus), communicating to them the fullness of his essence but not his hypostatic property of unbegottenness.

This is a crucial distinction, for what differentiates the three Persons of the Trinity is precisely their hypostatic origin: the Father is hypostatically "unoriginate" (*agennêtos*), the Son is eternally "begotten" or "generated" of him, and the Spirit "proceeds" eternally from him. Through this double act of generation and procession, the Father communicates to the Son and the Spirit the totality of his divine essence; and by virtue of *perichôrêsis*, the mutual communication of properties, each Person bestows upon the other every personal characteristic with the sole exception of their unique hypostatic origin. Thus each is all that the other two are, except that the unoriginate Father remains the sole cause of the Son and the Spirit, while the Son and Spirit retain their hypostatic distinctiveness denoted by the terms "generation" and "procession."

Photius took up this way of reasoning and developed his polemical anti-*filioque* stance around the assertion that the Spirit proceeds from the Father *alone*. Consistent with the thought of his Eastern predecessors, Photius insisted that the act of procession is a property of the Father's hypostatic being that is shared neither by the Son nor by the Spirit. He concluded that the only role the Son could play in the procession of the Spirit concerned the latter's *temporal mission:* the sending of the Spirit into the realm of human history to work out the divine economy of salvation. In his *Mystagogia*, however, Photius made a distinction between the divine essence (*ousia*) and the eternal, uncreated divine energies (*energeia*), affirming that the Spirit could be said to "proceed" from the Son in the sense that, by *perichôrêsis*, the Son, together with the Father, communicates the *charismata* of the Spirit to the world. Those *charismata*, however, are to be understood as uncreated *energies* (*energeia*) of the Spirit and not his hypostatic mode of being. Thereby Photius, while adhering strictly to the proposition that the Father is the unique *aitia* or cause of all

20 *Contra Arianos* I.45. D. Staniloae, "Le Saint Esprit dans la théologie byzantine et dans la réflexion orthodoxe contemporaine," in *Credo in Spiritum Sanctum* I, 663.

divine life, nevertheless laid the groundwork for a fresh Orthodox understanding of the role of the Son in the "bringing forth" of the Spirit, one that projected that role back into the immanent Trinity itself.

Photius' line of reasoning in fact goes back at least to St Athanasius. In his *First Letter to Serapion*, Athanasius describes the Spirit as being "given" (*didomenon*) and "sent" (*pempomenon*) by or from the Son within the framework of the divine economy. He goes on to affirm that the Spirit "is said to proceed from the Father, because from the Word, who is confessed to be from the Father, he shines forth (*eklampei*), is sent and is given."[21] While the verb "proceed" clearly refers to the eternal bringing forth of the Spirit within the immanent Trinity, and the last two verbs—"sent" and "given"—refer to the Son's communication of the Spirit to the world, the significance of the verb "shine forth" is not clear. As Joost van Rossum has shown, in its context the term is ambiguous: "It may refer to the divine 'theology,' or to the divine 'economy,' or, and what is perhaps most likely, to both at the same time."[22]

This ambiguity of expression in Athanasius led to a heated debate among Byzantine theologians during the twelfth and thirteenth centuries. The names most closely connected with the debate are those of Nicephorus Blemmydes (1197-1272) and Gregory of Cyprus, Patriarch of Constantinople from 1283-1289.

Ever since the Greek Roman Catholic theologian Leo Allacci (Allatius, †1669) attempted to co-opt Nicephorus Blemmydes as an advocate of union between the Orthodox and Roman Churches, scholars have usually held Blemmydes to be a firm defender of the *filioque* and other elements of Latin tradition.[23] While the unionist Patriarch John Beccus († 1282) was clearly a "latinophrone," the same cannot be said of Blemmydes. Although he was deeply concerned with the issue of reunion, Blemmydes remained a faithful representative of Byzantine theology, and particularly of its position on the procession of the Holy Spirit.

---

21 hêtis ek Patros legetai ekporeuesthai, epeidê para tou Logou tou ek Patros homologoumenou eklampei, kai apostelletai, kai didotai, *Ep. I ad Serapionem* 20, PG 26, 580A.

22 J. van Rossum, "Athanasius and the *Filioque: Ad Serapionem* I, 20 in Nikephoros Blemmydes and Gregory of Cyprus," in *Studia Patristica* XXXII (Leuven, 1997), 54.

23 See V. Grumel's well-known study, "Nicéphore Blemmyde et la procession du Saint-Esprit," *Revue des Sciences Philosophiques et Théologiques* 18 (1929), 636-656. For the history of the debate, together with an evaluation of Blemmydes' influence on Gregory of Cyprus, see the excellent study by Michel Stavrou, *Le Premier Traité sur la procession du Saint-Esprit de Nicéphore Blemmydès: édition critique, traduction et commentaire*, presented for the D.E.A. at the Dept. of Religions and Religious Anthropology, Sorbonne (Paris IV), in October of 1998.

This point has been made very persuasively by Michel Stavrou in his recent study of the question.[24] Byzantine theologians had long used expressions such as "the Spirit proceeds from (*ek / para*) the Father through (*dia*) the Son," or even "from the Father and (*kai*) the Son." While this referred chiefly to the divine economy, it could not avoid conveying the idea of "bringing forth" the Spirit *ad intra*. This is certainly the meaning of *ekporeuetai* in John 15:26, where the verb is clearly contrasted with the "sending" of the Spirit by the Son "from the Father" (*pempsô hymin para tou patros*). In his *Letter to James, Archbishop of Bulgaria*—otherwise known as *Treatise I on the Procession of the Holy Spirit*[25]—Blemmydes sought to defend the doctrine of the procession of the Spirit "from the Father by or through the Son."[26] To make the point that the formula is not compatible with the Latin *filioque*, he cites numerous Byzantine predecessors, including Athanasius and Cyril of Alexandria, Gregory of Nyssa and John of Damascus.

Nevertheless, recalling the passage cited above from Athanasius' *First Letter to Serapion*, Blemmydes argues that the verb *eklampei* refers to the inner life of the Trinity, God's eternal existence (*hyparxis*) rather than to the divine economy.[27] By describing the Spirit as the "energy of the Son" (*energeia tou huiou*) Blemmydes distinguishes between the being or nature of God (*hyparxis, physis/ousia*) and divine *energy*. With regard to the Trinity *ad intra*, the Spirit may be said to "proceed from the Father and the Son," not in terms of his personal existence but as the *eternal radiance* of the Father and Son.

> Thus, as the energy of the Son and Word of God, the Holy Spirit eternally shines forth (*aïdiôs eklampei*) from him, which is to say "through him," from the Father; but as gift he is sent and given by nature (*physikôs*).[28]

Michel Stavrou interprets this text as follows: "The Son is engendered from the Father as bestower of the Spirit... The divine energy which the Spirit dispenses is 'given by nature,' which means the giving is eternal and not dependent upon a created reality to receive it; it is the illumination which from all eternity bathes the perfect fullness of trinitarian life." And he adds the crucial point that this energy, dispensed by the Spirit, refers not to "being" considered in itself but rather in *relation* to another, as participation in the life of an "other."[29] It is

24 Ibid.
25 PG 142, 533-565.
26 Blemmydes uses the prepositions *ek* and *para* as synonyms when speaking of the Spirit's procession from the Father.
27 M. Stavrou, ibid., 36.
28 Treatise I, PG 541A; Greek text with annotations in M. Stavrou, ibid., IX, 15, 7.
29 Ibid., 38.

this essentially relational quality that enables the human person to participate in the divine energies to the point of *theôsis* or deification.

As Stavrou also notes, this section of Blemmydes' *Letter* clearly anticipates a further development in Byzantine reflection on the procession of the Spirit made subsequently by Patriarch Gregory II of Constantinople, more commonly known as Gregory of Cyprus, in his treatise *On the Procession of the Holy Spirit*.[30] This is the doctrine of the "eternal shining forth" (*aïdiôs ekphansis*) of the Holy Spirit from the Father by or through the Son.

Nicephorus Blemmydes, therefore, should be seen above all as a staunch defender of traditional Orthodox teaching regarding the procession of the Holy Spirit ("from the Father through the Son").[31] His highly nuanced trinitarian theology does allow him to employ language that with a superficial reading appears to support the Latin *filioque*. In fact, it does not. What Blemmydes accomplishes is to synthesize the thinking of such predecessors as Athanasius and Cyril of Alexandria and Gregory of Nyssa, in order to express a profound truth concerning the bringing forth of the Spirit within the Godhead. While maintaining absolutely the position that the Spirit in his essential and hypostatic being proceeds *from the Father alone*, Blemmydes allows for the Spirit to come forth or even to "proceed" from the Father *and the Son* as the "eternal radiance" or "shining forth" of the divine energies. Those energies pour forth eternally from the Father, through the Son and to the Spirit, who in turn bestows them on the created order. Yet that outpouring of the divine energies is not dependent on creation; it is rather an eternal manifestation. Accordingly, Blemmydes can accept the traditional Greek expression *ek tou huiou* while rejecting the "filioquist" theology which holds that Father and Son are both "causes" of the Spirit.

30 PG 142, 279-284. Stavrou, ibid., 39 and note 158. Cf. Gregory's *Homologia* (PG 142.242ff).

31 Recently some Orthodox theologians have suggested substituting the formula *a patre per filium / ek tou patros dia tou huiou* for *a patre filioque*. This formulation, however—found in St Basil, St Gregory of Nyssa, St Maximus the Confessor, and St John of Damascus, as well as in Patriarch Tarasius' formulation of the Creed at the Seventh Ecumenical Council (Nicea II, 787: *to pneuma to hagiou...to ek tou patros dia tou huiou ekporeuomen*)—was proposed at the "unionist" Councils of Lyons (1274) and Ferrara-Florence (1438-1443) as a virtual equivalent of the *filioque*. It has recently been proposed as well by the "Clarification" of the Roman Catholic reading of the *filioque*, "The Greek and Latin Traditions Regarding the Procession of the Holy Spirit," (*L'Osservatore Romano* no. 38 [13 Sept. 1995]). The susceptibility of the phrase "by" or "through" (*per / dia*) the Son of a "filioquist" interpretation has made Orthodox theologians wary of accepting it as a compromise formula. (See B. Bobrinskoy, "Le 'Filioque' Hier et Aujourd'hui," 22). In any case, the preposition "through" cannot be interpreted as "causal" but rather as "manifesting" the Spirit in the form of divine *energies* within the immanent Trinity as within the framework of salvation history.

The major contribution made by Gregory of Cyprus was to clarify the intuition, suggested already by Gregory of Nyssa, concerning the eternal mediation of the Spirit by the Son. With the Cappadocians and Blemmydes, the Cypriot, in his Tomus of 1285, distinguished between divine essence, energy and hypostatic being. The Father is the unique source of all divine life, and through his own hypostasis he confers on the Spirit and the Son their particular personal mode of existence as well as the fullness of the divine essence.

Up to this point, Gregory is merely repeating the thought of his predecessors. But he goes on to distinguish between the "cause of existence" (*hyparxein exein*) of the Spirit, which is the Father, and the existential quality of the Spirit (*hyparxein*) as he rests eternally on the Son. This leads him to posit an eternal and active "shining forth" or "manifestation" (*aïdiôn ekphansin*) of the Spirit *by the Son*. This eternal manifestation, however, is not to be confused with procession as expressed by the *filioque*, since it concerns the uncreated *energeia* or *charismata* of the Spirit and not his essence or hypostatic existence. Since the "energies" are common to all three *hypostaseis*, the formula *dia tou huiou* properly conveys the thought that the eternal manifestation of the Spirit also comes forth "through" or even "from" the Son.

While the *hypostasis* of the Spirit is derived uniquely from the Father through eternal procession, Gregory of Cyprus affirms that the uncreated *energeia* of the Spirit are brought forth from the Son through eternal manifestation (*ekphansis*).[32] This crucial distinction between the eternal *procession* of the Spirit from the Father and the eternal *manifestation* of the Spirit from or through the Son, marked a significant step beyond the thought of Photius, who restricted the mediating function of the Son to the temporal mission of the Spirit.

From this point on in Byzantine thought, a particular reading of the *filioque* clause became in principle acceptable. With Gregory Palamas, it remained necessary to distinguish between the Spirit's procession *kat' hyparxin* from the Father and *kat' ekphansin* or *kat' energeian* from the Son. But theoretically, insofar as this distinction was rigorously maintained, it had become possible for the Orthodox to confess the Spirit "who proceeds from the Father and from the Son." Because no such distinction was made in Latin theology, however, and the West continued to posit a *double cause* in the

32 M. Orphanos, *op. cit.*, 25ff; J. Meyendorff, *Byzantine Theology*, 92-94; and the art. by D. Staniloae (note 16 above). Gregory of Cyprus' contribution is discussed in detail by Aristeides Papadakis, *Crisis in Byzantium. The Filioque Controversy in the Patriarchate of Gregory II of Cyprus (1283-1289)* (Crestwood, NY: St Vladimir's Seminary Press, 1997).

procession of the Spirit, it was impossible for the Eastern Churches to adopt the interpolated form of the Nicene Creed. Some other solution to the *filioque* problem was needed, and this remains the case to the present day.

What, then, are the implications of the *filioque* for the question of Nicene christology? Orthodox reaction to the *filioque* has always been based on the undeniable tendency of the clause to compromise the principle of the monarchy of the Father. But its implications are equally problematic with regard to the person and work of the Son.

By confusing the unique hypostatic properties of the Father (generating or begetting) and the Son (generated or begotten), the interpolation inevitably posits a "double cause" for the hypostasis of the Spirit. Since by *perichôresis* everything proper to one hypostasis is fully shared by the other two with the sole exception of origin, the *filioque* in effect eliminates all hypostatic (personal) distinction between the Father and the Son, while clearly subordinating the Spirit as the object of the double procession. Thereby the hierarchical relationship of the three hypostases is destroyed. Moreover, the Spirit is deprived of full consubstantiality when, in Augustine's terms, he is reduced to a *nexus amoris*. Such a reduction—from an Orthodox perspective—deprives the Spirit of both hypostatic integrity and consubstantial fullness. He is no longer *homoousios* with the Father and the Son, and therefore he can no longer be "worshiped and glorified together" with them.

To the Orthodox mind, the consubstantiality of the three Persons precludes any form of ontological priority relative to *nature*. If we can speak of a "hierarchy" within the Trinity, it is to be understood in strictly existential terms: a hierarchy of existence but not of essence. Acceptance of the *filioque* according to its traditional Latin interpretation would abolish this crucial distinction and lead to a conception of Father, Son and Spirit which differs radically from the image presented by the self-revealing "economic Trinity."

The Eastern Churches' reaction to the Latin position was based on their orthodox understanding of the ontological priority of *personhood*. Since the unity of the Trinity is assured by the monarchy of the Father, the Father as a unique *hypostasis* can alone be the origin or source of the other two persons, the Son and the Holy Spirit.

Furthermore, the doctrine of the *filioque* posits not only two principles of origin within the Trinity, but, as it were, *two moments* as well. In a first a-temporal moment, the Father, as the unique principle of origin, brings forth the Son through the act of generation. Then, in a second a-temporal moment, the Son and the Father together as a combined principle of origin bring forth the Spirit through an act of procession. Consequently, the Son's existence has logical ("a-temporal") priority over that of the Spirit, as the Father's has over that of the Son. The result is to affirm the heretical Arian view that "there was when he [the Son] was not"; and the same must be said of the Spirit.

From an Orthodox perspective, then, the *filioque* effectively destroys the monarchy of the Father by positing a second principle of procession; it destroys the eternal generation of the Son, whose mode of existence is determined not by filiation but by his participation with the Father in bringing forth the Spirit; and it destroys the hypostatic equality of the Spirit by subordinating him to the other two persons.

A final Orthodox objection to the *filioque* also concerns the crucial distinction between person and nature. Both generation and procession—however we may understand the mystery they designate—are possible only as *acts of love grounded in personal freedom*. This means that the begetting of the Son and the bringing forth of the Spirit cannot be functions of abstract, impersonal nature; they can only be activities of the Father *as person*. For if the generation of the Son and the procession of the Spirit were functions of nature, then they would result from "ontological necessity." They would no longer be what Scripture and ecclesial experience reveal them to be, namely, manifestations of a personal communion in love.

Whether or not we agree with Sergius Bulgakov and others that the *filioque* is directly responsible for papal dogma and Catholic ecclesiology,[33] there can be little doubt that it represents to Orthodox eyes a heretical distortion of divine revelation that bears as fully upon the image of the Father and Son as it does upon that of the Spirit.

There are two possible responses to the problem. On the one hand, we could dismiss the whole affair as a meaningless debate over abstract theological concepts that are inherently incapable of expressing the ineffable mystery of divine life. Accordingly, we would limit our "God-talk" to "what God does" in the framework of salvation-history, and simply refuse to engage in speculation concerning the inner being of the Trinity. This appears to be the approach adopted by many Protestant theologians.

On the other hand, we could accept with Christian tradition of both East and West the conviction that God does in fact reveal himself—his will, but also his personal being—within the domain of human history, and that his self-revelation permits us to discover him to be the ultimate source and end of our own existence. To the Orthodox, only this second approach is acceptable,

33 See B. Bobrinskoy, "Le 'Filioque' Hier et Aujourd'hui," 10f; English tr., 136f.

because it is the only one that conforms to the witness of Scripture and the liturgical-sacramental experience of the Church.

If we agree that knowledge of the immanent Trinity is both possible and necessary for salvation (Jn 17:3), then a solution to the *filioque* problem is of utmost importance. In recognition of this, recent patristic study by Orthodox scholars has demonstrated a willingness and a desire to press beyond centuries of polemic in order to discover the breadth of common ground that in fact does exist between traditional Western and Eastern thought concerning christology and pneumatology. If the debate has often seemed sterile and frustrating, it has nevertheless proved highly salutary in two major ways.

First, it has led Orthodox theologians to rediscover the implications of Eastern trinitarian theology for God's work of salvation within the created order. As the Greek Fathers fully understood, there can be no reflection on the immanent Trinity that does not begin with and bear directly on the economic Trinity. Knowledge of God is and must be *saving* knowledge that bestows eternal life. But if it is true that such knowledge concerns the inner life of the Trinity as much as it does God's saving acts within the world, then the Nicene Creed remains even today an indispensable instrument of our salvation. For it remains *the* authoritative statement of the universal Church concerning both inner-trinitarian relationships and the significance of those relationships in working out the divine economy "for the life of the world and its salvation" (Liturgy of St John Chrysostom).

Second, and conversely, the debate has led Western Christians to reassess their own views concerning the relationship between christology and trinitarian theology, as well as their understanding of the limits of divine revelation. To take a pertinent example: in the mid-1980s Dr. Martha Stortz of the Pacific Lutheran Seminary pointed out that

> "Luther's explanation of the creed is oriented toward the work and not the person of Father, Son, and Spirit... For Luther what God *does* is more important than who God *is*... As Lutherans reassess the relationship between Son and Spirit, as they grapple with problems such as the *filioque* clause, they will be thinking not simply about what God does...but who God is. This may well be the next reformation within the church that is always being reformed."[34]

Such a welcome statement makes it clear that the difficult and often contentious debate surrounding the *filioque* question can, by God's infinite

34 "Lutherans and the Holy Spirit," a paper presented to the NCCC-USA Consultation on the Holy Spirit, Boston, Oct. 1985, 22.

patience and grace, produce significant steps toward genuine unity within the divided body of Christendom. Further evidence of this has been provided in more recent times by the Lutheran (ELCA) decision to allow individual parishes to suppress the *filioque*, as well as by the Roman Catholic "Clarification" of the issue, published in 1995.

5. Conclusion

The chief argument for the abiding relevance and active retention of the Nicene Creed within the Church and its mission today has to do with its enduring *soteriological* value as the most authoritative—because it is the most biblical—of all confessional statements. The Creed confirms the scripturally revealed truth, "startling, even shocking" as it may be, that the man Jesus is personally identical with the eternally begotten Son of God, the second Person of the Holy Trinity. This it does by reproducing in confessional form the pattern of revelation—the "katabatic-anabatic" movement of humiliation and exaltation—found in liturgical and kerygmatic passages throughout the New Testament.

This pattern of revelation, through which God realizes his saving *economia* within the world, makes it clear that christology can have substance only insofar as it issues directly from trinitarian theology. For only God himself, in the person of the eternally begotten Son, can assume human nature with its manifold existential properties, and "deify" that nature. This he does by liberating the children of God from death by the life-giving power of his resurrection, by endowing them with the sanctifying grace of the Holy Spirit, and by enabling them through his ascension to participate in the glory which he shares with the Father from all eternity (Jn 17:5).

Trinitarian theology itself, however, must conform to God's self-revelation. Therefore it must be grounded in the apostolic *paradosis* or tradition of the Christian community that focuses on the *experience* of God within human life. It must be grounded, in other words, in the early Church's witness to the active, loving and saving presence of Father, Son and Spirit *within history,* that is, within the framework of the divine economy. Only on this basis can theological reflection proceed to delve into the ultimate mystery of the immanent Trinity.

To the mind of the ancient Church that produced the Nicene Creed, reflection on the nature of the triune God and the interrelationships of the divine Persons was guided both by tradition and by the living presence and inspiration of the Holy Spirit within the conciliar assembly. The Creed, then, although produced in a climate of polemic, was received and promulgated not only as a "legitimate" interpretation of Scripture, but also as *the authoritative statement of faith* of the One, Holy, Catholic and Apostolic Church. Its authority was understood to derive solely from God himself, who in the Person of the Spirit guided formulation of the Creed and "presented" it, as it were, as a true reflection of the inner life of the Trinity and of its saving work within the world. To the Orthodox mind, this understanding of the *inspired* quality of the Creed, that faithfully reflects divine truth through human language and concepts, gives it a timeless relevance and explains why it is still considered to be an indispensable expression of the Church's faith.

Recent study of the *filioque* issue has gone far to deepen the pneumatological reflection of various Christian traditions and has served to draw them in the direction of a common appreciation—which may ultimately lead to a common proclamation—of the Church's ancient trinitarian faith.

On the one hand, Orthodox theologians who have engaged in this process of dialogue have come to a new appreciation of Augustine's teaching, and they now generally acknowledge that neither he nor the Latin tradition in general posited the Son as a "second and *equal* cause" of the Holy Spirit. Through a more nuanced approach to the theme of "double procession," they can accept that Augustine never intended to question either the consubstantiality of the three Persons or the monarchy of the Father as the principal source and cause of the other two hypostases.[35] As a result, some Orthodox specialists in the area have recently stressed the positive value of a certain reading of the *filioque:* to affirm the participation of the Son in the eternal as well as the temporal manifestation of the Spirit; to recover the Western emphasis on the Spirit as the bond of love between the Father and the Son, an idea taken up and developed in the East by St Gregory Palamas; and to underscore the mutual interaction of Father and Son in the Pentecostal outpouring of the Spirit upon the Church.[36]

Then again, by virtue of the modern *filioque* debate Protestant and Catholic theologians are becoming increasingly aware of both the richness and the limitations of their own trinitarian teachings. They show a growing appreciation for contemporary Orthodox positions, based on the reflection of Greek Fathers such as Gregory of Nyssa and Gregory of Cyprus, that attribute to the Son a central role in the eternal bringing forth of the Spirit by the act of *ekphansis* or "manifestation." Most importantly, they evidence a growing concern to reintegrate into the trinitarian theology of their respective confessions

35 See *de Trin.* XV.17, 29.
36 See B. Bobrinskoy, "Le 'Filioque' Hier et Aujourd'hui," 16-18; English tr., 141-143.

affirmations that are consistent with the Nicene confession concerning the immanent Trinity, God in his innermost being.

As the debate continues, both "camps" will need to make certain concessions (which is not to say "compromises"). We Orthodox must carefully reevaluate our traditional charges that the *filioque* (1) subordinates the Spirit to the Father and Son, (2) vitiates the monarchy of the Father as the unique "cause" of divine life, (3) leads to ecclesiastical heresy and papal dogma, and (4) depersonalizes the Spirit, making of him a *dynamis* more appropriate to quasi-sectarian charismatic groups than to the liturgical-sacramental community of the Church. To just what extent, we must ask, in the practical existence and piety of the Western Churches, has the *filioque* played a role that renders it unacceptable? Can it or can it not, from an Orthodox point of view, be accepted as a *theologoumenon*, a legitimate theological opinion but without the weight of dogmatic authority? Questions such as these need further serious and concerted reflection on the part of Orthodox theologians.

The burden, however, falls especially on Western Christians. For the real problem with the *filioque* is one of *ecclesial authority*. No one today questions the fact that the clause was interpolated arbitrarily by a local synod into the normative confessional formula of the universal Church. Whatever its merits or shortcomings, such an interpolation does violence to the very nature and function of the Creed. Therefore the Orthodox can only request that all Christian Churches affirm, as did Pope John-Paul II in 1981, that the authentic form of the Creed is the uninterpolated version, and that they act in consequence by removing the *filioque* clause altogether.

Further steps in that direction have recently been taken by the Congregation for the Doctrine of the Faith, in its year 2000 Declaration, "*Dominus Iesus. On the Unicity and Salvific Universality of Jesus Christ and the Church.*" Many non-Roman Catholics, including Orthodox Christians, reacted with dismay at the firm reiteration by the Declaration that the "unicity and unity" of the Church are expressed only by the Catholic Church "governed by the Successor of Peter and by the Bishops in communion with him."[37] Equally significant, and in a much more positive vein, is the fact that the Declaration begins with a translation of the "Symbolum Constantinopolitanum." This is the Nicene-Constantinopolitan Creed in its original formulation *without the*

37 The "single Church of Christ…which our Saviour, after his resurrection, entrusted to Peter's pastoral care…constituted and organized as a society in the present world, subsists in [*subsistit in*] the Catholic Church, governed by the Successor of Peter and by the Bishops in communion with him" (IV.16).

filioque.[38] The third article reads: "I believe in the Holy Spirit, the Lord, the giver of life, who proceeds from the Father. With the Father and the Son he is worshipped and glorified..." It is this version which is described by no less an authority than the Congregation for the Doctrine of the Faith as expressing "the fundamental contents of the profession of the Christian faith." The omission of the *filioque* here is certainly not fortuitous. We can only hope that it signals growing acceptance on the part of the Magisterium of the original version of the Nicene-Constantinopolitan Creed (C).

It is on the basis of this hope that we would reiterate our appeal that the Roman Catholic and other Western Churches remove the *filioque* from the Creed once and for all. Such a request, however, should be accompanied by serious effort on the part of Orthodox theologians to pursue their study of the history of the debate and to discover the value inherent in the Western position.

Approached with mutual good will and in a common, dedicated quest for truth, the *filioque* may yet prove to be less a *skandalon*, a stumbling block in the way of common confession of Christian faith, than a focal point around which Eastern and Western traditions can meet in mutual belief and shared witness. The basis for that meeting, however, remains the Symbol of Faith of the ancient, undivided Church. And that fact alone makes clear the enduring value and relevance of the (original) Nicene Creed.

38 This was first brought to my attention by Rev. Aaron Archer, to whom I am grateful for several exchanges on this issue.

10

Chalcedonian Christology and the Humanity of Christ

1. An "A-symmetrical" Christology

If the relevance of Nicene christology has been called into question in recent decades, no less a protest has been raised against the christological perspective represented by the debates and decrees of the fourth Ecumenical Council held at Chalcedon in 451. At the celebration of that council's fifteen-hundredth anniversary in 1951, an impressive number of publications appeared in its honor.[1] They set a tone in contemporary christological reflection that continues to reverberate into this new millennium. In this chapter we want to assess that tone and explain why to Orthodox ears it sounds somewhat discordant.

Since 1951, many scholars of major Christian traditions, including Orthodox, have questioned the completeness or adequacy of the Chalcedonian model, claiming that it emphasizes the divinity of Christ to the point that his humanity is thrown into question. This is an ages-old debate, but since the 1950s Western theologians in particular have wanted to complement the "descending" christological model with an "ascending" one. Terms to express this concern are often borrowed from the German Protestant tradition. The aim is to stress less a *Theologie von oben* and more one *von unten*, giving preference to a christology "from below" rather than one "from above."

Some have suggested that we scrap the Chalcedonian model altogether, since it rings of "monophysitism," the ancient doctrine that holds Christ to possess a single (divine) nature. Although the decrees of Chalcedon defended precisely the *two natures* of Christ against widespread monophysite tendencies, its formulation of "one person (*hypostasis*) in two natures (*physis/ousia*)"

---

1 For bibliography and a perceptive evaluation of some of this material, see the article by Fr. Gregory Havrilak, "Chalcedon and Orthodox Christology Today," *St Vladimir's Theological Quarterly* 33/2 (1989), 127-145.

sounds to many of our contemporaries like a one-sided compromise that concedes too much to those who see in Jesus of Nazareth a "god in the flesh" rather than a full participant in human nature and human destiny. In Gerald O'Collins' words, Chalcedonian christology presents a Jesus who "looks like a man, speaks like a man, suffers and dies like a man. But underneath he is divine, and this makes his genuine humanity suspect."[2] In other words, from this point of view Orthodox christology must be characterized as "crypto-monophysite" insofar as it affirms that in his earthly incarnation, Jesus Christ remains *essentially* what he had been from all eternity, namely "of one *divine* nature."

Such a christology also seems open to the charge of "docetism" (from *dokein*, "to seem, appear"): Jesus only "appeared" to assume flesh, the fullness of human nature. In reality, he remained wholly and uniquely divine. The "incarnation," then, is an illusion based on one of two models which can be described as "Cerinthian/Nestorian" or "Gnostic/Monophysite." According to the first, the divine "Christos," emanating from the Godhead, descended at Jesus' baptism and dwelt within him (the descending, indwelling "dove" of Johannine tradition) until the moment of the crucifixion, at which time the heavenly Christos ascended while the man Jesus suffered and died. The second model, representing true "docetism," holds that the "man" Jesus of Nazareth was in reality "God in disguise," that he only "seemed" to be a human being, whereas in reality his nature was and remained wholly divine. He was God and not man. According to this model, Jesus neither "took flesh" nor died on the cross; he merely appeared to do so.

Orthodox theologians would firmly deny that the christology of the Eastern Fathers represents either one or the other of these models. As Georges Florovsky, John Meyendorff and many others have demonstrated, Chalcedonian christology faithfully develops the image of "*one* person in *two* natures," humanity and divinity united—without confusion, change, division or separation—in the unique hypostatic reality of the "God-man."

Why, then, do Protestant and even certain Catholic theologians persist in taxing Orthodoxy with "monophysitism"? Why, in other words, do they have such difficulty with the notion that humanity and divinity can be truly and fully united in a single Person? The usual Orthodox response to that question is based on the assumption that these Western theologians "rationalize" the mystery of Incarnation to the extent that, to their minds, a true "hypostatic union" becomes inconceivable; its classical formulation is merely an abstract

2   G. O'Collins, *What are They Saying About Jesus?* (NY: Paulist Press, 1977), 2.

theory with no grounding in fact. Consequently, the Orthodox conclude, many Protestants in particular structure their christology according to the Cerinthian/Nestorian model noted above: an *essential* difference remains between the "historical Jesus" and the "eternal Son of God, the Lamb slain from eternity," and therefore the man Jesus can in no way be identified with a "Person" of the Holy Trinity.[3]

True as this assessment may be, it does not really answer the question as to why Protestant theologians in particular are so reluctant to accept the "descending" Chalcedonian model of christology. It does not really account for their persistent substitution of a "theology from below" for the traditional trinitarian-incarnational theology of the Eastern Church Fathers, a "theology from above" that begins and ends with divine initiative and divine intervention.

If the present christological debate were transposed to the fourth and fifth centuries, we could perhaps rank the Orthodox with the Alexandrians and the Protestants with the Antiochenes. But in today's context, those are not the appropriate categories. Protestant theologians seem to be reacting against a "theology from above," the classical "descending" model, because they are convinced that such a model seriously jeopardizes the true humanity of Christ and consequently *undermines the Church's theology of redemption*. As all Christians would agree: if Jesus is not fully *human*, then his "death" has no genuine redemptive or saving value *pro nobis*. Yet while we as Orthodox insist that Jesus' humanity was and remains true and complete, and, to our mind, we adequately express that conviction with Chalcedonian terminology, other Christians remain convinced that classical christology does not in fact adequately express Christ's true humanity and consequently must be replaced, or at least complemented, by other formulations that represent in the clearest terms a "theology from below" which unequivocally proclaims Jesus' total solidarity with sinful, suffering human beings.

Wherein lies the disagreement, and our inability to draw the same conclusions regarding the meaning of classical christological statements?

In the first place, it seems that the current debate has missed the point by focusing uniquely on the issue of "christology": the person and work of Jesus of Nazareth, including questions of preexistence, incarnation, ascension, and the relation between "the man Jesus" and "the eternal divine Logos." The real problem, however, is not an Orthodox denial of Jesus' true humanity, but

---

3 See the quotation from John Cobb's article at the beginning of ch. 9 above (source: *SVTQ* 28/3 [1984], 174).

rather a lack of understanding on the part of non-Orthodox as to what constitutes *human nature*. The problem, in other words, concerns not so much christology as *anthropology*.

Orthodoxy can affirm an "a-symmetrical" christology, holding that the subject of the God-man is the eternal divine Son, without in any way compromising the plenitude of the human nature (the "true humanity") he assumed. That is, the Logos can "assume flesh," can participate in the fullness of human existence—with the exception of actual sin (understood as a lack, a negation)—because our humanity, our human nature (*ousia*) is "truly itself," it realizes its full potential, only by its *participation in divine nature* rendered accessible in and through the divine energies.

The distinction between "divine essence" and "divine energies," worked out especially by Gregory Palamas but representing the Orthodox theological consensus, is crucial to this question. On the one hand, we must confirm the patristic insistence that a human person can never "know," can never participate epistemologically or ontologically, in the divine *ousia*. Yet the divine nature itself, according to Eastern theology and mystical experience, is present—and in an ineffable but real way becomes *accessible*—in the divine energies.

If this is accepted, it means that what the Orthodox perceive to be the (typically Protestant) difficulty with "understanding"—with grasping intellectually and expressing dogmatically the ultimately unfathomable mystery of God incarnate—is not at all due to the fact that Orthodox christology is defective or incomplete. It is due rather to an inadequate *anthropology*, widespread in Protestant theology, that fails to grasp the true significance of the patristic formula (variously stated by Irenaeus, Athanasius, Basil the Great and others): "God [the eternal divine Son] became man [as Jesus, Christ and Savior], in order that man might become god"; i.e., that human persons might participate ontologically in divine life.

This participation of human life in the divine, on the level of "essence" as well as "existence," is possible only through the divine energies. Accepting the "essence-energy" distinction, we can affirm that "human nature" and "divine nature" are not two utterly different or opposed realities. In fact there is *continuity* between humanity and divinity, precisely in the realm of the divine *energeia*. This can be spelled out in the following way.

Man is only truly "human"—in the likeness of the humanity assumed and perfected by the eternal Son of God—insofar as his humanity is determined by the divine energies; that is, insofar as the "fruits of the Spirit" (Galatians 5:22, understood as Spirit-endowed *charismata* rather than as self-acquired "virtues") transform the fallen human nature *of a particular person* into the true Humanity of the God-man. Christ's redemptive and saving work, in other words, must be understood as one of *restoration*. His "recapitulation" of human nature through the incarnation serves to *restore* that nature from its fallen state to its original state of "perfection."

It is possible to make this affirmation, however, and to declare that "God became man so that man might become god," only insofar as our anthropology is correct, accurately reflecting the nature and destiny of the human creature: man created in the divine image and fallen through the misuse of freedom, is called to assume the divine "likeness" (perfection) through a life that fully manifests the divine energies as "fruits of the Spirit." "From the beginning," our humanity is "laid up in Christ." Adam before the fall is truly human, in that he embodies and manifests the true humanity of the archetypal God-man. And it can also be affirmed that "potentially" the Son of God is the "God-man" even prior to creation, a potentiality that is actualized in the womb of the Virgin. True "humanity" is thus a reflection—in the realm of creation and embodied in the created human person—of the eternal divine-humanity of the Son. Accordingly, we can affirm that there is indeed *continuity* between authentic ("prelapsarian") humanity and divinity, since the true measure of humanity is the God-man himself, the Subject of whose hypostatic union is the eternal divine Son of God: one Person, uniting in himself the fullness of humanity and divinity.[4]

Thus the eternal Son can be understood as "first Adam" as well as "last Adam": he is the eternal source and paradigm—thus the archetype—of all that is authentically "human."

Expressed in other terms: rather than measure Christ's divinity by the norm of our humanity ("theology from below"), we can only grasp the mystery of the incarnation of the preexistent Logos, and understand the meaning of that incarnation for our salvation, insofar as we measure our humanity by

4 Such "continuity," of course, implies neither that man is an "emanation" of God or that human nature is on a continuum with God. As Fr Paul Wesche expressed it to me in a letter, dated Nov. 9, 1988, "There is affinity between God and man in that man is created fundamentally in the image of the Triune God as 'person,' so that as 'person' or *hypostasis*, man is created to live in communion with God. It is the character of 'person' to 'be with,' to be 'open' to others so as to be able to 'receive' others without being destroyed or destroying the other, and above all it is the character of person to love, which is the essence of 'communion.' But even as person, man is still 'created being.' Since human nature is fundamentally 'personal,' man is able to receive the divine Life of God, even though man is created (that is, to me, the marvel), and it is this Life filling the human *hypostasis* that makes man 'godlike,' or that deifies him."

the norm of his divinity. The Word "became flesh," but only to realize the full potential of that "flesh" for participation in divine life.

This means, however, that the Word must remain *essentially* divine in his incarnation (thereby excluding 19th century "kenoticism," the idea that he totally divested himself of divine properties as well as divine pre-rogatives). The *Subject* of the incarnate hypostasis must therefore be *divine*, in order to restore humanity to its authentic condition determined by its participation in the divine energies. Accordingly, the destiny of each human hypostasis, through sacramental incorporation into the Body of the God-man, is to become itself a "god-man," whose *subject* is "deified" by the divine energies.

Despite criticisms leveled against this Orthodox doctrine of *theôsis* or "dei-fication" of the human person, the teaching does not by any means represent an "exalted" view of human nature. It takes fully into account human sin, the fallenness of the human creature. Yet it also sets in relief the biblical revelation of the ineffable love of God for humankind. Salvation cannot be understood only in the narrow terms of liberation from self, from evil powers and from death. "Salvation" in the fullest sense leads to the acquisition of *life* through grace. Acquisition of the "fruits of the Spirit" (the divine energies) is a free gift of God (to be understood as both an objective and a subjective genitive: stem-ming from God and consisting in the gift of God's very life). But it is a gift granted only in response to a repentant heart that longs insatiably for "the one thing needful." That longing, strengthened by repentance and obedience, is the one indispensable condition for the reception of saving grace; it is the "way to perfection" that the Fathers call *synergy*.

Soteriology, then, concerns the saving work of God-in-Christ, to accom-plish within each human hypostasis the process of *theôsis*. Accordingly, to be properly understood, anthropology—like christology—must be conceived and formulated "from above"; for humanity is "true" or authentic only insofar as it bears, reflects and participates in the divine life of the Triune God.

"Do not wonder that I said to you: You must be born from above (*anôthen*)" (Jn 3:7).

2. One Hypostasis: Fully Human, Fully Divine

The argument that Orthodox christology minimizes Christ's full humanity and therefore jeopardizes his saving work is often expressed in a way that reveals a fundamental misunderstanding of the theological language used in tradi-tional, and specifically Chalcedonian, formulations. A typical example of this appears in Charles Möller's article on Chalcedonian and "neo-Chalcedonian" theology from the mid-fifth through the sixth centuries.[5]

Möller raises the question: "How can the human nature of Jesus be perfectly consubstantial with ours if it is devoid of a human hypostasis?" The question itself betrays what German theologians like to call "falsche Voraussetzungen," erroneous or indefensible presuppositions.

In the first place, Jesus does not "have" a human nature in the sense of a possessed (inherent or acquired) object or quality. Consequently, "human nature" cannot be "devoid of a human hypostasis." A nature does not "possess" a hypostasis; rather, a hypostasis is characterized or qualified by the nature. Then again, Möller's question betrays a basic confusion regarding the traditional theological terms used to designate humanity and divinity in the God-man. It distinguishes between "Jesus" and the "Son" as between two natures: "Jesus" refers to humanity, while "Son" refers to divinity. (The error here is similar to that of Theodore of Mopsuestia, who distinguished essentially between the *verbum assumens* [the heavenly Word] and the *homo assumptus* [the earthly Jesus], and thereby laid the foundation for Nestorian dualism.) To Möller, it would seem, the incarnation produces a sort of symbiosis between the two natures. "Jesus" and "the Son," however, are not two distinct natures. They are names that depict the hypostatic union between humanity and divinity, accomplished through the historical incarnation. Both names, "Jesus" and "the Son," refer to the *one hypostatic reality of the God-man*, who unites in himself the fullness of divinity and humanity, as "first" and "last Adam."

Prof. Möller's question is, of course, rhetorical. In order to answer it, the misconceptions it is based upon need to be cleared up. It is important to do so, since his position is so widely shared among non-Orthodox theologians today. Perhaps we can formulate an appropriate response in the following way.

The eternal divine Son, consubstantial with the Father and existing as a distinct hypostasis within the tri-unity of the Godhead, assumes flesh (*sarx egeneto*, Jn 1:14). He becomes man—and a specific man—as (not "in"—that would be Cerinthian again) Jesus of Nazareth. The actualized humanity (i.e., the human nature) which the Son assumes is received from the Virgin Mary through his incarnation in her womb (and therefore she is venerated as "Theotokos" or "Mother of God"). The Son, therefore, is *one* with Jesus. There can be no hypostatic distinction between Jesus and the Son, just as

---

5 Ch. Möller, "Le chalcédonisme et néo-chalcédonisme en Orient de 451 à la fin du VIe siècle," in A. Grillmeier, *Das Konzil von Chalkedon*, vol. I (Würtzburg: Echter-Verlag, 1951-62), 697; quoted in Fr Gregory Havrilak's article [note 1, above].

there can be no mere symbiosis between the "divine Son" and the "human Jesus." What the Son assumes, namely human nature, he assumes for all eternity. Hence the importance of St Ignatius' conviction that Christ "rose in the flesh" (*Smyrn.* 3.1). From the moment of the incarnation he remains forever the God-man: the eternal divine Son who *is* Jesus of Nazareth, crucified, resurrected and exalted into glory.

The divine Son, co-eternal with the Father, has existed *en archê* and *ap' archês* (Jn 1:1; 1 Jn 1:1). This means that the divine *hypostasis* of the Son has existed co-eternally with the Father. At the incarnation, the one hypostasis of the Son *assumed* humanity, uniting it inseparably and eternally ("from that moment on") to his divinity. Therefore there remains *one* hypostasis, fully divine and fully human. The humanity is in no wise diminished simply because there is no independently existing "human hypostasis." The categories "divine" or "human" refer to *nature*, whereas a hypostasis is a *person*: integrally unified and God-centered, with the capacity for self-transcendence through communion with the *plêrôma* of the triune Godhead.

Thus the expression, frequently used in Orthodox as well as non-Orthodox circles: "The Son became incarnate in the *person* of Jesus of Nazareth," is wrong. It is a glaring example of modern Nestorian dualism. There neither is nor ever was a "person" or hypostasis called "Jesus of Nazareth" who was in any way independent of or separate from the eternal Son of God.

The problem, it seems, lies in the inability of theologians such as Prof. Möller to fathom the patristic, and particularly Cappadocian, notion of "hypostasis." "Consubstantiality" implies hypostatic distinction: the Son is of "one nature" with the Father, but he is hypostatically distinct from him. The Son possesses his own personal quality of existence within the *essentially* undivided Trinity. By asking, "How can the human nature of Jesus be perfectly consubstantial with ours...?," Möller implies that a distinction exists between "our (human) nature" and "Jesus' (human) nature." But the whole truth—and saving efficacy—of the incarnation lies in the fact that Jesus' human nature *is* our human nature. And it is precisely *our* human nature, assumed in its fallen condition and brought to perfection ("restored") by being united to his eternal divine nature in the one divine *hypostasis* of the divine Logos. The humanity which Christ assumes is thus "taken up" into his divinity and is itself *deified*. Therefore the *hypostasis* of the God-man must remain the one *divine hypostasis* of the eternal Logos: the *Subject* of the God-man can be none other than the eternal Son of God, whose single, unique hypostasis unites in itself divine and human natures, in order to deify humanity by assuming it into the fullness of his divinity and imparting to it the fruits of his victory over sin and death.

The question, then, "How can the human nature of Jesus be perfectly consubstantial with ours if it is devoid of a human hypostasis?" is meaningless. It misuses theological language to create a false problem. Any hypothesis, in fact, that affirms the true humanity of Jesus by postulating a "fully human hypostasis" is misguided and pernicious, however noble the motives of its proponents may be. This is because the *hypostasis* of the God-man is, was, and shall forever remain the preexistent divine Son. (Attempts to do away with the concept of preexistence, by the way, like the attempts to establish an independent "human hypostasis" in order to safeguard Christ's humanity, lead invariably to forms of Adoptionism or Nestorianism; that is, to fundamental distortions of the image of Christ as that image is revealed in Scripture and Tradition.)

There can be, therefore, only one hypostasis: that of the eternal Son of God, who assumed human nature in order to deify it through intimate association or communion with his divine nature. This means that the expression "hypostatic union" refers not to the "union of two hypostases," one human and one divine. It refers rather to the *union of two natures* within the one hypostasis of the preexistent Son, who at a moment in history *became*, and forever remains, the God-man.

3. Jesus Christ: The Archetype of Our Humanity

If it is properly understood and expressed, Chalcedonian christology does not at all jeopardize the full humanity of Christ, as so many modern commentators fear it does. In fact it affirms his humanity in the fullest and most positive way. For it is only by becoming "fully man" that he who is "fully God" could assume the plenitude of our humanity, to purify it from sin, to resurrect it from the dead, and to exalt it into the glory which was his with the Father from the beginning.

Thereby Christ—the "first and last Adam," the true "Anthropos"—both reveals and recreates authentic humanity, which is in fact a *divine-humanity*. He grants to human hypostases the possibility to participate in that which constitutes his very life: true humanity and true divinity united in a single hypostasis. That participation in turn transforms fallen human nature into *his* human nature. At the same time, because our participation in him is hypostatic and not merely essential—we commune in his Person, in his Body, and not merely in an abstract nature—we have access to his divinity and can participate fully in it. Through such participation—in his humanity and in his divinity—our own humanity is restored to the "Adamic" state in which it was created.

Yet our humanity is also deified, so that it bears within it the potential for divine life. Just as his humanity was from the beginning "potential," becoming actualized only through the incarnation, so within the context of our own historical existence our humanity remains "potentially" divine. Although our participation in him through faith, love and sacramental communion is a real participation, it retains a proleptic quality. It will be realized as a fully "deified humanity" only after our passage through death and our reception into the Kingdom of God.

The divine Son is therefore the *archetype* of our humanity, who bears, reveals and communicates to us true and perfect human nature and thereby restores us to perfect human "personhood." Like divinity itself, human existence is personal, hypostatic existence. Just as the God-man through the incarnation unites human nature to his own divine nature, so our salvation as human hypostases consists in uniting his divine nature to our human nature.

This deifying process is certainly nothing we can accomplish for and by ourselves. "Synergy" from our side means mere openness to grace, whereas all saving and transforming power belongs to Christ. The revealing and actualizing of our true humanity—and the deification of that humanity through participation in the divine energies—occur wholly through his initiative and his saving power. If the end of human existence is to commune eternally in the plenitude of trinitarian life, that end is made possible only through his death and glorification, and by the indwelling and sanctifying grace of his Spirit.

To realize that end in and for us, however, the Son of God must be and forever remain the God-man, *uniting in his undivided personal existence both divine and human nature.* Thereby the Creator-Word can reveal and recreate human beings as they were meant to be: personal existences marked by transparent openness to divine love and grace, who embody fully both the image and the likeness of God.

11

Jesus Christ: The "Face" of the Spirit

1. Rediscovery of the Spirit

The last three decades of the past century were marked by an extraordinary and surprising rediscovery of the Holy Spirit. From Protestant Pentecostalism to the charismatic movement that has influenced to a greater or lesser degree all Christian traditions, there has been a shift away from a uniquely Christ-centered theology, a "christomonism" as it has been called, and toward a serious quest to understand better the person and work of God as Spirit. Even the Seventh Assembly of the World Council of Churches, held in Canberra in 1991, chose a specifically pneumatological theme: "Come, Holy Spirit. Renew the whole creation!"

The results of this refocusing of theological reflection have been promising, but in many ways they have also been disconcerting. Pentecostalism and the charismatic movement, in many of their expressions, tend to disconnect from a traditional trinitarian theology and to place a one-sided stress on the phenomena associated with the Spirit, such as speaking in tongues, prophetic utterance, and healing miracles. At the Canberra Assembly, the Orthodox reacted with no little dismay when the "spirit" invoked in one notable presentation appeared to be a *stoicheion,* a Pauline "elemental spirit of the universe,"[1] more akin to the pagan spirit of this world than to the Holy Spirit of God. In the intervening years, it seems, little progress has been made toward recovering a traditional trinitarian approach to the mystery of the Spirit, one that pays full respect to the biblical and patristic witness.

If theology is to have substance, if it is to be truly reflective of the person of God and of his presence and purpose in this world, then that theology must be grounded in God's own self-revelation, particularly as it comes to expression in the Church's canonical Scriptures. For it is only there that we

1   Gal 4:3, 9; Col 2:8, 20.

can hear the authentic voice of the Church's first witnesses, and enter into their experience of the living Lord.

The Eastern Church Fathers liked to point out that the *prosôpon*—the "face" or personal identity—of God the Father is revealed by the Son, whereas the *prosôpon or* "face" of the Son is revealed to us by the Spirit. But the Spirit himself has no other divine person to make him known. Does he indeed have a "face," a personal identity? Ecclesial experience confirms that he does. The following remarks discuss the basis for that belief, particularly as it is found in the Holy Scriptures.

2. Christological Pneumatology

Orthodox liturgical tradition preserves remarkably few prayers addressed directly to the Third Person of the Holy Trinity. In addition to the familiar invocation, "O Heavenly King," and the compline canon of Pentecost in Slavonic tradition (which today is rarely, if ever, sung), the most significant is perhaps the exapostilarion of Pentecost: "Most Holy Spirit, who proceeds from the Father and, through the Son descended upon the untaught disciples, save and sanctify all who acknowledge Thee as God." The framework of this petition is and must be *trinitarian*.

The ancient supplication, *Marana tha* ("Our Lord Come!"), referring to the "parousia" of Christ in glory, is a primitive liturgical element that serves as a "Christ-epiklesis" (Rev 22:20; 1 Cor 16:22; *Did.* 10.6). St John of Patmos concludes his apocalypse with the cry, "The Spirit and the Bride say, Come!... Amen. Come, Lord Jesus!" If the Church invokes the coming of Christ as Judge and Redeemer, she does so only in the power of the Spirit. Similarly, if she invokes the descent of the Spirit to renew the whole of creation, she does so only through the power and authority of Christ. Each epiklesis, addressed either to the Spirit or to the Son, is ultimately addressed to God the Father, from whom the Son is eternally generated and the Spirit eternally proceeds. In the poignant image of St Irenaeus which we recalled in the last chapter, the Son and the Spirit are the "two hands" of the Father, by whom all things are made and through whom all creation is renewed.

Christian theology and ecclesial experience, therefore, know the Holy Spirit to be the "third Person" of the triune God. According to the Nicene-Constantinopolitan Creed, the Spirit is to be honored as "Lord and Giver of Life," titles properly attributed only to divine being. If the Spirit is "worshiped and glorified together" with the other persons of the holy Trinity, this is because he is "consubstantial" *(homoousios,* sharing a common nature, substance, or essence) with the Father and the Son. Neither an emanation from God nor a separate divinity, the Spirit ineffably yet essentially *is God.*

In order to approach the mystery of the Spirit as God, Orthodox scholars have recently produced a number of exegetical studies that stress the intimate relationship between the Spirit and the Son. These investigations focus both on the "immanent Trinity," the inner life of God, and on the "economic Trinity," God's design and operations within the created world. Gradually, there has emerged what is called a "pneumatological christology." According to this perspective, the Spirit "prepares, determines, constitutes and communicates" the mystery of Christ.[2] From the incarnation, through his baptism and earthly ministry, culminating in his work as the resurrected and exalted Lord, the Son stands in an intimate and reciprocal relation to the Spirit. On the one hand, the Son is "sent" by the Spirit to assume human form in the Virgin's womb (Lk 1:35; Phil 2:7), he is driven by the Spirit into the wilderness to be tempted by the devil (Mk 1:12) and he is empowered by the Spirit to fulfill his messianic ministry (Lk 4:14; Mt 12:18; cf. Jn 3:34). On the other hand, the Son "sends" or communicates the Spirit, to function primarily as a Teacher of Truth and an Advocate or Defender on behalf of the faithful (the *allos paraklētos* of Jn 14:16; 16:7, 13-15; cf. Mk 13:11). Christology is fundamentally pneumatological in that the very being of the incarnate Word is the being of the Holy Spirit, and the saving mission of Christ consists in restoring the life-giving grace of the Holy Spirit to all of creation in accordance with the Father's purpose. That purpose is shared fully by the Son and the Spirit, since the divine hypostases are perfectly united in their common will.

A complementary emphasis to this pneumatological christology focuses on the significance of the person of Christ in the shaping of the biblical image of the Spirit. This "christological pneumatology," as it might be called, attempts to demonstrate how the mystery of the Spirit is revealed, constituted and communicated by Jesus, the Son of God; and it stresses the way apostolic writers tended to shape their depiction of the Spirit according to their image of Jesus. Especially in Johannine tradition the image, "face" or person of the Paraclete or Spirit of Truth is made visible—that is, perceptible and open to human participation—by reflecting Jesus' own personal traits and his revelatory, saving work. Just as the Son reveals the "face" or personal image of God the Father (Mt 11:27; Jn 1:18; 17:4, 6, 26), so Jesus reveals the Spirit as the one who continues Jesus' own revelatory and "paracletic" or intercessory

---

2   This is the language of Boris Bobrinskoy. See his article "The Holy Spirit—in the Bible and in the Church," *The Ecumenical Review, 41 / 3* (1989), 357-362, and esp. his *Communion du Saint-Esprit,* Bellefontaine, 1992, 19-70.

functions within the eschatological age of the church.[3] To see what relevance
these complementary functions may have for helping us to discern the "face"
of the Spirit, the personal image of this most intimate yet most hidden aspect
of divine life, we need to turn to the Scriptures themselves. There we need to
pay attention to the gradual development of the spirit-concept in the religious
consciousness of Israel, as well as to the great shift in that consciousness that
occurred in the wake of the experience of Pentecost.

3. The Spirit in the Old Testament and Intertestamental Judaism

From the primitive *ruach-Yahweh*—a mysterious, capricious and semi-autono-
mous divine power—the image of Spirit matured in Israel's perception until,
with the classical prophets, it came to denote God himself: the mode of God's
loving, blessing and saving presence among the remnant of his people.[4]

The earliest stage of recorded reflection on the nature and function of
Spirit is that of the "J-E" (Jahwist-Elohist) writings, produced between the
eighth and ninth centuries BC. Here the divine *ruach* (wind, breath, power)
appears as an occasional charismatic force that fills selected persons, such as
the judges and ecstatic prophets, and guides or drives them to accomplish
specific tasks within Israel's salvation history. The work of the *ruach-Yahweh*
is basically twofold: *revelatory* and *soteriological*. It inspires ecstatic prophecy,
it pronounces and executes judgment on Israel and the nations, and directly
(as a chastising wind) or indirectly (by empowering human agents) it serves to
defend God's people against their enemies. Depicted as an independent
entity, yet at the same time as a kind of divisible fluid that can be distributed
or transferred as God wills (e.g., from Elijah to Elisha), *ruach* is essentially a
mode of divine activity within Israel and among the nations. Nothing is said
of its "nature"; no hint is given of its inner qualities and characteristics, except
the indication that it is basically impersonal, a mere instrument in the hands
of the righteous Lord, who wields it as he will.

With the growth of classical prophecy, from the eighth century through
the post-exilic period, *ruach* becomes an expression for the presence of God
himself in Israel's history. In Jeremiah's vision, spirit remains a destroying
agent of divine wrath. Here and elsewhere it also preserves its function as the

---

3   See J. Breck, "'The Lord is the Spirit.' An Essay in Christological Pneumatology," The *Ec-
    umenical Review* 42.2 (April 1990), 114-121; and especially *The Spirit of Truth* (New
    York: St Vladimir's Seminary Press, 1991).
4   Biblical references for this section can be found in *Spirit of Truth*, 5-41.

defender of the people against hostile forces both from within and from with-out Israel's borders. Nevertheless, the chief function of *ruach* in this period is to serve as the *vehicle of God's self-revelation*. With the exilic prophets and the priestly tradition, the Spirit of the Lord manifests Yahweh's personal presence and will among the people, even his various moods and attitudes.

At this stage, Spirit acquires as well an *eschatological* function. According to the salvation oracle, Jeremiah 31:31-34, God is preparing a "new cove-nant" for his people, written upon the heart rather than on tablets of stone. Ezekiel takes up this theme and declares that this end time promise will be fulfilled through the sprinkling of water for purification, together with bestowal of a "new heart": "I will put my Spirit within you, and cause you to walk in my statutes..." (Ezek 36:22-32). This sanctifying work of the Spirit for moral transformation "at the level of the heart" is complemented by the resuscitation he performs in the prophet's vision of the valley of dry bones (ch. 37). Here God raises up the desiccated remnant to reconstitute a holy people through the infusion *of ruach,* the divine breath that creates new, eschatological existence. This is a new creation animated by the Spirit of the living and life-giving Lord. As such, it recalls and fulfills the original creation of Genesis 1, where the Spirit "hovers" over the cosmos in a profoundly maternal gesture that brings life and harmony out of primeval matter.

The post-Davidic period in Israelite history produced the enthronement hymn, Psalm 2, and the closely related royal song, Psalm 109/110. Here the king is anointed by the *ruach-Yahweh.* Thereby he becomes a bearer of the Spirit, a *pneumatophore* who foreshadows the "new David," the eschatological Anointed One or Messiah. According to post-exilic and intertestamental tra-dition (Zech 4; the Dead Sea Scrolls), Israel came gradually to expect the coming of a pair of messianic figures, a priestly as well as a political or royal messiah. But already by the close of the exilic period itself, in the late sixth and early fifth centuries B.C., Deutero-Isaiah (Isa 40-55) knew of an out-pouring of the Spirit on another eschatological figure: the *ebed-Yahweh* or Servant of the Lord. This Servant, destined to suffer vicariously for the sins of the people (Isa 52:13-53:12), would also "bring forth justice (*mishpat*)" in the earth. That is, he would lead the people to authentic faith and to true worship of Yahweh as Lord of all creation.

Post-exilic prophecy, however, stresses above all the *inspirational* and *teaching* function of the Spirit. From a spirit of prophecy in the earliest tradi-tion, the divine *ruach* now serves both to *communicate* the Word of God through prophetic oracles and to lead the people to the proper *interpretation* of those oracles. The Spirit thus assumes a *hermeneutic* role within Israel, inspiring the prophet to speak the Word of the Lord and the people to under-stand and obey that Word. In this period as well, the Word itself becomes the active agent of revelation and regeneration. Spirit and Word operate together, to manifest divine life in the people's midst, and to work a moral and spiritual regeneration in both their individual and their collective social life.

Israelite prophets of the post-exilic period came to perceive the Spirit as a "personal" reality, as the mode of divine *presence* within creation: God dwells among his people *in the Spirit*, to speak his judging and redeeming Word. The Spirit is thus the inspirational power behind the Word and the instru-ment of its communication. Yet it is the Word itself that provides content and direction to the Spirit. The *ruach-Yahweh* is perceived as the Spirit of the Word, the source of divine revelation. Yet he is also known as the agent of sanctifying divine grace. Thus Spirit in this period assumes multiple func-tions—revealing, teaching, chastising, sanctifying—all of which serve to actualize the Word of God in the people's midst and for their salvation.

The increasing unity of function, or intimate complementarity, between Spirit and Word is confirmed by the fact that in pre-Christian Judaism the hypostatized figure of Sophia or Wisdom assumes and unites in herself the roles of both Spirit and Word. In the Wisdom Psalms, Sophia acquires a *teaching function* as the source of true instruction (Ps 31/32:8-11), communi-cating the essence of knowledge and virtue, namely "fear of the Lord" (Ps 32/33:18-22). Sophia assumes as well the creative role of both Spirit and Word (Ps 103/104:24,30). Although she remains hidden, her secrets are revealed to an obedient few (Sir 1:6; 6:22; 51:19), and she bestows her glory on those who seek her (Sir 4:13; 14:27).

With its identification of Wisdom and Torah or divine Law, "Jesus ben Sirach" (Ecclesiasticus) laid the foundation for the development of Rabbinic Judaism. The identification of Wisdom with Spirit in the "Wisdom of Solo-mon," on the other hand, provided the bridge between the spirit-concept of Hebrew thought and the image of Spirit as the creating, sanctifying and renewing divine power bestowed on the Church at Pentecost. Yet in the Wisdom of Solo-mon as well, the primary roles of Spirit are revelatory and soteriological. Wisdom is the prophetic Spirit of God who sustains creation, imparts moral knowledge for the discernment of righteousness and unrighteousness (Wis Sol 6:17-20; 9:11), sanctifies the just (7:7, 22f), and renews all things (7:27). In each genera-tion, she passes into "holy souls" to make of them "friends of God" and "proph-ets" (7:27). Like the Spirit of classical Hebrew prophecy, the Sophia-Pneuma indwells and sanctifies the faithful, leading them along the "way of truth" (6:14; 7:28; 8:9, 16; 9:9f) to life beyond the grave (1:15; 10:10; 15:8-16).

During the late prophetic period, we can say that the Spirit was the inspirational *power*, the Word was the vehicle of *expression*, and the Truth was the *content* of divine revelation. By the first century before Christ, the figure of Wisdom had assumed each of these roles. In addition, she was recognized to be the source of sanctification and the bestower of immortality.[5] The one role of Spirit and Word she did not appropriate, however, was that of the eschatological fulfillment of the divine plan for the salvation of God's people. Although she sanctifies the just and renews the people's faithfulness to God, she is never associated with national regeneration or with the New Covenant, as is the Spirit (Jer 31:31ff; cf. Ezek 36:22ff).

From the earliest period in Israel's recorded history, Spirit was known and experienced as the powerful mediator of the divine Word (cf. Num 24:2ff). The Spirit seizes the prophet with the single intention of compelling him to speak oracles of the Lord. As the chastising divine breath or cosmic wind, ruach guides Israel and the nations toward fulfillment of their respective destinies, revealed by God through the voice of his human agents. In the post-exilic age, Spirit becomes the very presence of God himself in history, but a presence whose unique purpose is to accomplish through the Word that which he intends (Isa 55:10f). Finally, Spirit communicates and actualizes the spiritual regeneration of God's people under the New Covenant; and he does so by serving as the instrument of the Word, by which all of the elect shall "know the Lord" (Jer 31:34).

4. The Spirit in the New Testament

Each of these functions of the *ruach-Yahweh,* the Spirit of the Lord, foreshadows and prepares the New Testament revelation of Spirit as Revealer, Teacher, Defender, Sanctifier, and Giver of Life.

In the experience of the early Church, as in post-exilic tradition, the Spirit and the Word, the divine Logos who appears in history as Jesus of Nazareth, operate together to produce a single "economy of salvation." Together they reveal the will, the purpose and the love of God the Father, and perform within the community of faith the work of regeneration and sanctification.[6]

5   The witness of Wis Sol is uneven in regard to the relation between Spirit, Word and Wisdom. At times Wisdom is identified with Spirit (1:4ff; 7:7; 9:17) or with Word (9:1f); at times she is in some sense independent (cf. 9:17, where the Holy Spirit "sent from on high" bestows Wisdom upon the just).
6   Sanctification by Christ: Rom 6:12; 1 Cor 1:2, 30; Eph 5:26; Heb 2:11; (9:13f); 10:10, 14, 29; 13:12. Sanctification by the Spirit: Rom 15:16; 1 Thess 4:7f; 2 Thess 2:13; 1 Pet 1:2. In a liturgical context, 1 Cor 6:11 stresses the joint operation of Christ and the Spirit

According to St Paul, the love of God is poured out into the hearts of believers "through the Holy Spirit which has been given to us" (Rom 5:5). This outpouring, an effect of the perpetual Pentecostal experience of the Church, bestows *huiothesia,* adoption of the faithful as children of God. Existing henceforth in the freedom of the Spirit, they beseech and glorify God in prayer with Jesus' own term of endearment, "Abba! Father!" (Rom 8:15; Gal 4:6). Receiving the Spirit as a foretaste (*arrabôn,* 2 Cor 1:22; 5:5) or first fruit (*aparchê,* Rom 8:23) of the eternal kingdom, they are objects of a new creation (*kainê ktisis,* Gal 6:15; 2 Cor 5:17), constituted as "members of one another" (Rom 12:5) within the body of the Church, of which Christ is the Head (Col 1:18; cf. Eph 4:15). By the Spirit, each member of Christ's Body is empowered to utter the primordial confession of faith, "Jesus is Lord!" (1 Cor 12:3; Phil 2:11). And by the Spirit, God the Father reveals the glory of the age to come, prepared for those who love him (1 Cor 2:9).

The title "Spirit of Christ" is rare in the New Testament (Rom 8:9; 1 Pet 1:11; cf. Gal 4:6, "Spirit of the Son," and Phil 1:19, "Spirit of Jesus Christ"), but the association between the two is evident throughout the apostolic writings. Earlier we noted the many instances in which the Spirit "prepares, determines, constitutes and communicates" the incarnate Word. The converse occurs as well: repeatedly the Spirit is depicted as the personal manifestation of the Son within the life of the believing community. To "be of Christ," filled with the life-giving power of the glorified Lord, is a quality of existence realized through the indwelling presence of the Spirit of Christ, and is equivalent to "Christ in you" (Rom 8:9-11).

Within the Christian community selected persons are endowed with special *charismata* or *pneumatika,* gifts of the Spirit for the upbuilding of the household of faith (1 Cor 12:1,4ff). The fruit of the Spirit (*karpos tou pneumatos,* Gal 5:22f), however, is to be cultivated by every believer and takes the form of diverse Christian virtues: love, joy, peace... Such virtues operate on the level of personal being, effecting a transformation from the domain of the flesh to the domain of the Spirit, where life in the Spirit means deliverance from the threat of death and eternal corruption. For Paul, this life in the Spirit is "realized eschatology," a very real foretaste of eternal life in the Kingdom of God.

Turning to the Synoptic tradition, we find in the Gospel of Mark an image of the Spirit descending upon Jesus at his baptism to anoint him as Messiah and to inaugurate his public ministry of preaching and healing. In the infancy

in Christian baptism: "You have been washed... sanctified... justified in the name of the Lord Jesus Christ and in (or by, *en*) the Spirit of our God."

narratives of Matthew and Luke, the operation of the Spirit in the life of Christ begins with his conception in the womb of Mary. There the Spirit overshadows her whom Orthodox tradition venerates as "Theotokos," the "God-bearer" or "Mother of God." The Spirit hovers over the Virgin as he hovered over the primeval waters (Gen 1:2), to bring forth a new creation, the incarnation of Emmanuel, "God with us" (Mt 1:23). By the finger of God (Lk 11:20), identified by the evangelist Matthew as the Holy Spirit (12:28), Jesus casts out demons, and thereby he manifests his power over the lesser powers of sickness and corruption. Working within the apostolic community, the Spirit exercises a "paracletic" or forensic role, defending the faith of believers before the tribunal of a hostile and unbelieving world (Mk 13:11, and parallels).

The Synoptic witness to the Spirit culminates in the "trinitarian" formula of Mt 28:19, where Jesus exhorts his followers to ground their apostolic mission in the sacrament of baptism: "Go," Jesus commands, "and make disciples of all nations, baptizing them in the name of the Father and of the Son and of the Holy Spirit." Whereas the book of Acts generally prescribes baptism "in the name of (the Lord) Jesus," Matthew's witness attests to the established use of a genuinely trinitarian formula in the region of Antioch by the third quarter of the first century.[7] Together with the Father and the Son, the Spirit who gives birth to the Church on the day of Pentecost fills and sustains the community of faith. Nevertheless, like St Paul the Synoptic tradition refrains from attributing to the Spirit any distinctively personal characteristics. It describes his operations but reveals nothing of his "face."

Johannine tradition, on the other hand, indicates more clearly than any other New Testament source how the *prosôpon* or personal image of the Spirit can be perceived among the body of believers. In the first Epistle of John, Spirit appears as a divine gift that indwells (*menei*) the believer and the community as a whole, to reveal the presence of God among and within his people (1 Jn 3:24; 4:13). The work of the Spirit is expressed by the verb *ginôskô*, "to know" with a knowledge acquired through personal experience.[8] "We know" that God abides in us and we in him, the author declares. It is this mutual indwelling manifested by the gift of the Spirit that constitutes the Church as a community of faith.

7   Or even in the second quarter, if the recently discovered fragments of Matthew ch. 26 have been correctly dated to 55-65.
8   Οἶδα on the other hand, designates an intuited knowledge that is not dependent on immediate experience. See I. de la Potterie, "Οἶδα et γινώσκω: Les deux modes de la connaissance dans le Quatrième Evangile," *Biblica* 40 (1959), 709-725; and ch. 7 above, "The Function of Πᾶς in 1 Jn 2:20."

The Spirit in 1 John also exercises a crucial teaching function. Designated by the baptismal term *chrisma* (anointing/unction, 2:20, 27), the Spirit communicates to the faithful the truth (*alêtheia*) concerning Jesus' divine origin and saving mission. The author is attempting to combat a heretical denial that Jesus Christ is the Son of God.[9] He does so by appealing to the work of the Spirit, received through baptismal anointing, that "confirms" within believers the fundamental truth that Jesus is indeed the Christ (the promised Messiah) and Son of the Father (2:22-24), and that this Son of God is "the Savior of the world" (4:14).

This revelatory, teaching function of the Spirit in 1 John is attested to once again in the enigmatic passage, 5:6-8:

> This is he who came by water and blood, Jesus Christ, not with the water only [alluding to his baptism?] but with the water and the blood [the crucifixion?]. And the Spirit is the witness, because the Spirit is the truth. There are three witnesses, the Spirit, the water and the blood; and these three agree [lit., are one].

Both Revealer and Teacher of Truth, the Spirit is here identified as the primary witness to the baptism and crucifixion of Jesus Christ, the Son of God, just as he is witness to the gift of eternal life granted to the Church through the Son (5:11-12).

In the Gospel of John these same functions of the Spirit are elaborated and developed in several directions. Here the Spirit descends upon Jesus at his baptism and remains with him (1:32f), indwelling him as the divine power that will enable him to utter the very words of God (3:34). If 1 John depicted the Spirit as witness in a baptismal context, the Fourth Gospel shows him to be the operative power behind baptismal regeneration, described as rebirth through water and the Spirit (3:5; cf. 7:38f). As such, the Spirit is the Life-giver (*to zôopoioun*, 6:63) who unites believers to Christ, the ultimate source of life itself ("I am the resurrection and the life," Jesus declares to Martha as she laments the death of her brother Lazarus. "Those who believe in me, though they die, yet shall they live," 11:25).[10]

Indication that the Spirit is to be understood as a divine entity, personally distinct from the Father and the Son yet essentially united with them, is

9   Scholarly opinion is divided over the question whether the antichrists are docetists, early Christian gnostics who denied the fleshly reality of Jesus' earthly life (as 1 Jn 4:2 would suggest), or whether they were Jews who denied the basic Christian confession, "Jesus is the Son of God" (4:15; cf. 5:1).

10 Compare the apparent regenerative work of the Spirit identified as *sperma* in 1 Jn 3:9: "No one born of God / commits sin, / for his seed (*sperma*) dwells in him. / And he is not able to sin, / because he is born of God." The Greek text forms a perfect a:b:c:b':a' chiasm, with its focus on the central reason for the sinlessness of Christians: the Spirit (*sperma*) dwells (*menei*) in them.

nowhere more clearly given than in the discourse Jesus held with his disciples in the upper room on the eve of his death. Here the Spirit is invested with three distinct titles: the traditional designation "Holy Spirit," together with "Spirit of Truth" (found in 1 Jn 4:6, the *Dead Sea Scrolls* and *Testaments of the Twelve Patriarchs*), and "Paraclete." This last title, *paraklêtos*, is attributed to the Spirit only derivatively. In 1 Jn 2:1-2, Jesus himself appears as the "heavenly Paraclete," exercising a function of intercession on behalf of the sins of the faithful, in a role that clearly parallels Jesus' ministry as High Priest in the Epistle to the Hebrews. Jesus is Paraclete insofar as he serves as an advocate or defense attorney on behalf of sinful humanity before the judgment seat of God the Father. Yet like the great High Priest of Hebrews, Jesus not only makes intercession; he serves as both Advocate and Expiation for those who seek reconciliation with the Father (1 Jn 2:1f; Heb 7:25ff; 9:11-14).

In the Spirit-Paraclete passages of John's Gospel (14:16f, 26f; 15:26f; 16:7-11, 13-15), *this work of advocacy and intercession is transferred from Jesus to the Spirit*. As Spirit of Truth, he sustains the apostolic community and defends them—not before the righteousness of God, but before the hostility of an unbelieving world (cf. 16:2; Mk 13:11). As Paraclete, this same Spirit assumes Jesus' eschatological role as world-judge, convicting the world of "sin, righteousness and judgment" (16:8).[11]

Johannine tradition thus knows of two divine Persons that exercise the forensic role of "Paraclete": Advocate, Comforter and Witness. On the one hand, the exalted Christ as "heavenly Paraclete" continues his expiatory work on our behalf by making perpetual intercession for our sins before the Father (1 Jn 2:1f). As our High Priest, he prays for our union with the Father (Jn 17) and, in the language of Hebrews, he offers mediation in the heavenly sanctuary through the offering of his own blood, to secure for us "an eternal redemption" (Heb 9:12-14). On the other hand, the "earthly Paraclete," the Spirit of Truth, communicates to the believing community the life-giving grace and power of Christ's sacrifice, by defending the faithful against a hostile world (Jn 16:7ff; Mk 13:11, par.) and leading them into "all the Truth" (Jn 16:13).

The Spirit's role within the divine economy is solely to communicate the life-giving Word of God and to sanctify the faithful by uniting them to him who is Wisdom, Word and Truth.

11 The forensic language here is intentional, perhaps even ironic. Jesus in the Fourth Gospel is on trial, defending himself against the unbelieving Jewish authorities, yet convicting them at the same time as children of the devil (8:44). After the resurrection, the faithful are likewise on trial, yet their witness, accomplished by the indwelling Spirit (14:17; 15:27), has the similar effect of condemning their accusers.

Accordingly, St John the evangelist presents an image of the Spirit that is fashioned directly upon the image of the Logos himself. In 5:25-29, he reflects the traditional view of the Son of Man, the eschatological judge who will come in the "final hour" to vindicate the righteous and condemn those who refuse to believe. In 16:7-11, however, this role of world-judge passes from the coming Son of Man to the Spirit-Paraclete. *The eschatological judgment by the glorified Son of Man is thereby rendered historical through the activity of the Spirit.* It is the Spirit who convicts the world of "sin, righteousness and judgment." That is, he convicts unbelievers of denying the person and revelation of the Word of God, Jesus Christ.

Nowhere more than in the Farewell Discourses of the Fourth Gospel do we find developed the intimate relationship—both personal and economic—between the Spirit and the Son. Both Jesus and the Spirit are divine "persons," who share the very nature of God (Jesus: 1:1, 18; 10:30; 20:28 / the Spirit: 4:24). Both are *sent* from the Father (3:17; 5:30; 8:16; 14:24; 17:8 / 14:16, 26); the Son *comes* from the Father (8:42; 13:3; 16:27, 30; etc.) and the Spirit *proceeds* from the Father (15:26). (Holy) Spirit is the life-breath of Jesus (20:22). The disciples *know* or will know both Jesus and the Spirit (6:69; 7:17; 8:32; 10:14, 38; etc. / 14:17), although "the world" knows neither (1:10; 3:10; 8:14; etc. / 14:17).

The most significant correlation in Johannine tradition occurs between the respective revelatory-teaching functions of Jesus and the Spirit. Each *dwells in* the Christian (6:56; 15:4f / 1:32f, 14:17; 1 Jn 2:27; 3:9), as does the "word" of Jesus or of God (5:38; 15:7; 1 Jn 2:14); yet neither speaks his own words or on his own authority (14:10; etc. / 16:13). Both Christ and the Spirit, as *parakletoi*, convict the world of sin and unbelief (3:18-20; 5:22-30; 7:7; etc. / 16:8-11). Their chief function for the Church and the world, however, is to reveal the Truth which Jesus himself embodies and communicates as the way to eternal life (14:6 / 14:26; 16:12-15). Both Jesus and the Spirit teach (6:59; 7:14-17, 28; 8:20; 18:19f, / 14:26; cf. 16:13; Jn 2:27). Just as Jesus' revelatory activity is described as "true teaching," so the work of the Spirit is to "teach" and "guide" the disciples into the fullness of Truth (14:26; 16:13). Thus the Spirit will bear *witness* to Jesus (15:26; 16:8-11; 16:14; cf. 1 Jn 5:6-9), as Jesus bears witness to himself (8:14, 18; but cf. 5:31) and to God (3:31f; 12:44f; 18:37). Again, neither Jesus nor the Spirit speaks on his own authority. As the Son speaks the words of the Father, so the Spirit speaks those of the Son (3:34; 5:36; 7:16f; 8:28; 12:49f; 14:10, 24; / 16:13-15). Both the Messiah and the Spirit will announce or reveal *panta*, an eschatological term which signifies "the things to come," or "the fullness of Truth" (14:25f, / 16:13; cf. 1 Jn 2:20, 27, and ch. 7 above).

Among the eschatological gifts Jesus leaves to his disciples is the gift of "peace" (14:27; 16:33), closely associated with bestowal of the Spirit (14:26f; 20:19-21). Twice Jesus is described as the source of "living water," which is the Spirit himself (4:10, 14; 7:39); and if Jesus' words give life (5:24; 6:63, 68; 8:51; cf. 11:43), then it is the Spirit who is the "life-giver" (6:63). The revelation communicated by the Spirit to the glorification of the Son is a proclamation that has its source in God the Father. By bearing witness to the Son in this age, the Spirit continues the revelatory work of the ascended Lord, thus pointing the way to eternal life or consummate knowledge of the Father (16:14f; 17:3).

Johannine tradition depicts the revelatory and soteriological functions of the Spirit within the Christian community as standing in direct continuity with the salvation-ministry of Jesus. Neither here nor elsewhere in the New Testament can the Spirit be understood or experienced apart from the risen and glorified Christ. The very identity of the Spirit is in fact so closely united to that of the Son that we may speak with the apostle Paul of "the Spirit of Christ" (Rom 8:9-11). It is in and through this Spirit that the inner transformation of the believer is accomplished "from glory to glory" (2 Cor 3:18). The revealing, sanctifying and saving work of Christ thus provides the orientation, the content and the meaning of the Spirit's mission. As Spirit of Truth, he is in his very essence the Spirit of Christ, fulfilling Christ's own work, through which we receive life in our mortal bodies "through the indwelling Spirit" (Rom 8:11). And this inestimable gift, this ineffable transfiguration, "comes from the Lord, who is the Spirit" (2 Cor 3:17).[12]

12 The precise meaning of Paul's affirmation *ho de kyrios to pneuma estin* has always perplexed commentators. The consensus rightly sees in this verse an allusion to Exodus 34:34. R. Bultmann, *The Second Letter to the Corinthians* (Minneapolis, MN: Augsburg, 1985), 89; F.F. Bruce, *I & II Corinthians* (Grand Rapids, MI: Eerdmans, 1971), 193; et al., conclude that in the Exodus passage *kyrios* is equivalent to *pneuma* (Bruce: "The Lord in that text means the Spirit"). This can hardly be supported exegetically. Still less convincing is the conjecture of J. Héring, *La seconde épître de Saint Paul aux Corinthiens* (Neuchâtel: Delachaux & Niestlé, 1958), 39, that 2 Cor 3:17 should be emended to read *hou de ho kyrios, to pneuma estin*. The key to this passage lies rather in 2 Cor 3:6-8, where the *diakonia tou pneumatos* signifies the life-giving New Covenant, as opposed to the former Covenant based on the written code that kills. The affirmation, "the Lord is the Spirit," refers to the *content* of that New Covenant: it is through the Lord (Christ) that the Covenant is realized; it is he who bestows "freedom in the Spirit" (since it is he who removes the "veil") and grants us participation in the transfiguring splendor of his own glory (3:18). As in the doxology of 13:13 (cf. 1 Cor 12:3ff; Rom 5:1-5; 8:26f), Paul clearly distinguishes between Christ and the Spirit. Yet in each instance the Spirit does nothing other than actualize within the personal and ecclesial life of believers the New Covenant established by Christ. The Lord *is* the Spirit, then, insofar as the Lord (Jesus) alone determines the orientation of the Spirit's activity and provides it with content.

Taken together, the various biblical witnesses to the Spirit—and particularly the Johannine witness—lead to a single basic conclusion: that *the "face" of the Spirit, like that of the Father, is revealed to us in the face of Jesus Christ.*

The patristic doctrine of *perichôrêsis (circumincessio,* coinherence or interpenetration) holds that attributes common to one divine *hypostasis* are shared by all, with the single exception of origin.[13] The Father is uniquely "unoriginate," the Son is uniquely "generated," and the Spirit is uniquely brought forth by an act of "procession." Yet the three *hypostases* share all other attributes and functions equally: attributes of wisdom, knowledge, love, power; functions of will, thought, purpose, and work. Within the divine economy, this includes their activity of reciprocal revelation. The Father sends and reveals the Son through the incarnation (Matthew-Luke) and the baptism in the Jordan (Mark), while the Son reveals and manifests the Father through his own spoken word and healing acts ("He who has seen me," Jesus tells Philip, "has seen the Father," Jn 14:9).

Similarly, the Spirit both reveals and is revealed by the Father and the Son. On the one hand, from the period of early prophecy until the time of Jesus' baptism, Israel knew the Lord and his Messiah through the presence and operation of the Spirit. Within the eschatological age of the Church, the Spirit continues to manifest the Son, while "giving access" to the Father (Eph 2:18). On the other hand, God made known the presence and power of his *ruach* throughout Israel's long history, from the empowering of charismatic rulers to the outpouring of the Spirit on the day of Pentecost. Yet the true revelation and manifestation of the Spirit occurs through the activity of the Logos himself, the divine Son, who sends the Spirit from the Father and grants to him "the things concerning himself," which the Spirit in turn will proclaim to the community of faith (Jn 16:13-15).

In regard to the Spirit, however, this reciprocal revelation goes a step further. For the "face" of the Spirit is made visible, it is provided its specific contour or profile, by the face of Jesus. The presence of Spirit within the Church is the presence of the risen and glorified Lord. The *pneuma* that fills and animates the body of believers is Christ's own life-breath, breathed upon the disciples on the evening of Easter Sunday (Jn 20:22). And yet that Spirit remains a distinct reality, a personal existence who "receives from" the Son all that is necessary to continue the Son's revelatory and saving work in the new age of the Church. The face of the Spirit, then, is none other than the face of Jesus;

13 See Verna Harrison, *"Perichoresis* in the Greek Fathers," *St Vladimir's Theological Quarterly* 35/1 (1991), 53-65. With regard to the immanent Trinity, the term implies mutual indwelling and self-giving in love (p. 64f).

yet the Spirit remains the "other Paraclete" (Jn 14:16f), intimately united with the Son, yet personally distinct from him.

It would be generations, even centuries, before the Church would baptize philosophical language of Hellenistic provenance, in order to articulate what in the canonical writings remains inchoate: that the Spirit exists with the Father and the Son in a relationship of essential unity and hypostatic distinctiveness. In the Fourth Gospel, just as in the writings of the apostle Paul, Spirit remains the Spirit of God (3:5) or the Spirit of Christ (20:22). Nevertheless, from the perspective of Eastern patristic tradition, that tri-unity between the Spirit, Christ and God (the Father) can only be properly understood as one which is grounded in a personal communion of love, shared equally among the three divine *hypostases*.

5. Conclusion

An Orthodox pneumatology, grounded in the witness of Scripture, must be essentially christological: it is the person and mission of Christ, the eternal Word, that determine, constitute and communicate the mystery of the Spirit.

"I will pray the Father," Jesus declares, "and he will give you another Paraclete, to be with you forever, even the Spirit of Truth" (Jn 14:16f). He will "teach you all things, bringing to remembrance all that I have said to you" (14:26). "He will not speak on his own authority, but whatever he hears he will speak... He will glorify me" (16:ff). Assuming Jesus' own role as eschatological judge, the Spirit-Paraclete "will convict the world of sin, righteousness and judgment" (16:8f) because of its unbelief. "He will bear witness to me," to vindicate the Truth which Jesus has proclaimed. And he will make of Jesus' disciples witnesses to that same Truth, so that through their proclamation Jesus' saving work might be brought to completion (15:27; 3:16-18).

An intimate and inseparable relationship exists between Pascha and Pentecost, between the victory of Christ over death and the actualization of that victory within the life of the Church. The one Spirit—who inspires true confession of Christ, bestows *charismata* upon the community for its upbuilding in faith, and supplies the believer with the fruits of his sanctifying grace—is none other than the Spirit *of Christ*. The "communion of the Holy Spirit" in the Pauline benediction (2 Cor 13:13) is nothing less than communion *in Christ*, a sacramental fellowship that offers participation in the Lord's own death and resurrection. The inspirational work of the Spirit is nothing other than an actualization *of the Word of God* through preaching and hearing with faith. And if our ecclesial experience confirms that Christ, the Son of God, dwells within us to work out our salvation, it is only by virtue of the Spirit which he, Christ, has given to us (1 Jn 3:23f).

Within the inner life of the Holy Trinity there exists hypostatic distinction between the Son and the Spirit, but essential identity. Within the work of the Trinity *ad extra* there is a temporal distinction between the manifestation of the Word and the manifestation of the Spirit, between the Incarnation and Pentecost; but there is teleological identity. The Spirit, sent by the Son, comes with a single purpose: to fulfill the mission of the Son within the time of the Church.

Christology and pneumatology, therefore, are inseparable. They represent complementary reflections on a single transcendent mystery: the trinitarian mystery, in which the Son and the Spirit together reveal and make accessible the "face"—the loving, saving presence—of God the Father. "No one comes to the Father but by me," Jesus declares (Jn 14:6). And the apostle Paul adds, "through him (Jesus Christ), we...have access in one Spirit to the Father" (Eph 2:18).

Eastern patristic writers stressed the point that the Spirit has no other divine hypostasis to reveal him to the world. This does not mean, however, that he remains totally hidden. For in this present age it is *our vocation* to bear witness to him. It is our task to make him known here and now, both to one another and to our militantly pagan culture, and to do so through faithful witness to Christ and by works of love wrought in his name.

Yet as the Fathers also insisted, revelation of the face of the Holy Spirit will ultimately and fully occur only within the Kingdom of God. It is there that the "face" or divine image of the Spirit will shine forth in the faces of the saints: persons such as ourselves, whose very being is changed, transfigured into the glorious Body of Jesus Christ.[14]

14 See Vladimir Lossky, *The Mystical Theology of the Eastern Church* (New York: St Vladimir's Seminary Press, 1976), 173.

12

Prayer of the Heart:
Sacrament of the Presence of God

*In Part I of this book we emphasized the point that the primary aim of biblical in-
terpretation is to acquire* knowledge *of God. Christian life and experience confirm that there are other means by which we come to know God and to attain
intimate, personal communion with him. The most important of these is* prayer,
*both personal and corporate or liturgical. For either form of prayer to be appropri-
ate and fruitful, it must ultimately derive from and conform to Holy Scripture.
This, once again, is because of the normative or canonical value of the biblical
witness. To pray to the true God in a language that is truly appropriate*
(theoprepês), *we need to return constantly to the most basic source of God's
self-revelation, which is the Church's canonical writings. Otherwise we risk
paying homage to a god of our own making, and our prayer becomes nothing more
than a form of auto-idolatry.*

*In the realm of prayer, as in the realm of dogmatic theology, developing tradi-
tions within the Church must be rooted in and shaped by the canonical Scriptures.
We address our prayer to the Father, through the mediation of the Son, and in the
power of the Holy Spirit. As this final chapter attempts to make clear, prayer is
essentially a divine activity, accomplished by God, working through his "two
hands," the Son and the Spirit. This trinitarian operation is particularly evident
in the* hesychast *tradition or "prayer of the heart." Such prayer, particularly dear
to Orthodox Christians, illustrates once again that Scripture derives from living
Tradition, while it serves as the canonical or normative expression of that
Tradition.*

1. Hesychia *and Prayer of the Heart*

The deepest sadness and the greatest joy in Christian life are caused by an
innate *longing for God*, a passionate quest for intimate and eternal communion
with the Persons of the Holy Trinity. Such longing brings sadness, because in
this life it goes largely unfulfilled. Yet rather than lead to frustration, it can produce an ineffable joy, nourished by the certitude that ultimately nothing can

separate us from the love of God in Christ Jesus, that our desire for union with him will ultimately be answered beyond our most fervent hope. This profoundly spiritual longing is often called "bright sadness" or "joyful sorrow" (*charmolupe*). In Christian mystical experience, it is the impulse that leads, through ascetic struggle and purification, to *theosis* or "deification."

Each of us, without exception, bears within the inner recesses of our being the "image" of our Creator. Fashioned in that divine image, the holy fathers declare, we are called to grow toward the divine "likeness" (Gen 1:26f). In the words of St Basil the Great, the human person "is an animal who received the command to become god,"[1] that is, to become a participant in the very life of God through the deifying power of the divine energies or operations of the indwelling Spirit. The motivating force behind this sublime vocation is *eros* or *epithymia*, an intense longing or deep affective desire for union with the Beloved. Perverted by sin, that longing becomes narcissistic, and the soul goes whoring after other gods, idols fabricated in her own image. Purified by grace, the soul is redirected toward the original Object of her love. Like the Prodigal, she turns back home, in repentance and compunction (*penthos*), to discover the Father waiting for her with open arms. The love that inspires her return, however, is a response to the prior love of God. "This is love," the apostle tells us, "not that we loved God, but that he loved us, and sent his Son as an expiation for our sins" (1 Jn 3:10). Acquisition of the divine likeness, then, is predicated entirely on divine initiative. The longing of the soul for eternal life, like that life itself, is a gift of grace, wholly dependent on the object of the soul's affection.

The first prayer of thanksgiving after communion, in the Liturgy of St John Chrysostom, declares: "Thou art the true desire and the ineffable joy of those who love, thee, O Christ our God, and all creation hymns thy praise forever!" The longing for communion with God is a major incentive to prayer, which may be described as "conversation" with God at the level of the heart. Prayer in the first instance involves praise and glorification of God, and it includes personal supplication as well as intercession on behalf of others. Prayer marked by the intense longing that leads to union with the Divine, on the other hand, requires *silence*. In addition to the scriptures, the liturgy, and other sources of revelation recognized by the Church, Christian mystical tradition has always known another avenue of divine self-disclosure: God reveals himself in the silence of the heart. In his letter to the Magnesians, St Ignatius

1   Quoted by St Gregory Nazianzus, *Oration* 43. Cf. Basil's *Treatise on the Holy Spirit* IX.25: the human vocation is *theon genesthai*.

of Antioch declared, "There is one God who manifested himself through Jesus Christ his Son, who is his Word, proceeding from silence."[2] St Isaac the Syrian expressed a similar thought with his familiar statement, "Silence is the sacrament of the world to come; words are the instrument of this present age."[3] Revelation that conveys knowledge of God normally requires words, as do petitions that address needs and conditions of our daily life. Prayer uttered out of the deepest longing for God, however, demands silence.

Yet silence, at least in present times, seems to be the most difficult of virtues to acquire. We fear it, and we run from it in a relentless search for noise and distraction. A stroll on the beach requires the companionship of a Walkman. At the workplace, or waiting on the phone, or shopping for groceries, we expect to be "entertained" by music — any music, so long as it focuses our attention outside ourselves and away from the inner being. Silence means a void, a dreadful emptiness that demands to be filled. What we choose to fill that void with most often produces not only noise but agitation through overstimulation. Sensory overload is addictive. It becomes an escape from the present, from the self, from God. Like any addiction, it is pathological and life-threatening. From the news media to MTV to contemporary works of art, American culture is marked by an insatiable hunger for stimuli that divert our attention from "the place of the heart," the place of inner silence and solitude. To some degree, however, this has always been the case. When Adam was cast forth from the Garden, he lost more than life in paradise. He lost the gift of silence, and with it he lost "the language of the world to come."

In human experience prayer offers the way to recover that language, for authentic prayer transcends human language and issues in the silence of God. It is this intuition, confirmed by ecclesial experience, that led ancient spiritual guides to develop what is called "hesychast" prayer. The term *hesychia* signifies inner calm, stillness, silence. It describes not so much a method as an attitude, a disposition of mind and heart, that facilitates remembrance of God and concentration upon him to whom prayer is directed.

In its earliest expression, hesychast prayer took the form of jaculatory petitions, single words or phrases fired like an arrow toward God. "Marana tha!," "Our Lord, Come!" may be one of the earliest examples, together with Peter's cry as he sank in the waters of the Lake of Galilee, "Lord, save me!"[4] These

---

2 *Mag* VII.2.
3 *Letter* no. 3. Recall the ancient hymn, sung in Byzantine tradition at the Great Entrance of the Holy Saturday Liturgy: "Let all mortal flesh keep silence..."
4 1 Cor 16:23, Rev 22:20; Mt 14:30.

and similar petitions could be spoken aloud in the church assembly or repeated silently by someone praying in solitude. From virtually the time of the resurrection, however, special emphasis was placed on the Name of Jesus, as having unique, life-giving power. "There is salvation in no one else [but Jesus Christ], for there is no other Name under heaven given among men by which we must be saved."[5] The name "Jesus," given by the angel at the Annunciation, signifies "God is salvation." Therefore it was very naturally taken up and incorporated into such brief, frequently repeated petitions.

Gradually, out of the experience of the desert monastics during the fourth and fifth centuries, there grew a more or less fixed formula that we know as "the Jesus Prayer": "Lord Jesus Christ, Son of God, have mercy on me, a sinner."[6] In this classic form, it combines a doctrinal confession ("Jesus is Lord") with a supplication that seeks forgiveness and healing.[7] Because some persons receive the grace by which this simple formula is gradually internalized, becoming rooted in the innermost sanctuary of one's being, it is virtually synonymous with "prayer of the heart."

The Jesus Prayer is often said to have originated in the context of the hesychast movement associated with St Gregory Palamas and Athonite monks of the 13th to 14th centuries. "Palamism," however, must be seen as the culmination of a long tradition which begins with the Holy Scriptures and the frequent invocations of the Name of Jesus they contain (Mk 10:47; Acts 4:12; Rev 22:20; etc.). In one form or another the Jesus Prayer was practiced by anchorites of Syria, Palestine and Egypt during the 4th and 5th centuries. It flourished on Mt Sinai under the spiritual direction of St John of the Ladder from the 6th century, then on Mt Athos from the 10th century. Only

5 Acts 4:12. See the monograph by Bp. Kallistos Ware, "The Power of the Name," (Fairacres, Oxford: SLG Press, 1974).

6 *Kurie Iesou Christe huie tou theou, eleêson me* [*ton hamartolon*]. K. Ware, "The Jesus Prayer in St Gregory of Sinai," *Eastern Churches Review* IV/1 (1972), 12 and note 44, locates the origin of the "standard" formula in the *Life of Abba Philemon* from 6th-7th century Egypt, but without the final phrase, "a sinner." It existed in many other forms, the most primitive of which, as he notes, may have been simply invocation of the name: "Lord Jesus." See especially his contribution "Ways of Prayer and Contemplation. I. Eastern," in *Christian Spirituality. Origins to the Twelfth Century*, ed. Bernard McGinn, John Meyendorff, and Jean Leclercq (New York: Crossroad, 1985), 395-414. This is an excellent study both of the history of the development of the Jesus Prayer and of its spiritual significance.

7 The Greek term for "mercy" (*eleêson*) is closely related to the word for "oil" (*elaion*). The petition "have mercy on me," like the *Kyrie eleêson* that serves as a leitmotif of the Eastern liturgies, is in effect a request that God anoint the individual or community with "the oil of gladness." It recalls the wine and oil applied by the Good Samaritan in Jesus' parable (Lk 10:34), with its properties of purification and healing.

some four hundred years later did the Prayer become the focus of the controversy between Gregory Palamas († 1359) and Barlaam the Calabrian. By the 15th century the Jesus Prayer had become the cornerstone of much Russian Orthodox piety, finally inspiring the nineteenth-century classic known as "The Way of a Pilgrim."[8] During the second half of the preceding century, Nicodemus of the Holy Mountain ("the Hagiorite"), together with his friend Macarius of Corinth, enshrined traditional teaching on the Jesus Prayer in five tomes entitled the *Philokalia* (first translated into Russian by Paisy Velichkovsky as *Dobrotolubiye*).[9] The complete collection contains sayings from the fathers on prayer, beginning with Anthony the Great († 356) and concluding with Gregory Palamas, thus embracing more than a millennium of Eastern contemplative tradition. The title of the work, "Philokalia," signifies "love of beauty." The expression conveys the truth about the divine life and purpose which the heart learns through practice of the Prayer. God is love; but he is also the source of all that is truly beautiful, resplendent with divine glory. Such beauty, the Russian philosophers held, "will save the world."

2. The Biblical Foundation of the Jesus Prayer

In answer to the Pharisees' question as to when the Kingdom would come, Jesus replied, "The Kingdom of God is not coming with observable signs...behold, the Kingdom of God is within you" (Lk 17:20-21). While most modern commentators take the Greek expression *entos hymon* to mean "among you," "in your midst" — that is, as present in Jesus' person — patristic interpreters tended to render it "within you." From this point of view, the Kingdom is a mystical reality, a divine gift to be cherished and cultivated within the inward being, in the depths of the secret heart. Access to that inner reality is provided by prayer, particularly continual prayer that centers upon the divine Name.

8 The most well-known English translation of this work is by R.M. French (London, 1954). Numerous other editions have appeared in recent years. The first four chapters consist of a spiritual biography of a handicapped Russian peasant, who undertakes a spiritual pilgrimage toward (the heavenly) Jerusalem. It recounts his experience with the Jesus Prayer, which he learns to interiorize through constant repetition guided by a spiritual father. The last three chapters ("The Pilgrim Continues His Way") offer an in-depth meditation on the nature of hesychast prayer.
9 For a useful overview of the respective contributions of Macarius and Nicodemus, see K. Ware, "The Spirituality of the Philokalia," in *Sobornost* 13/1 (1991), 6-24.

Such prayer, however, must never be treated as a technique, a christianized mantra, whose use enables one to attain a particular spiritual end. Prayer, as St Paul insists, can never be manipulated, since in its essence it is not a human undertaking at all. "We do not know how to pray as we should," he declares, "but the Spirit himself intercedes for us with groanings too deep for words" (Rom 8:26). True prayer occurs when the Spirit addresses the Father, "Abba," in the temple of the human heart. Prayer, therefore, is essentially a divine activity. Yet like every aspect of the spiritual life, it demands *synergeia* or cooperation on our part. To attain *theoria*, the contemplative vision of God, one must proceed by way of *praxis*, active struggle toward purification and acquisition of virtue through obedience to the divine commandments.

Prayer, then, is not merely a gift; it is work. It demands patience, persistence and ascetic discipline. It also demands the constant vigilance known as *nepsis* or "watchfulness." The Hebrew sage admonished, "Watch over your heart with all diligence, for from it flow the springs of life."[10] "Watch!" Jesus commanded His disciples at the close of his apocalyptic warnings. "What I say to you, I say to all: Watch!" (Mk 13:33-37). Such watchfulness raises a bulwark against demonic images (*phantasiai*) or thoughts (*logismoi*), enabling the mind and heart to concentrate on "the one thing needful" (cf. Lk 10:42). More than by any other virtue, we cooperate with God in the activity of prayer through "nepsis." This is the attitude of sober vigilance exemplified by the five virgins who welcomed the Bridegroom, and by the maiden who awaited her lover: "I slept, but my heart kept watch."[11]

Prayer, then, requires our cooperation with the Spirit of God through "a watchful mind, pure thoughts, and a sober heart."[12] With this conviction, the fathers turned to Holy Scripture in order to discern various levels of prayer that can be attained in the spiritual life. A key passage is 1 Timothy 2:1, "First of all, I urge that petitions, prayers, intercessions, and thanksgivings be made on behalf of all." To the patristic mind these represent four stages or orders of prayer, from the most elementary to the most sublime.[13] The apostle first names "petitions" or "supplications" (*deêseis*). These include confession of

10 Prov 4:23, New American Standard translation.
11 Mt 25:1-13; Song 5:2.
12 From the "Evening Prayer to Christ" of the Byzantine Compline service.
13 Examples of this kind of exegesis can be found in many sources. On the question in general, see esp. *The Art of Prayer*, ed. Igumen Chariton of Valamo (London: Faber, 1966), with an excellent introduction by Kallistos Ware; and *Unseen Warfare* (by Lorenzo Scupoli, ed. by Nicodemus of the Holy Mountain, revised by Theophan the Recluse), (Crestwood, NY: St Vladimir's Seminary Press, 1978).

sins, together with requests for spiritual cleansing and wholeness. Their thrust is basically negative, seeking liberation from all that impedes progress toward perfection. Second, he speaks of "prayers" (*proseuchas*), meaning positive requests for the gifts and fruit of the Spirit, for virtue and the attainment of righteousness. The third order or level consists of "intercessions" (*enteuxeis*). At this stage, one turns from one's own spiritual concerns to focus on the needs of others through intercession; this is in essence a prayer of mediation that seeks another's salvation. Finally, one reaches the level of "thanksgivings" (*eucharistias*), in which the heart rises toward God in joyous adoration, offered in response to his saving grace.

Yet as the fathers insist, the four stages exist simultaneously in the spiritual life. Thanksgiving must be complemented by ongoing repentance and petition for the forgiveness of sin, just as intercessions on behalf of others go hand in hand with prayers for one's self. Beyond these four levels or orders of prayer, however, there is another about which we can say virtually nothing; yet we shall have to return to it when we raise the question of the way hesychast prayer is internalized. This ultimate form or degree is known as *kathara proseuchê*, "pure prayer," that issues from the ineffable experience of union with God, in peace, love and joy. Although it defies any attempt to express it with words or images (all of which inevitably deteriorate into *logismoi* and *phantasiai*), it is the truest prayer of all, the utterance of the Spirit himself. As unitive prayer, it is both the goal and the fulfillment of *hesychia*.

A key element in hesychasm is frequent repetition: continual prayer as a means to uninterrupted and ever deeper communion with God. The psalmist declared, "I keep the Lord always before me; / because he is at my right hand, I shall not be moved" (Ps 15/16:8). The apostle Paul exhorts his followers to "pray without ceasing" (*adialeiptôs proseuchesthe*, 1 Thess 5:17), urging them to persevere, seeking constancy in prayer (*têi proseuchêi proskarterountes*, Rom 12:12).[14]

Both the object and the content of such repetitive prayer is the divine *Name*. According to Hebrew thought, a name bears or expresses the essence of the person or thing that bears it. By extension, knowing the name of an adversary gives some measure of control over him. The patriarch Jacob wins the struggle with the angel of God, then immediately seeks to learn his name. Although the angel refuses to divulge it, he bestows upon Jacob the new name "Israel," prophetically announcing the salvation of God's elect people (Gen 32:27-29). Jesus gains power over demons by asking their name: "Legion is my

---

14 The same idea is expressed in Col 4:2, "Be constant in prayer"; and he adds, "being watchful (*grêgorountes*) in it with thanksgiving."

name," he/they reply, "for we are many" (Mk 5:1-20). In this same encounter, the demons identify Jesus by name, adding a christological confession that even his disciples are incapable of making: "What is your concern with me, Jesus, Son of the Most High God?" The name reveals one's authentic identity, the innermost reality or truth (*alêtheia*) of one's being. Accordingly, Moses seeks to learn the name of God at the theophany on Mount Sinai. As he will with Jacob, God refuses to give his Name. Instead, he affirms the truth of his being: "I AM" (*ego eimi*, Exod 3:13-15).[15] In philosophical language, this is an existential rather than an ontological identification. Nothing is revealed of the divine essence, the inner being of the Godhead. Rather, God declares that he *IS*: Yahweh is the God who is present and active within human life and experience.

Yet the Name he does reveal to Moses conveys all the truth about God that can ever be known or expressed. "I AM," he declares. "This is my Name forever." In the person of the incarnate Son, God continues to manifest himself as "I AM." The revelatory formula "Be not afraid!" is often coupled with the added word, "I AM." Translations that render *ego eimi* as "It is I," do a great disservice. They obscure the point that in encounters with Jesus—whether they occur to the disciples on the Lake of Galilee (Mt 14:27), or in the Upper Room on the night of his betrayal (Jn 14:6), or during a resurrection appearance (Lk 24:39, *ego eimi autos*)—the designation "I am" signals a theophany, a manifestation of divine life and purpose. God's being is revealed by his acts, and beyond those "mighty acts" nothing can be known of him. "I AM the Alpha and the Omega, says the Lord God, who is and was and is to come, the Almighty!" (Rev 1:8).

Prayer of the heart focuses upon the divine Name because that Name itself is a personal theophany, a manifestation of God in Trinity. By invoking the Name of Jesus, with faith and love, the worshiper ascends Mount Sinai in the grace and power of the Holy Spirit, to stand in awe before the divine Presence. Byzantine theologians developed this image of ascent, the passage of the soul through divine darkness to the uncreated light, on the basis of the primal experience of God as *personal*. Within the "immanent Trinity," the inner life of the Godhead, the three Persons exist in an eternal communion of love, united in a common nature and a common will. Accordingly, the Trinity *ad extra*—the "economic" Trinity which is present and active within creation—reveals itself as three personal realities who bear the "names" of Father, Son and Spirit.

15 The designation "I AM" is the equivalent of "*ho on*," "He who exists." This is another form of the divine Name, invoked in the final blessing of the Byzantine office ("Christ our God, the Existing One, is blessed..."), and inscribed on icons of the Holy Face.

Since the name bears and manifests the reality of the one who possesses it, prayer must address God precisely by these revealed Names. Orthodox Christianity, therefore, is obliged to retain the traditional language of God's self-disclosure, and to refrain from resorting to functional designations such as "Creator," "Redeemer," and "Sanctifier." "Inclusive language," while appropriate to eliminate a masculine bias that has affected many of our translations, cannot properly apply to the Godhead. This is not only because God is "beyond gender." It is primarily because functional "names" such as these, so prevalent in church usage today, lead inevitably to confusion and distortion, that is, to "heresy." (However unpopular the label "heresy" might be, it remains a useful term insofar as it implies a serious distortion of the most basic elements of revelation.) Eastern tradition opposes "inclusive" or "functional" designations for God for the fundamental reason that *the three divine Persons share a common will and activity.* The Father is Creator; yet he is the author of redemption and sanctification. The Son is Redeemer; yet he is the agent of creation and the mediator of sanctifying grace. The Spirit is Sanctifier; yet he is the *spiritus creator*, who actualizes within ecclesial experience the redemptive work of the Son. As St Gregory Nazianzus declared, the Persons of the Godhead can only be distinguished in terms of their *origin*: the Father is eternally "ungenerated," the Son is eternally "generated," and the Spirit eternally "proceeds" from the Father. Prayer, then, cannot properly address God with "functional" language, since such language inevitably obscures the revealed identity of each divine Person.[16]

16 Masculine "names" have traditionally been attributed to the first two divine Persons, and, by association, to the Spirit as well. This usage is preserved today by Orthodox and many other Christians, and is defended on grounds of revelation: in the Old Testament (rarely), but especially in Jesus' own teaching, God is made known as "Abba," Father; the Logos becomes incarnate as a male; and the Son and the Spirit come forth from the Father, who is identified as the "source" (*pêgê*) or "principle" (*archê*) of all life, both created and uncreated. In antiquity, with very little knowledge of reproductive biology and a patriarchalist environment, the acts of "generation" and "bringing forth" ("causing to proceed") were understood as uniquely male functions. Today there is growing appreciation for the maternal aspects of God's relation to the world and human persons — and Orthodox theologians themselves are actively exploring the implications of feminine images used of the Spirit in early Syriac Christianity. If orthodox Christians of all stripes insist on retaining masculine names for God, it is because Scripture itself employs such gender-specific designations. God is indeed "beyond gender"; and all such gender-related names must be seen as analogies. But the limits of human language are not expanded by shifting analogies away from the biblical images, to speak both of and to God as "Mother." This carries pagan overtones that seriously distort God's self-disclosure as it is given in the biblical witness.

The name invoked by prayer of the heart is thus a *personal* name, one that reveals both the identity and the purpose of the One who bears it. Most frequently this is a name of the Son of God, the Second Person of the Holy Trinity. The child born of the Virgin receives the name "Jesus," "God is salvation"; yet he is also designated "Emmanuel," meaning "God is with us" (Mt 1:23; Isa 7:14). As the risen and exalted One, he receives the Name above every name: "Kyrios" or "Lord," the Name of God himself (Phil 2:10-11). To St Paul, even the title "Christos" or Christ, which originally signified "the Anointed One" or "Messiah," has the force of a proper name: "I have been crucified with Christ; it is no longer I who live, but Christ who lives in me" (Gal 2:19-20). In each case, the name conveys not only the personal identity of the incarnate Son; it also designates his divine "operation" as savior, revealer, ruler or liberator. To invoke the Name is to invoke as well the saving power inherent in that Name.

Bishop Ignatius Brianchaninov, a widely respected spiritual leader and recently canonized saint of nineteenth-century Russia, held that the Prayer of Jesus, focusing on the Name, is a "divine institution," established by the Son of God himself.[17] He grounds this assertion in Jesus' extraordinary promise made to his disciples in the Upper Room on the night of his Passion (Jn 14:13f): "Whatever you ask in my name, I will do it, that the Father may be glorified in the Son; if you ask anything in my name, I will do it." Later on Jesus adds: "If you ask anything of the Father in my name, he will give it to you. Hitherto you have asked nothing in my name; ask and you will receive, that your joy may be full" (16:23f). In a similar vein, the author of Hebrews exhorts his listeners: "Through [Jesus] let us continually offer up a sacrifice of praise to God, that is, the fruit of lips that confess his name" (Heb 13:15). Confession of the name of Jesus is here identified as "a sacrifice of praise," offered by human lips in gratitude for the life-giving sacrifice accomplished by our great High Priest on the altar of the Cross. A generation later such power had been attributed to the Name of Jesus that the unknown author of the Shepherd of Hermas could declare, "The Name of the Son of God is great and without limit; it upholds the whole universe."[18]

The New Testament also records the ancient linkage made between the divine Name and the appeal for "mercy." St Luke recounts Jesus' parable in which the tax collector casts his eyes to the ground and beats his breast,

17 See the opening chapter of his remarkable little book, *On the Prayer of Jesus* (London: Watkins, 1952): "Praying by the prayer of Jesus is a divine institution...instituted by the Son of God and God Himself," p. 2-3.
18 *Similitudes* 9.14.

imploring, "O God, have mercy on me, a sinner!" (Lk 18:13). The blind man identified by St Mark as "Bartimaeus" ("son of Timaeus") defies the attempts of the crowd to silence him and cries out, "Jesus, Son of David, have mercy on me!" (Mk 10:47). From here it was a very short and natural step to formulate the familiar petition, "Jesus, Son of God, have mercy on me, a sinner!" Thus the New Testament itself can be considered the primary source of both corporate liturgical worship and individual devotion. The *Kyrie eleêson* of the communal Liturgy has as its counterpart personal invocation of the Name of Jesus, coupled with the petition, "have mercy on me!"

3. The Hesychast Way of Prayer

Hesychasm (*hesychia*) may be described as a tradition of prayer, based on inner discipline (*askêsis*), that leads to contemplation of the divine Presence. Although certain streams of that tradition are associated with a vision of the Uncreated Light, its true aim is to establish communion, in the depths of the heart, with the Persons of the Holy Trinity.

Hesychasm seeks ultimately to attain *theosis* or deification, through participation in the energies or operations of God. These consist of divine attributes, such as love, wisdom, justice, beauty. Attainment of this sublime end involves us in an "antinomy," the apparent paradox of *synergeia* or cooperation with God. On the one hand, human effort is necessary, to respond to divine grace with faith and ascetic effort. This engages us in "unseen warfare" with sin and temptation, principalities and powers. On the other hand, grace remains a free gift, totally independent of any merit or accomplishment on our part. "Synergy" consists of divine initiative and human response. The human element, however, is limited to repentance, a constant turning back to God with a broken and contrite heart.[19]

The apostle Paul declared the body to be "a temple of the Holy Spirit within you" (1 Cor 6:19). Hesychast tradition knows that temple to be "the place of the heart." According to biblical thought, the heart is the center of all life, somatic, psychic and spiritual. It is the organ of reason, intelligence, and

---

19 Hesychast tradition understands repentance to involve "guarding the heart": "Be attentive to yourself, so that nothing destructive can separate you from the love of God. Guard your heart, and do not grow listless and say: 'How shall I guard it, since I am a sinner?' For when a man abandons his sins and returns to God, his repentance regenerates him and renews him entirely." St Isaiah the Solitary (5th century), "On Guarding the Intellect" [text 22], *The Philokalia* vol. 1 (ed. G.E.H. Palmer, Philip Sherrard, Kallistos Ware), (London & Boston: Faber, 1979), p. 26.

therefore of knowledge of God. As such it is the most intimate point of encounter between God and the human person.

Hesychast prayer is grounded in a theology of the heart. The recently canonized Bishop Theophan Govorov (1815-1894), known as "the Recluse," expressed the essence of the hesychast way in the following simple yet profound assertions:

> The heart is the innermost person. Here are located self-awareness, the conscience, the idea of God and of one's complete dependence on Him; and all the eternal treasures of the spiritual life.

> [True prayer] is to stand with the mind in the heart before God, and to go on standing before Him ceaselessly, day and night, until the end of life.[20]

Here there is neither enthusiasm nor quietism,[21] but total sobriety, with a complete integration of the spiritual faculties. Yet once again, although attainment of this state of integration demands an ongoing struggle against the "passions," the inclinations of the fallen self, it remains wholly dependent on the work of the Holy Spirit. The quality and intensity of prayer that leads to abiding communion with God are bestowed only by the Spirit. Prayer of the heart is a charismatic prayer in the genuine sense of the term. "We do not know how to pray as we ought..." But the Spirit, as a free gift, makes prayer possible. "The love of God has been poured out into our hearts through the Holy Spirit given to us," Paul affirms (Rom 5:5). And the chief work of the Spirit is to quicken authentic prayer within us. In the words of the great seventh century Syrian mystic, Isaac of Nineveh:

> When the Spirit takes up His (in Syriac, Her) dwelling place in a man, he never ceases to pray, for the Spirit will constantly pray in him. Then neither when he sleeps nor when he is awake will prayer be cut off from his soul; but when he eats and when he drinks, when he lies down or when he does any work, even when he is immersed in sleep, the perfumes of prayer will breathe in his heart spontaneously.[22]

How does one acquire such prayer? The answer, once again, lies less in the acquisition of techniques than in the dynamic of "longing," in a spiritual

20 Theophan the Recluse, *The Art of Prayer*, pp. 190 and 63.
21 On the difference between "quietism" and the "quiet" or "calm" of hesychia, see K. Ware, "Silence in Prayer: The Meaning of Hesychia," *Theology and Prayer*, ed. A.M. Allchin (Studies Supplementary to Sobornost, no. 3), (London: Fellowship of St Alban and St Sergius, 1975), p. 21f.
22 *Mystic Treatises* by Isaac of Nineveh (tr. A.J. Wensinck; Amsterdam, 1923; 2nd ed. Wiesbaden, 1967), p. 174.

attitude of love for God and the intense desire to commune with him. There are, however, certain steps one can take to create the outer and inner conditions that facilitate genuine prayer, including prayer of the heart. These include achieving a certain measure of silence and solitude, to hear the voice of God and become aware of his presence.

The *Apophthegmata patrum* or Sayings of the Desert Fathers, include a familiar story of St Arsenius (354-450) that stresses the importance of silence and solitude for acquiring inner prayer. Arsenius sought from God the way to salvation, and a voice replied, "Flee men! Flee, keep silent, and be still, for these are the roots of sinlessness."[23] This does not, however, imply rejection of others or isolation for its own sake. Nor does it mean that one no longer listens to others or seeks communion with them. Silence and solitude are inner qualities that imbue all speech and all personal relationships with peace and attentive love. They serve to cultivate a level of spiritual transparency that enables the voice of God to be heard and his presence to be felt, whatever the ambient conditions might be.

With regard to the Jesus Prayer itself, however, two points need to be stressed above all. First, we cannot force the prayer. As a gift of the Holy Spirit, it cannot be manipulated. Any attempt to use the Prayer as a mantra, or to exploit it as a psychological tool for relaxation or for any other proximate goal, will inevitably lead to spiritual shipwreck. And second, to progress along "the way of hesychast prayer," it is imperative that one be continually guided by a spiritual master. Today we are faced with a dearth of *startsi*, spiritual elders who can guide the seeker by virtue of their own experience with prayer and ascetic discipline. To a limited extent, books can serve as a substitute: hence publication and translation of the *Philokalia*, *The Art of Prayer*, *The Way of a Pilgrim*, and many other important works that convey the distilled wisdom of centuries of experience. Books, however, need to be used with discretion. Even if their content is *nihil obstat* in the eyes of God, it is always possible for the reader, because of sin, weakness or ignorance, to misconstrue and misuse their wisdom. Any serious quest for attainment of prayer of the heart needs to be guided by an authentic spiritual elder.

This said, however, it is possible—and highly desirable—for any Christian to make sober and genuinely pious use of the Jesus Prayer. Without attempting to "produce" prayer of the heart, one can nevertheless incorporate

---

23 Arsenius, 1.2; PG 65 88BC. Cf. St John Climacus, *The Ladder of Divine Ascent* 27 (PG 88 1100A), quoted by K. Ware, "Silence in Prayer," p. 13: "Close the door of your cell physically, the door of your tongue to speech, and the inward door to the evil spirits."

the usual formula, or a shorter version of it, into personal prayer at any time and under any circumstances. Even when it is called upon occasionally, the Name of Jesus manifests its grace and healing power.

When they speak of the actual internalization of the Jesus Prayer, the spiritual masters usually distinguish three stages: oral or verbal, mental, and prayer of the heart. The novice (like the Russian pilgrim) begins with frequent, unhurried repetition of the prayer, adopting a regular rhythm which may or may not be associated with breathing.[24] One may, for example, form the words "Lord Jesus Christ, Son of God," while inhaling, then exhale with "have mercy on me, a sinner." Posture can also be an important factor in acquiring a fruitful rhythm and intensity of prayer. Often it is recommended that one sit on a low stool and fix both the gaze and the mental attention literally on the place of the heart, the center or left side of the chest. Pain can often occur as a result of the cramped position. This can have a positive effect insofar as it concentrates attention. If it becomes a hindrance or burden, or is ever sought for its own sake, then it should be avoided as a temptation or even deception (*planê*). As with all things, discernment is crucial.

The Russian Pilgrim was instructed to pray the Jesus Prayer frequently, finally several thousand times each day. This is more than most people can manage; it can even be dangerous if it expresses an unconscious compulsion, a need born of "religiosity" rather than sobriety and a genuine desire to commune with God. Here the crucial element is moderation.

Often one finds that use of a *chotki* or prayer cord helps considerably in focusing attention and establishing a rhythm of repetition.[25] While it can be used carelessly, like conversation beads, it should be integrated into the practice of prayer consciously and with respect. Like prostrations and the sign of the cross, it permits involvement of the physical body in the activity of worship.

24 Far too much has been made of the role of the breath in hesychast prayer. While coordinating the prayer with the breath can be useful for some, for others it is a distraction and an obstacle. This, too, needs to be decided with the guidance of an experienced teacher. St Theophan the Recluse notes: "The descent of the mind into the heart by the way of breathing is suggested for the case of anyone who does not know where to hold his attention, or where the heart is; but if you know, without this method, how to find the heart, choose your own way there. Only one thing matters—to establish yourself in the heart." *The Art of Prayer*, p. 198.
25 The Orthodox prayer cord is usually made of black wool thread, tied in a chain of complicated knots and ending with a cross. It often contains 100 knots, but that is variable. One seldom uses it to count the number of prayers said. Rather, it serves to focus the mind through a bodily gesture and adds the faculty of touch to the experience of prayer.

Gradually as the Prayer is repeated, it begins to transcend the verbal level and root itself in the mind. One continues to pray with the lips. But the Prayer seems to take on a life of its own, whether one is awake or asleep. Many experiences are known such as that of a Roman Catholic contemplative sister who slowly regained consciousness after a serious automobile accident. Before she actually came to, those around her saw her lips forming the words of the Jesus Prayer. Here again we are reminded of the words of the Song of Solomon: "I slept, but my heart kept watch..."

Once the Prayer is imprinted on the mind, it appears to "pray itself" spontaneously. The writers of commercial jingles understand all too well the psychological mechanism involved here. With the Prayer, of course, there is a far deeper dimension, one that embraces the entire being, suffusing mind, heart and body with a sense of peace and joy. This is the bright sadness that radiates from the faces of saints depicted in authentic iconography. It is not merely the psyche's response to repetition. It is a gift of the Holy Spirit, that calls forth compunction and penitence, love and devotion for God, and at times, the cleansing, healing grace of tears.

The authors of the *Philokalia*, and countless others with them, know of a still deeper level of prayer called *kathara proseuchê* or "pure prayer." This ultimate stage is reached when the Prayer literally "descends from the mind into the heart." There, as the voice of the Spirit himself, it makes its dwelling place within the inner sanctuary. Then the Prayer is no longer "prayed" as a conscious, deliberate act. It is received, welcomed and embraced as a manifestation of divine Presence and Life. The Prayer now associates itself with the rhythm of the heart, producing without conscious effort a ceaseless outpouring of adoration and thanksgiving. From prayer of the lips to prayer of the mind, it has become "prayer of the heart."

But once again, such prayer is a gift and must always be respected as such. Many have actively sought it, through heroic "praxis," in the hope of being blessed with the divine vision and knowledge known as *theôria*. Some have been granted the gift almost at once. After only three weeks, St Silouan of Mount Athos was so blessed. St Symeon the New Theologian († 1022) struggled and implored God for years before he received the gift of pure prayer. And many saints, of course, never do. That determination, like salvation itself, must be left entirely in the hands of God. Nevertheless, there is virtue in seeking the gift, whether or not it is accorded, as long as it is sought out of love for God and longing for union with him, and not for the sake of the experience itself. In this regard, discernment of one's motives can also be made most surely and most effectively through the guidance of a spiritual teacher.

4. The Fruit of the Jesus Prayer

The depth and authenticity of prayer are known by its fruits. We can gauge the truth of our own prayer by the effects it has on our personal life and relationships. With respect to the Jesus Prayer, we can conclude by noting four such effects.

In the first place, practice of the Prayer promotes what is referred to today as *centering*. Within the spiritual life, this means focusing on "the one thing needful" (Lk 10:42). Yet this ability to "center" is itself a gift, one granted in a relationship of "synergy" between God and the human person. Mary of Bethany welcomes Jesus into her home and places herself at his feet in the position of a disciple. While her sister Martha busies herself with domestic affairs, Mary seeks what is essential. She centers upon the Word of God, and receives an invaluable legacy, "the good portion that will not be taken away."

The Prayer of Jesus can serve to focus thought during periods of meditation. Once it becomes an integral part of worship, regardless of its degree of internalization, it produces an ability to concentrate, to center, that provides depth and richness to all prayer.

A second purpose of the Prayer, and fruit borne by it, is acquisition of the *memory of God*. Great mystics of the Christian East from Diadochus of Photice (5th century) to Gregory of Sinai (14th century) used the expression "Memory of God" as equivalent to invocation of the Name of Jesus or "Prayer of the Heart."[26] The concept of "memory," in Hebrew thought as well as Greek, signifies more than recollection, the recalling of a person or an event. *Anamnesis*, as its use in the Liturgy suggests, signifies "reactualization." Through the anamnetic quality of the Liturgy, the saving events of Christ's death and resurrection are rendered present and "actual" in the experience of the worshiping Church. Repetition of the Prayer of Jesus can have this same anamnetic effect. By it, one "remembers" God in the sense of rendering him present; or rather, one opens the mind and heart to his presence, otherwise obscured by thoughts, images, and other distractions. To preserve the memory of God is to hold oneself continually in God's presence, with fear and trembling, but also with the certitude that Jesus remains with us "until the end of the age."

Practice of the Prayer of Jesus can also bear fruit of *self-sacrificing love*. We are becoming aware today that much self-sacrifice within the Church is the result of religious addiction, a compulsive need to help, heal and save others,

26 See K. Ware, "The Jesus Prayer in St Gregory of Sinai," p. 17.

however appropriate or inappropriate our actions might be. Self-sacrifice can in reality be the unconscious sacrifice of one's family, of friends, and of one's well-being, all in the name of "fixing" or "rescuing." These are destructive behaviors; and often our own discernment is not adequate to distinguish them from genuine expressions of *diakonia*. Yet the fact of such compulsive behaviors should never be allowed to obscure Christ's call to take up one's cross, to go the extra mile, to sacrifice one's own interests out of love and concern for another.

In ways that are not explainable but are a constant in Christian experience, invocation of the Name of Jesus can bring order, harmony and clarity of vision out of our inner chaos. It can restructure our unconscious priorities, so that love is no longer self-serving but is freely offered from "a pure heart and a sober mind." Perhaps the Prayer decreases our level of anxiety by causing both mind and heart to surrender to him who is the Wisdom, Word and Power of God. But this kind of reflection can lead us into sterile "psychologizing." It would be more accurate to say that the love which issues from practice of the Prayer is a fruit of the Spirit, together with "joy, peace...and self-control" (Gal 5:22). Both a "gift" and a "fruit," that love itself is the power of God, for reconciliation, growth and healing in every personal relationship.

The fourth effect or fruit of the Prayer of Jesus leads us back to where we began, to the concept of *longing*. Longing for God, the intense inner desire of the heart that seeks eternal union with him, is the driving force and the sanctifying grace of the spiritual life. It provides the courage and strength to assume the ascetic way toward *theôsis*, the vision of God and participation in his divine life. Repetition of the Name of Jesus enhances that longing, again by centering upon what is essential.

In his first *Mystical Treatise*, St Isaac of Nineveh declared,

> The highest degree of silence and inner calmness (*hesychia*) is reached when a person, in the intimate depths of the soul, converses with the divine Presence, and is drawn in spirit to that Presence. When the soul is transfigured by the constant thought of God, with a watchfulness that does not fade either by day or by night, the Lord sends forth a protecting cloud, that provides shade by day and sheds a radiant light by night. That light shines in the darkness of the soul.

That transfiguring Light is the presence of the Holy Spirit himself, bestowed in baptism, but constantly renewed through the exercise of inner, contemplative prayer. The Prayer of Jesus is a gift, superficially accessible to all, but internalized in the hidden depths of the heart by only a few. If one feels called to pursue "the hesychast way," it is important to remember that ceaseless prayer must never be sought for its own sake, not even for its perceived spiritual benefits.

Received with thanksgiving as an expression of divine love, the Prayer of Jesus can be offered up as a "sacrament" of the divine Presence. Through it, "God is with us," in an intimate and unique way, to bless, guide, heal and transform the "secret heart" from stone to flesh and from flesh to spirit. But like every sacramental aspect of life in the Body of Christ, the Prayer can be true to its purpose only insofar as it serves to glorify God, and to increase both our faith and our joy in his unfailing presence with us.

Prayer, then, as much as the interpretation of Scripture, depends on the working of God within the mind and heart. The sacred, canonical writings of the Church, as we have seen, took shape within the community of faith as the normative expression of its belief and guide of its moral conduct. Those writings, in other words, emerged from within Holy Tradition, which is the Church's experience of and response to God's saving presence and activity in her midst.

Yet the same can be said of prayer, both liturgical and personal. Prayer also emerges from within the life and experience of the Church and constitutes a vital element of Holy Tradition. Scripture is the primary medium of God's self-revelation, and thus it serves as the Church's canon or rule of truth. Prayer, on the other hand, is the life-breath of the Church, her soul or animating principle, that creates and sustains our most intimate communion with God. As Scripture derives from the eternal Word or Son of God, so prayer ultimately derives from the indwelling Spirit, who "intercedes for us with sighs too deep for words" (Rom 8:26). Just as the Son and the Spirit serve as the "two Hands of the Father" in view of the world's salvation, so Scripture and Prayer serve as complementary sources of Christian life and faith. Scripture provides the most basic content of Prayer, whereas Prayer articulates the deepest meaning of Scripture: *lex orandi lex est credendi.*

Biblical interpretation, therefore, can fulfill its task faithfully only insofar as it issues from a life of prayer. This truth, self-evident to the Church Fathers, means that we can move from the literal to the spiritual meaning of Scripture only by means of *theôria*, the insight and inspiration offered by the Holy Spirit to one who prays. As Evagrius insisted, prayer is the indispensable source and ground of genuine theology. It is no less the source and ground of responsible, faithful and fruitful interpretation of the Word of God.

Appendix

Mary: Mother of Believers, Mother of God

This review article, originally published in Pro Ecclesia *vol. 4, no. 1 (1995), 105-111, complements chapters 8 and 10 above, on the Virgin Theotokos and the humanity of Christ. It concerns the vital significance of Mary as "locus" of a true incarnation and her role in the mystery of redemption. We reproduce it here as a further example of the way in which Orthodoxy grounds its traditional dogmatic teachings in the witness of the canonical Scriptures, while recognizing that the biblical witness itself both derives from and shapes Holy Tradition.*

Edward Schillebeeckx and Catharina Halkes, *Mary: Yesterday, Today, Tomorrow.* Forward and Introduction by Marianne Merkx; tr. John Bowden (NY: Crossroad Publishing Co., 1993); 88 pages.

The two essays contained in this important little book are significant less for what they conclude about the mother of Jesus than for the christological presuppositions they reveal. Although the authors did not intend as much, each essay raises from a different perspective the critical issue of Jesus' identity as both son of Mary and Son of God.

If the person and role of Mary are undergoing an impassioned yet chaotic reassessment in feminist and other theological circles today, it is due in large measure to a prevailing christology that has simply done away with the Church's traditional understanding of "incarnation." If it is no longer theologically correct to speak of Jesus as the "God-man," the Second Person of the Holy Trinity, who assumed the fullness of human nature in the womb of Mary—if Jesus is to be understood as God's "dearest son" (Schillebeeckx, p. 33) rather than as the *Monogenês*, the unique and eternal divine Son of God—then the images of Mary as "mother" and "virgin" must be rejected as relics of a patriarchalist and (celibate) clericalist order that deserves to go under once and for all. This would mean, however, that we have to jettison as well the traditional designation of Mary as Theotokos or "Mother of God," and with it the christology that title implies.

This is what is at issue in the present "quest for the historical Mary," that Edward Schillebeeckx and Catharina Halkes have embarked upon. Less directly than the authors' more familiar writings, yet just as acutely, these essays raise the question of the relevance, indeed, of the very truth of Christian orthodoxy. Their considerable merit is that they oblige the reader to confront and respond to that more basic question in light of the ongoing debate concerning the identity of Mary of Nazareth.

The authors are well-known Dutch Catholic theologians and professors emeriti of the University of Nijmegen. Their theme is Mariology since Vatican II: how their own views have changed in the intervening years, and how they assess the traditional Roman Catholic images of Mary as "Holy Virgin" and "Mother of the Church."

In her lucid introduction, Marianne Merkx, Study Secretary of the Edward Schillebeeckx Foundation, describes a "generation of silence" surrounding the person of Mary since the Council, due to a reaction in Roman Catholic piety and theological reflection against the traditional view of Mary that overly stressed her identity with her son, particularly in the work of redemption. Schillebeeckx, a specialist in dogmatic theology, and Halkes, an influential feminist theologian, attempt to provide a renewed image of Mary based exclusively on Scripture (although Halkes relies as well on insights from the psychology of religion and depth psychology). They do so out of a concern to reclaim Mary as a "sister" rather than "mother," a person "on our side" in the mystery of redemption, rather than on the side of the Redeemer. Their ostensible targets are the traditional images of Mary as "holy virgin," chaste and submissive, the model of the "good" Christian woman; and Mary as "Mother of the Church," the co-redemptrix whose exalted status separates her from common humanity and jeopardizes the uniqueness of her Son's salvific role.

Protestants and the Orthodox would generally reject this popular interpretation of these titles and agree that a reassessment of Catholic Mariology is long overdue. Problematic is the consequence which effectively abandons the ancient images of Mary as "Theotokos" (Ephesus, 431) and "Ever-Virgin" (Protoevangelium of James, Athanasius, dogmatic decrees from the fifth century), as well as the more recent (and to most non-Roman Catholics unacceptable) papal dogmas of the Immaculate Conception (1854) and the Assumption (1950).

Schillebeeckx opens his article with reflections on the significance for Mariology of the Vatican II document Lumen Gentium, which situated Mary in the context of "ecclesiology" rather than "christology and redemption." Although

Pope Paul VI yielded to traditionalist pressure and concluded the third session of the Council by proclaiming Mary "Mother of the Church," the majority rejected the related title "co-redemptress," thereby removing her from the domain of "objective redemption." Schillebeeckx prefers the expression "companion in redemption," which places her "on our side" in God's saving work. "Mary," he declares, "is the active prototype of the communion of saints redeemed by Christ" (p. 21); thus he favors the feminist designation of Mary as "our sister."

His chief concern, however, is to develop a "*pneuma*-christological Mariology, purely on a New Testament basis" (p. 25). To do so, he examines a number of biblical texts which, to his mind, presuppose a basic distinction between the (anarthrous)[1] spirit of God, a "creative power," and the (articular) Holy Spirit. Because his exegesis reflects an all too common misreading of the texts, and serves to ground his entire approach in reassessing the person and function of Mary, it would be worthwhile to examine it in some detail.

Schillebeeckx begins his argument by declaring that "the 'virgin birth of Jesus', also for historical, biblical and theological reasons, is now interpreted by many theologians in a different way from the literal and biological sense..." (p. 25). In other words, traditional incarnational theology—that rests upon the conviction that God became (a) man as the person of Jesus of Nazareth, through a union of divine and human nature in a single hypostasis or person (the "hypostatic union")—is to be rejected as untenable in the age of modern science (although, we should note, the Church Fathers never used biological categories as such when speaking of the mystery of "God in the flesh"). The incarnation, we may assume, is rather to be understood as the translator of John 1:14 in the New Revised Standard Version (*NRSV*) would have it: "we have seen his glory, the glory as of a father's only son, full of grace and truth." Glory, grace and truth, according to this rendering, are predicable of any male child who has no male siblings. The implication, of course, is that although in some unspecified way "the Word became flesh," Jesus himself is the biological son of Joseph. Accordingly, the term "incarnation" should be understood as a simple metaphor, expressing the notion that God's Word came to expression in Jesus' teaching.

This implied conclusion is based on Schillebeeckx's distinction between *pneuma hagion* with and without the article. With, it signifies the Paschal gift of the Holy Spirit; without, it refers rather to "God's creative power" (p. 26f). From here, he concludes that the anarthrous use of the expression in Luke 1:35, "the angel said to her: holy spirit will come upon you," is equivalent to

1 I.e., omits the article.

its use in 1:15 and 41, in reference to John the Baptist and Elizabeth. There, he maintains, it signifies "a provisional gift of prophecy"; and in 1:35 it is synonymous with "power of the Almighty." In neither case is it to be understood as though "the Spirit takes over the role of the man in producing a child; what we have here is God's unique presence in the origin of new life, the life of this human child Jesus" (p. 27).

Two points need to be made in regard to this exegesis of Luke 1:35. First (as Schillebeeckx is certainly aware), traditional incarnational theology denies categorically that "the Spirit takes over the role of the man in producing a child." The Spirit is never understood as a divine consort, a male counterpart in the process of procreation. The Byzantine liturgy expresses this unambiguously with its oft repeated phrase, "she who *without seed* bore God the Word." The real issue raised by Schillebeeckx's exegesis is not the identity of the *pneuma hagion*, but the identity of the one conceived in Mary's womb. It is not so much the "how" of the virginal conception that matters as it is the "who": the identity and origin of the one whom Mary bears.

If in this day of bipolar virtual entities and post-deconstructionism there remains any interest at all in what is known as the "literal sense" of the biblical text, then reasonable exegesis can only conclude that to the mind of the third evangelist—and to his underlying tradition—the one conceived in Mary's womb was the (unique) holy one, the Son of God, who alone was conceived by the Holy Spirit, the "power of the Most High." While this same Spirit "filled" Elizabeth and the son born of her, he is never depicted apart from Luke 1:35 (and the corresponding passage Mt 2:18-21, *ek pneumatos agiou*) as empowering a woman to "give birth without seed." This is the indispensable significance of Mary's virginity.

But it is further necessary to show that in Lukan usage, there is no distinction between the anarthrous and articular forms of *pneuma hagion*. This can be easily done by referring to a few key verses. In 2:25-27, for example, it is said that (anarthrous) "Holy Spirit was upon" Symeon, that revelation had been granted to him "by the (articular) Holy Spirit,...and he came by (*en*) the (articular) Spirit into the temple." Does it seem more likely that Luke is making an extremely subtle distinction between two (or three) distinct realities—"Holy Spirit" as divine power, contrasted with "*the* Holy Spirit" and "*the* Spirit" as divine entity(ies)—or that he is simply making three allusions to the same Spirit, who indwells, inspires and guides Symeon toward fulfillment of his longing to "see" the consolation of Israel?[2]

2   J.A. Fitzmyer says of v. 25: "The anarthrous use of *pneuma hagion* occurs here again, as in 1:15, 35, 41, 67... That it is to be understood of God's holy Spirit is clear from v. 26." *The*

In Luke 3:16, John the Baptist declares, "he will baptize you with (anarthrous) Holy Spirit and fire," a promise grounded in Jesus' own baptism, when, in 3:22, the (articular) Holy Spirit descends upon him in the Jordan River. In 4:1f, Jesus, full of the (anarthrous) Holy Spirit returns from the Jordan and is led "by (*en*) the (articular) Spirit" into the wilderness. If Luke had wanted to distinguish between *pneuma* as "divine power" and as "divine entity" (or "life," we might say "person"), would he not have used the article with the title "Holy Spirit" and leave "Spirit" anarthrous, thereby avoiding ambiguity? The evident conclusion is that he had no such distinction in mind.

Evil spirits likewise appear to be hypostatized in Luke's thought, whether articular or anarthrous (4:31-37 anarthrous; 10:20 articular; 11:24 articular). In 11:13, the Holy Spirit the Father will bestow on those who ask him, is anarthrous; yet it is clearly personified, referring to the same (articular) Holy Spirit who (!) is the object of blasphemy and who instructs the disciples what they are to say in the hour of persecution (12:10,12). Whereas the latter, by virtue of its function, might be considered a "provisional gift of prophecy," it/he too is clearly personified as the Lukan equivalent of the Johannine Paraclete, the Spirit of Truth (Jn 14:26-27; 16:7-15).

Finally we may note the parallelism between "the (articular) promise of my Father" and the (anarthrous) "power from on high" which the resurrected Lord will send upon his disciples (Lk 24:49); and the fulfillment of that promise/power in Acts 2:4, when the (anarthrous!) Holy Spirit filled those in the house on the day of Pentecost. Note the parallelism here as well: "they were all filled with the (anarthrous) Holy Spirit // ...just as the (articular) Spirit gave them utterance." In each case, reference is to the Holy Spirit of God, the manifestation of personal divine life and presence, and not merely to some "provisional gift of prophecy."

A distinction between the articular and anarthrous usages of proper nouns, in any case of *pneuma* (*hagion*), holds no more for the evangelist Luke than it does for the apostle Paul. Paul is surely referring to one and the same reality in Phil 2:1, when he speaks of "any communion in the (anarthrous) Spirit," and in 2 Cor 13:13, when he invokes upon the community "the communion of the (articular) Holy Spirit."

For his development of a *pneuma*-christological Mariology Schillebeeckx relies on a distinction that simply does not exist. The venerable but specious argument that biblical authors distinguished fundamentally between a spirit

Gospel According to Luke I-IX (New York: Doubleday, 1981), p. 427. The fact that the Spirit in these contexts often plays a prophetic role is no reason to assume that the evangelist distinguishes between the Holy Spirit of God and some independent spiritual influence.

(of prophecy) and the Holy Spirit by using the article only for the latter, has led to a great deal of bad exegesis and should be abandoned.

In Schillebeeckx's case, the aim is clearly to avoid attributing a "biological" role to the Holy Spirit in the conception of Jesus. But beneath that lies the theological "bottom line" of his reflection that perceives Jesus of Nazareth to be a human being (only). Therefore he can speak so approvingly of the admittedly touching sermon by Phie Peeters (pp. 43-46), which denies the virgin birth on grounds of a curious romanticism that virtually ignores the biblical text ("Christians have almost forgotten that the couple, Mary and Joseph, loved each other and that God wanted a human child as the fruit of that love."). And therefore he can lavish praise on the Nijmegen taxi-driver ("a real theologian!") who declared, "God in human clothes is too much for me" (p. 30). He has been too much for many people, not least of all brilliant and dedicated theologians of the Church. But therein lie both the mystery and the cross of Christian faith.

The second essay in this volume is the more personal and highly perceptive article by Catharina Halkes, "Mary in My Life." For several decades, Catharina Halkes has devoted herself to developing "a critical theology of liberation" that addresses the plight of women suffering from "psychological and sexual oppression, infantilization and structural invisibility as a result of sexism in the churches and society" (from Merkx's introduction, p. 6). Her article, "Mary in My Life," was written to complement Schillebeeckx's presentation originally given at a symposium on Mary, held for members of his order in 1990.

Halkes opens with an autobiographical sketch of her earliest experiences with Mary, presented as the "chaste and lowly virgin," as the ideal "mother," and consequently as a model for emulation. Gradually, she declares, "Mary became a shadow in my life" (p. 48). The shadow was one of rage: not at the person of Mary as such, but at what she perceived to be both pious and dogmatic caricatures of Mary's person and function. This is captured in a single page (49), where Halkes recites a litany of hostile feelings, including "anger," "helplessness," "shame," "agitation," "distance," "alienation," "perplexity," "indignation." Her personal experience, coupled with insights from Latin American liberation theology, led her over the years to produce a number of writings on Mary, in which she came to envision her as "first among believers," as a woman on the side of women, one who is a *sister* rather than a mother.

Traditional images of Mary, on the other hand, are to be discarded as theologically inappropriate, the bitter fruit of the Church's ambivalence "about human sexuality, and especially about the *sexuality of women*" (p. 59, emphasis hers). Mary, consequently, is presented always "as a reference to something or someone else"; she is, in effect, a "hyphen being." "Mary represents humanity as the feminine and subordinate partner. A Mariology which is based on this serves as a legitimation of traditional sexual attitudes rather than as a source of liberation" (p. 62). The crucial element in any *new* Mariology, then, is "liberation" from male stereotypes of women that the Church and its theologians have transferred to Mary, thus making of her a symbol or archetype of the feminine ideal: subservient, chaste, and "an inspiring model for women."

Once again, Protestant and Orthodox Christians (together, of course, with many Catholics) would resonate in perfect harmony with Halke's rejection of a "supernatural Mary who dwelt with her child in the clouds and thus lost contact and solidarity with our humanity" (p. 52). Those of us from non-Roman confessions, in any case, are highly suspicious of any tendency to view Mary from the perspective Schillebeeckx so incisively criticizes: *de Maria numquam satis,* "one can never speak highly enough of Mary." That well-meaning phrase has spawned in Catholicism an image of the mother of Jesus that indeed separates her from the common mortal and attributes to her a role in redemption that properly belongs to her Son alone. We can feel sympathy, then, and even gratitude, that these two eminent and influential Catholic theologians are attempting to redress the imbalance and rediscover the Mary of Scripture. But again, as with Schillebeeckx, the tendency in this present article is to make of Mary *only* our sister, the first of believers. Although Halkes uses the language of "incarnation," the relation between Mary's "virginity" and the birth of Jesus are severed to such an extent that it is meaningless to speak of "the Word become flesh," except as a metaphor, a symbol void of content.

In her "theological quest for a 'new' Mary," Halkes asserts that "Mary calls for liberation from the image that men have formed of her" (p. 59). But like Schillebeeckx, she proceeds to ground that liberation in a somewhat strained exegesis. Referring to the Synoptic tradition, she argues that "the evangelists are concerned with the proclamation of Jesus as the Messiah, whose natural mother and brothers are *contrasted with* the family of God (Mark 3:31-35)" (p. 60, emphasis hers). While this is true, at least from the Markan perspective, it does not support her thesis that Marian reflection is grounded more in "symbolic form" than in "historical form"; nor is it sufficient to conclude that in Johannine tradition Mary appears in the form of "theological symbolism," as though that were all there is to it. For her conclusion is not merely that

Scripture offers little on which to build a "Mary of history" (a point with which few would argue), but that the Church's traditional images of Mary as "virgin, bride and mother, queen of heaven, and comforter of the needy" are only adequately explained in terms of the psychology of religion and depth psychology (p. 61—Halkes refers to a well-known study by E. Drewermann on the role of religious archetypes in shaping Marian dogma in Roman Catholicism).

An adequate exegesis—one that accepts as canonical and therefore as authoritative both the infancy narratives and Mark 3—would find in the biblical texts themselves grounds for each of these titles, perhaps even that of "queen of heaven." The virgin mother of the birth stories is also she who responds to the call of God with her *fiat*, who intercedes before her Son (Jn 2), and who by implication has heard the word of God and kept it (Lk 11:28; cf. 8:21). These latter passages are not intended by Jesus or the Gospel tradition to demean Mary but, as the patristic and liturgical tradition of the Church has held, to emphasize for the reader/hearer of the Gospel that Mary is (first) among those who have responded in faith to God's word, and that she is in fact the archetypal "believer." This is why the Byzantine lectionary appoints Luke 10:38-42 for Marian feasts that are not directly grounded in Scripture itself: like Mary of Bethany, the mother of Jesus assumes the posture of a disciple, to receive "the one thing needful." But she also assumes the nurturing role of "comforter," reflected not only in the pious image of the *pieta*, but also in the reciprocal covenantal bond Jesus forms between his mother and the Beloved Disciple at the foot of the cross (Jn 19:26f).

Schillebeeckx will argue that such titles originally belonged to the Holy Spirit and were only subsequently transferred, first to the Church then to Mary. Historically speaking, there may be some truth to this claim. If that transference was made, however, it is due less to the mechanism studied by depth psychology than to the *living experience* of the community of faith, in which Mary is sister and mother, the first of all believers and nurturing intercessor on behalf of all believers. It is on the basis of this experience that the Church, in its doctrine and liturgy, extrapolates from the biblical text to proclaim Mary as "first in the communion of saints" and thus "queen of heaven." From the perspective of *sola scriptura*, such an extrapolation is hardly permissible. As an expression of ecclesial experience, however, it constitutes an essential element of what Christians from East and West have regarded as Holy Tradition. And as such, it is integral to Christian life and faith.

This said, however, we can only applaud Halke's effort to liberate Mary—and thereby all women—from the deformations to which certain theological currents have subjected her. Women have undeniably suffered from sexist, patriarchalist attitudes within the Church; and the appeal to a distorted Mariology to support such attitudes needs to be identified for what it is and discarded once and for all.

Perhaps Halke's key statement is this: "For me, Mary has become the image of the person who in Christianity came closest to the divine by being completely filled with the Holy Spirit" (p. 74). Precisely! But when she specifies what that "filling" means, she, like Schillebeeckx, effectively rejects "incarnation" by rejecting the biblical meaning of Mary's virginity. Virginity, she holds, is "an attitude of being open and available to the divine mystery..." (p. 75). True; but the immediate question is, what then distinguishes Mary's virginity from the chastity required of every faithful Christian?

In fact, Halkes makes the common mistake of confusing "virginity" and "chastity." Consequently, she takes as a simple metaphor the biblical affirmation that Mary was a virgin when she conceived her child Jesus. Mary, then, cannot meaningfully be spoken of as "Theotokos" or "birth-giver of God." She is reduced to our "sister," the "mother of all believers," who corresponds to the Old Testament image of Abraham as "father of all believers." Ironically, however, both Halkes and Schillebeeckx (cf. pp. 34-38) place such stress on Mary's invisibility in the Gospels and her unawareness of the significance of her birth-giving, that the title "mother of all believers" itself is devoid of meaning. Mary ponders; but does she in fact "believe"? Reading these two essays, one would hardly think so.

In her introduction to this book, Marianne Merkx declares, "Many people, above all women, have suffered under the old image of the virgin and the mother. Fortunately this image has been shattered...." One can only wonder who has benefited from this kind of shattering. Can women truly "be themselves" and claim the God-given grace, authority and power which is manifestly theirs, by "shattering" (losing or rejecting) the image of Mary as the bearer of Life, the Mother of God, the image and fulfillment of personal integrity, receptivity, purity and holiness? If she is our sister and the mother of all believers, she is so not primarily because of her response to the divine invitation, but because of the mystery of the incarnation itself. Her significance lies in what God, through his own divine initiative, has accomplished in and through her "for the life of the world."

Presenting Mary (merely) as "sister" and "mother of believers," these essays in fact transform her into the image of the liberated woman, rather than recover her traditional and vastly more significant role as an icon of transfigured humanity. Reduced to "the model of the radical believer"

(Halkes, p. 77), she is restricted to a role far more "symbolic" than anything traditional(ist) piety may have imposed upon her. This is what raises the crucial question of the relation between Mariology and christology, and obliges us once again to determine where our loyalties—and the source of our salvation—actually lie.

The question of the truth and relevance of Christian orthodoxy—which has historically informed each of our confessional traditions—is as significant and vital today as it has ever been. Can there be an authentic "liberation theology" which is not grounded in the unshakable conviction that the eternal Son of God "became flesh" as Jesus of Nazareth, that through the death and resurrection of the "God-man" death has been overthrown, bondage to sin and corruption has been broken, and eternal life has been made accessible to all those who receive it in faith and love?

If we reject, or reinterpret into oblivion, the biblical witness to the virgin birth, the actual "incarnation" of the Son of God—however scandalous and incomprehensible that mystery might seem—then we effectively reject the gift of life that his suffering death offers to us. The insight of Gregory of Nazianzus, affirming the *ontological* aspect of the incarnation, is still pertinent: "What is not assumed is not healed, but what is united to God is saved" (Ep. 101 *ad Cledonium*).

Despite Halke's claim that "We take the incarnation seriously..." (p. 53), she in fact does not—any more than does Schillebeeckx—at least not in a way that allows for that actual assumption of human nature (human being, existence, life) which God's saving work in Christ depends upon. This is why these essays, articulate and well-reasoned as they are, ultimately fail. They fail the Church and they fail all those, women and men, who long for authentic liberation and the gift of life.

Nevertheless, we must be grateful for this little book, since it obliges us to come to terms with the relation between Jesus and Mary in our own faith and in the faith of the Church. The conclusion to be drawn from the very failings of these essays is that *christology and Mariology are inseparable*. Apart from her son, Mary has no ultimate meaning for us, either as believer or as mother or as sister.

Her "meaning" lies precisely in her willingness to accept the call to give birth to the eternal Word, the Son of God. Yet beyond that, it lies in God's own action in bringing about the miracle of "incarnation," making of Mary the Theotokos, the Virgin Mother of God, the mother of Jesus and our mother, through whom salvation has come to this world.